William Hazell's Gleaming Vision

A CO-OPERATIVE LIFE IN SOUTH WALES, 1890–1964

William Hazell's Gleaming Vision

A CO-OPERATIVE LIFE IN SOUTH WALES, 1890–1964

ALUN BURGE

First impression: 2014

© Alun Burge, 2014

This book is subject to copyright and may not be reproduced
by any means except for review purposes without the prior
written consent of the publishers

The publishers wish to acknowledge the support of
Welsh Books Council and the Wales Co-operative Centre

Cover design: Y Lolfa

The image on the cover of this book is taken from the original cover
of William Hazell's *The Gleaming Vision*, published in 1954 by the
Ynysybwl Co-operative Society.

ISBN:
978 1 78461 008 1 (softback)
978 1 78461 044 9 (hardback)

Published and printed in Wales
on paper from well managed forests
Y Lolfa Cyf., Talybont, Ceredigion SY24 5HE
e-mail ylolfa@ylolfa.com
website www.ylolfa.com
tel 01970 832 304
fax 832 782

Contents

List of Illustrations

Acknowledgements

FIRST MY THANKS GO to the family of William Hazell, especially Margaret and Bob West who opened up their home to me and helped make this project a reality. Their documents and memories have given this study a personal richness and have filled important gaps. I am grateful to Margaret, William's granddaughter, for permission to reproduce his publications including *The Gleaming Vision*.

Thanks go to Brian Davies of Pontypridd Museum, who first made me aware of the existence of *The Gleaming Vision*, and whose institution has one of the few copies of the book I have so far encountered. Chris Morrish, an ex-colleague and inhabitant of Ynysybwl, provided clues which helped me track down relatives of William Hazell. Neil Evans gave advice about sources of which I would otherwise have been unaware. Helen Thomas was an early collaborator who provided support and sources.

Huge thanks to Siân Williams and colleagues past and present in the South Wales Miners' Library. They provide a superb example of a public service institution which at times became my second home. Siân's engagement went far beyond that of Librarian.

Andrew Green and the staff of the National Library of Wales allowed me access to the *Co-operative News* in ways that made this study possible. Staff of countless libraries, museums and archives in South Wales provided support, including Pontypridd and Aberdare Museums; Aberdare, Pontypridd and Treorchy Libraries, Glamorgan Archives and the South Wales Coalfield

Collection at Swansea University Archive. At this time of cuts in public expenditure, they provide indispensable services. Gillian Lonergan in the Co-operative Library and Archive in Manchester is knowledgeable and helpful in equal measure. I am grateful to the Bevan Foundation for allowing me to draw heavily on my pamphlet which was published in 2012. Andrew Green, Chris Williams and Hywel Francis read drafts of this book and provided valued feedback. Chris originally suggested this undertaking and provided advice throughout. Andrew provided support in countless ways. Richard Bone and Elin Green worked magic with some of the images and I am grateful to Richard for the map. Lefi and colleagues at Y Lolfa provided support in bringing this book to publication.

Finally thanks are due to Layson Pope who has become an important part of my life in recent years – without him and his colleagues this book could not have happened.

Alun Burge, Norton, Good Friday, 2014

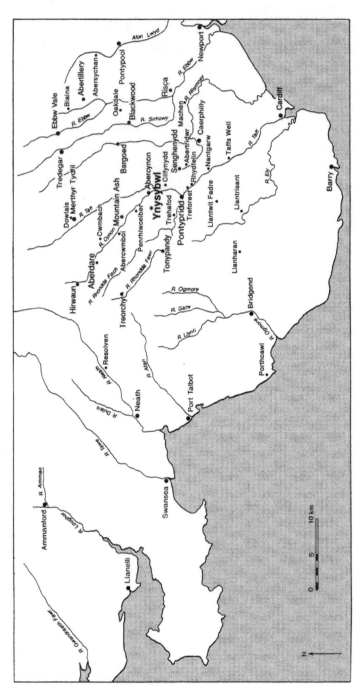

Map of the South Wales Coalfield

William Hazell's Gleaming Vision

T O DISCOVER A PREVIOUSLY unknown individual whose life illuminates a community, a society and a social movement is rare. When that ordinary working man is a writer and thinker as well as a man of action who had a powerful and articulate voice that still resonates over a half a century later, it is truly remarkable.

William Hazell (1890-1964) is a key figure to belatedly emerge from the South Wales coalfield. His lifelong commitment to the co-operative movement was inspired by his vision of co-operation as a means of building a better future. He epitomised the deep and loyal relationship that developed between the people of the valleys and their co-operative societies and which became a central part of their way of life.

In 1954 William Hazell wrote *The Gleaming Vision*, a history of the Ynysybwl Co-operative Society. The book is a window into a largely unrecorded co-operative world, which has been previously omitted from historical accounts of life in South Wales. It catalogued in close detail how ordinary people assumed responsibility for organising aspects of their economic and social lives to provide co-operative services for their own communities. A R Davies of the Co-operative Union described their endeavours as: 'a living, practical demonstration of what can be accomplished by an enthusiastic, self-governing local democracy of working men and women.'[1]

Hazell and other co-operative leaders considered their societies to be part of a national and international movement building a Co-operative Commonwealth, an economic and social system which was an alternative to capitalism, and which had a role that extended far beyond shops and trading. The title of his book, *The Gleaming Vision*, was intended to convey an aspiration of building a better future through co-operation. The picture on the cover, reproduced for this book, showed a group of people looking upwards towards the image of the co-operative stores under the banner headline "Yet Before Us Gleams the Vision of the Coming Brotherhood".

William Hazell is an authentic, but previously unrecognised working-class voice of the South Wales valleys. Although he lived and worked his adult life in Ynysybwl, a small village outside Pontypridd, his experience from the Great War until the 1960s typified the whole of the South Wales coalfield. He was characteristic of thousands of men and women who organised union branches and miners' lodges, branches of the Women's Co-operative Guild, workmen's institutes, trades and labour councils and co-operative societies. Like similar figures such as Sam Garland of Oakdale or Lewis Lewis of Blackwood, he was the backbone of labour organisation in the valleys. Their passing left little trace and they became lost to history, but in the first half of the 20th Century they were key figures in building the local labour movement and in shaping valleys society. While a few have been rescued from obscurity by coalfield histories, most have not. They were overwhelmingly members of the local Labour Party, which they also led, and often served as local or county councillors. Many of them were excellent organisers and accomplished public speakers. Some were sophisticated thinkers and could be considered intellectuals. While Hazell was all of these things, what sets him apart is his extensive writings.

In many of his values and ideals Hazell could be seen as a man before his time who could have slipped comfortably into the early 21st Century. Throughout his life he was gender aware and had an environmental consciousness. For example, in the early 1920s he wrote of the representation of women in the co-operative movement and of the environmental impact of industry. Some of his other perspectives also have contemporary resonance. While he was a living example of social solidarity, with a strong collectivist imperative, he saw the role of voluntary action as primary and was aware that too much state activity, or state intervention in the wrong areas, could be counterproductive and depress the human spirit. In other ways, however, he belonged firmly to the first half of the 20th Century. It is apparent from his published writings that he believed in God, co-operation, and the need for socialism. He lived his beliefs through his actions and expressed them via his writings.

A 'renaissance man', Hazell was a miner who grew into a polymath, and his writings covered a wide range of subjects, drawing on what he did, saw, read, thought or experienced. He was also an acute social observer and a chronicler of the life and history of South Wales, as well as a reporter on the co-operative movement. He had an eye for the detail of ordinary existence and used it to register the changes in people's lives. Over four decades his writings built into a compendium of valleys life as well as a commentary on national and international affairs.

Hazell's *Gleaming Vision* was a record of 65 years of collective entrepreneurship: an account of how one co-operative society expanded from a single village shop to become a large business undertaking with a million-pound turnover that stretched across and beyond the valleys towards Cardiff. It was William Hazell's only book, although it was his third history of a co-operative society, following shorter histories of the Ammanford and Tredegar Co-operative Societies, which were published as pamphlets in 1950 and 1951.[2] At the time of its publication there was every reason for Hazell, surveying over six decades of generally sustained growth, to convey confidence in the future. Co-operation was at its peak, coinciding with the ending of wartime rationing but before the growth of a consumer-driven society. Within a few years the face of British retailing would be transformed by market change, with a heavy impact on the co-operative movement, including the Ynysybwl Society.

The role of the Ynysybwl Society, and its economic and social prominence, was not exceptional. From Chepstow in the east to Pembroke Dock in the west dozens of societies pursued and achieved shared goals. Study of the co-operative movement provides the opportunity to reappraise previous interpretations of South Wales valleys society, its aspirations, and the ways they were pursued to achieve social change and build 'a new society'. Hazell and his colleagues in the Ynysybwl Co-operative Society, in common with those in other co-operative societies, saw themselves creating a world where the consumer was 'the ultimate person of importance'. The emphasis on the consumer as the primary agent ran counter to much of the ideology of the labour movement, not least in South Wales, which considered that the point of production, rather than that of consumption, was key. That local labour leaders, such as Hazell, could be both leaders of consumers as well as of producers, and lived these differences within their daily activist lives without any apparent contradiction, provides ample ground for explorations and explanations. It is remarkable that the co-operative movement, which was one of the most significant social movements in South Wales and which at its peak had approximately 300,000 members, has largely disappeared from our historical consciousness. The intention of this book is that in future no study of the social, political and economic life of industrial South Wales could be complete without taking into account the contribution of the co-operative movement.

The backdrop for Hazell's writing is a significant period in the history of the coalfield: the rapid growth of South Wales in the Edwardian era, with its positive expectations and aspirations; the rise of labour at a time of rapid political and economic change; the titanic industrial struggles of the 1920s, followed by the misery of the Depression; the upheaval of the Second World War, and the subsequent growing social and economic stability of the two decades from the end of the Second World War to the period of 'you've never had it so good' at the end of the 1950s. Throughout, Hazell picks up these and many other strands, and presents a view of South Wales which is in part familiar but also previously unrecognised.

Hazell was a member of the Ynysybwl Co-operative Society throughout his adult life and was its president for 30 years until his death. While co-operation came to dominate his life, at other times Hazell was, equally, a miners' lodge activist, a local councillor and a writer. He was also a husband, a father, and a committed Christian. This study seeks to weave the numerous strands into one life as he lived it. Although he always formally referred to himself as William, he was known as Bill.[3] He worked in Lady Windsor Colliery in Ynysybwl, and at various times was Chairman of the Miners' Lodge and Secretary of the Workmen's Institute, as well as being a local Labour councillor for almost 30 years. By knowing the man, his family, and his challenges within his society and times, it is possible to contextualize Hazell's commitment to co-operation, to see it as a reason for, and response to, his life and his circumstances. As well as being something which shaped his life, it also framed his life for those around him. Hazell the co-operator and his *Gleaming Vision* are therefore seen within the wider context of his family, his work, his health, and his other labour movement activities.

It is, of course, difficult to reconstruct the lives of ordinary people, particularly more than a half a century later. With a primarily localised role, they did not usually leave a sufficient imprint of their existence. Most published lives from the labour movement are of leaders who attained prominence in national office. It is remarkably good fortune that a diverse range of sources allow a detailed picture of the man in his times to emerge. Although Hazell did not write an autobiography, it is possible to track him through his activities in a range of organisations and the autobiographical detail in his publications. As well as three co-operative histories produced over a five-year period, Hazell is known to have written hundreds of articles, although his output was possibly much greater. He wrote for around 40 years, from the Great War at least until the end of the 1950s, covering most of the period of his time in South Wales. As well as providing a view of the world in which he lived, his writings allow us to get a sense of the man, his life and his thinking in a way that is possible for few very ordinary working men or women of that period. Some of his articles commented on the issues of the day and his experiences; others were written from an historical perspective. They have been drawn on extensively, often paraphrased or used verbatim, to illustrate his analysis, beliefs and actions. They provide an important backdrop that informs his Gleaming Vision.

The Gleaming Vision is hardly known, used, or referred to, even by labour historians of South Wales. This is surprising, particularly when compared with the well-known *A Village Workers' Council*, the history of the Lady Windsor lodge of the South Wales Miners Federation (SWMF), which is, in effect, a sister volume. *The Gleaming Vision*, together with *A Village Workers' Council*, provides a uniquely informed view of one South Wales village –

Ynysybwl – from the perspective of labour organisation, over a period of 60 years.

The Gleaming Vision was a period document. It was one of a large number of histories that were produced in the 1940s and 1950s by local labour movement organisations, such as miners' lodges, institutes, trades and labour councils, the Labour Party and co-operative societies to record their work in previous decades, their achievements, their local contribution to the building of the new society of post-war Britain, and their aspirations for the future.

As well as being of the early post-war period, *The Gleaming Vision* was also in keeping with the long tradition of co-operative commemorative volumes in being largely celebratory and consciously avoiding controversy or scandal in the Society's past. It was the longest history published by any local labour movement organisation in South Wales in the 20th Century and provided the most detailed account of a co-operative society in South Wales (which was referred to at times in the movement as 'South Wales and Monmouthshire'). It is also a rare book which does not appear in the catalogues of the National Library of Wales or the British Library.

Particularly important to understanding his life are family sources. A cache of family letters, dating from 1932 to 1977, including regular letters from William to his family members, were kept by his daughter Lilian, and from these it is possible to reconstruct a key period in his life during the mid-1930s. The letters allow an insight into the Hazell family, its members, and how they related. They are a unique source through which the lives and stresses of family members are articulated in their own words. They provide privileged access to normally closed worlds and demonstrate how extraordinary were these seemingly ordinary lives, or at least how these lives were made extraordinary by the circumstances through which they lived. It is common for the aristocracy, bred to assume their own importance, to keep records of their affairs; it is much less common for a series of letters of ordinary people from South Wales to have survived. Lilian and William's niece, Marjorie, both lived into their 90s and in conversations with this author drew on the family's received memory back to the beginning of the 20th Century, simultaneously providing continuity with the past and lending an immediacy to events over three-quarters of a century earlier.

Other significant sources are now inaccessible. Hazell's personal papers and collection of books, with a small number of exceptions, which could have provided invaluable information, have long since gone. Tragically, almost all the records of the Ynysybwl Co-operative Society, including its minute books, have been lost. In 1959, when the Ynysybwl Society was at its economic and social zenith, Hazell wrote as a dedicated local historian of the movement that he 'tears his hair and weeps' at the co-operative records that had been discarded 40 years earlier.[4] It would have been inconceivable for him to imagine that many society records, including those of Ynysybwl, which were then being carefully safeguarded, would later be discarded through structural changes in the movement.[5]

Sufficient of Hazell's articles have been located to confirm that he was a prolific writer on a wide range of subjects and for a variety of publications over four decades. To date, nearly 400 published articles have been identified. However, the full range of his work and the extent of his output cannot be fully assessed. In contrast to that other miner-writer, Bert Coombes of Resolven (who was almost an exact contemporary, also born outside the coalfield, and who arrived to work at around the same time), no archive of Hazell's work survived. For example, few copies exist of what was likely to have been the most prolific outlet for his writings, the Ynysybwl Co-operative Society's *Local Pages* section of the monthly national *Wheatsheaf* magazine (later renamed *Co-operative*

Home Magazine). Individual copies of that supplement – of which Hazell was editor – are extant for only September 1935 and June 1954 and it is therefore likely that hundreds, and possibly more, of his articles, news updates and reports from those pages have been lost. While co-operative sources have been searched extensively for his articles, other potential areas, such as publications related to the Labour Party, chapel, local government or the magistracy, have not been combed. Local newspapers have not been read, although four local press articles suggest that there may be still much more waiting to be uncovered. `

Another important source remains tantalisingly within sight, but just out of reach. A result of undertaking this work has been the discovery of the papers, including diaries, of John E Morgan, which cover much of the period from 1898 to 1959. Morgan, Secretary of Lady Windsor lodge for 45 years, author of *A Village Workers' Council*, and Secretary of the Ocean Combine Committee, was a close collaborator of William Hazell over decades. Only some of the early years of his extensive diaries, written in shorthand, have been transcribed and are therefore accessible. They are sufficient to reveal a unique and valuable source. The complete diaries may yet prove to be a belated treasure to emerge from the South Wales coalfield two decades after the effective closure of the coal industry and 50 years after the death of the diarist. They may provide currently immeasurable information on the work of the Unofficial Reform Committee, the Great War, the South Wales coalfield, and possibly greater insight into the politics, activities, ways of working and character of William Hazell.

Inevitably, there are gaps in the narrative. What led Hazell to come to the valleys of South Wales to work in the coal industry? Why did he end up in Ynysybwl? While it is possible to surmise, the answers to some questions may never be known.

Hazell was not one of the co-operators from South Wales

who went on to hold positions of national or international importance, such as (Sir) Tom Allen of Blaina, Aneurin Davies of Aberdare, (Sir) Jack Bailey of Miskin, Mountain Ash, or (Baron) T E Williams of Ynyshir. However, his writings gave him, and the Ynysybwl Society, a national prominence across the Co-operative Movement in Britain, where he was known as 'Hazell of Ynysybwl' and considered a 'very influential man'.[6]

As well as giving him national prominence in his lifetime, his publications are what draw Hazell to us now. His writings give extensive consideration to all aspects of the co-operative movement, including its values and principles and their application, structures, roles and dynamics. He was in the tradition of co-operative pamphleteers and lecturers of an earlier period and, as well as a co-operative thinker, he was an advocate and a propagandist. Ideas and beliefs are sometimes presented in sustained argument in one essay; often his credo and insights are built up from asides within broader pieces. His essays on co-operative history covered numerous subjects and issues that justified his description as 'the most energetic lay historian of the Welsh [co-operative] movement'.[7] He was committed to co-operative life and culture and, through his writings, explained the integral role they played in South Wales valleys society.

While some of the reference points in Hazell's life did not change over time – not least his unswerving commitment to co-operation – his outlook changed as he grew older. In 1957, aged 67, he wrote 'In the cocksure twenties, the hardening thirties and the dogmatic forties, one is so sure of all the answers; in the mellowing and tolerant sixties, before "crabbed age" sets in, one hesitates to prescribe...'[8]: While he was writing of co-operative education, his comments have a much wider applicability as is reflected in the nature of his writings. As his focus changed over time, losing its earlier sharper edge, so did his preferred outlets for publication. Many of his earliest articles, when he was a lodge official at Lady Windsor Colliery, appeared in the journal of the South Wales Miners' Federation, the *Colliery Workers' Magazine*. Subsequently his publications were mainly found in journals of the co-operative movement. Although Hazell was described as having 'an easy pen',[9] his was not polished writing. Although he could write effectively and had a powerful use of language, he could not easily sustain a book-length narrative and did not have the flow of the much better-known miner-writer B L 'Bert' Coombes. However, his lack of a smooth style was more than offset by the range and quality of the content, the timespan of his published work, the breadth of issues he embraced, his capacity to address issues that have resonance today, and the insights he conveyed.

For decades, from the 1920s to the 1960s, Hazell and the Ynysybwl Co-operative Society (YCS) were completely intertwined. Equally, YCS was not an isolated organisational entity: it can only be understood within the life of the village of Ynysybwl and the people whom it served, for the 'Co-op' was of them and about them. Only by appreciating its rootedness in the community, its location within the labour movement, and its direct or indirect links to, and interactions with, the miners' lodge, the Institute, the Trades Council and the Labour Party, is it possible to get a rounded sense of the role and position of the Co-operative Society. Of course, as its geographical ambit extended down to Pontypridd and beyond, so did the scope and nature of its relationships and hinterland.

Ynysybwl has already received considerable attention from historians, indeed, more attention than a place of its size would suggest, and compared with others in the South Wales valleys.[10] However, surprisingly, previous studies have given little or no attention to the Ynysybwl Co-operative Society, which was one of the main organisations in the village. This may be due, in large part, to what has been the invisibility of the co-operative movement in labour and general histories of South Wales and across Britain.[11]

In one of his articles Hazell emphasised the importance and significance of the title to biographies and autobiographies. Perhaps the nearest to a title that can be elicited from Hazell's own reflections on his life is that he had been 'on the anvil for most of his life, and taken many a hammering.' Certainly, in many ways his was a hard life. Equally, it was a reasonably typical one in terms of the hardships encountered by people of that generation.

I encountered the writings of William Hazell while researching the history of the co-operative movement in South Wales in the 20th Century. The writing of that history was put to one side to bring William Hazell to life. In the eight years that I have lived with William Hazell, getting to know the man and his ways, I have grown to admire and respect him as a man of integrity and principle. It would have been interesting to hear his comments on this 'attempt on his life'.

William Hazell believed that co-operation had a soul, which drew its inspiration from the needs and aspirations of ordinary people.[12] His message is one that has not been 'heard' for a long time. It is one that is long overdue.

CHAPTER 1

Starting Out

London

William Hazell was born on 27 August 1890 in St Pancras, London. His father Frederick was a shoeing smith and one-time secretary of the Amalgamated Farriers' Union. Frederick, aged 21, married William's mother, Eliza Jane Cook, aged 17, in 1879 in Westminster. They had five children, of whom William was the youngest. He had three older sisters, Annie then aged nine; Maude aged six; Nellie Beatrice aged three and a brother Frederick aged one.[1]

He described the house where he was born as 'one out of a million on the outskirts of an Empire's capital city'.[2] When he was a year old, his and two other families, totalling 15 people, lived at 138 Carlton Road, Kentish Town, in north London. He spent his early boyhood days in London 'within the sound of a London shoesmith's anvil', and attended a Board School. In the 1890s, William was taken by his parents in his father's trap to socialist demonstrations in Trafalgar Square, where he had his political baptism.[3] In 1895, this 'small London boy in Norfolk suit and spotless Eton collar clutched my father's hand tightly as we walked through [Highgate] Cemetery'. Hazell said he remembered 'somewhat mistily, my father staying for some meditative moments before a certain grave muttering, "Marx! Only twelve years ago!"' before moving to a 'kind of grey obelisk' where his father said 'You will read 'Adam Bede' some day, my boy, remember this grave then.' Years later, Hazell would visit Highgate Cemetery and the graves of Marx, George Eliot and Herbert Spencer again, but at the time he said he resented this cold winter visit as he had heard of much better places to visit, such as Madame Tussauds or the Zoo.[4] Young Hazell was also taken to the pantomime but the nearest he came to paradise was the colour, sound, motion and flames of Bonfire Night. Otherwise, he said, his memories of his city birthplace were 'fleeting and shadowy, as my parents moved soon after my unimportant advent – and kept moving.'[5]

A more important issue which he did not refer to in his writings was the loss of his mother at an early age. Eliza Jane Hazell died of typhoid in Hampstead aged 36 on 31 March 1898, when he was seven years old. His father Frederick, then aged 40, promptly went off to the Boer War as a sergeant farrier (as he did later in the Great War).[6] It is not known what happened to the children during this period. Possibly William went to one of his grandmothers, one of whom (his maternal grandmother), he described as his 'other-mother', who was a 'dear Victorian lady'.

William's life underwent an abrupt change in 1901, when he was 10 years of age. His father, then aged 43, married his second wife, Rose E Lily, whom he had met in a pub. Rose was 18 years younger than Frederick and what then comprised the family lived at 43 Coley Place, Reading. As William's sisters, who were by then all 14 years old or more, did not live at home William and his brother Fred shared with their two new step-brothers, Frederick and Arthur Watson, aged six and one. Fred senior and Rose subsequently had six children of their own, who would become half-brothers and sisters to William, the first of whom, Frank Alfred Stanley, was born in September 1903.[7] The family moved to Woking 'that delectable residential area of Surrey'. As a 13-year-old, William worked in a builder's firm, earning 10/- a week, where: 'My vocabulary was certainly enlarged and widened.' He then worked for a short period in the local Co-operative Society.[8]

This was a very unhappy period for Fred junior and William as their step-mother was unkind to them, withholding food and taking their money. Fred determined to leave home as soon as he could and went to live in Kent. William, too, left as soon as he was able and went to South Wales at any early age. According to Fred's daughter, Marjorie, 'they ran away'. This childhood experience left a solid bond between the two brothers. 'There was always a special feeling,' said Marjorie, with Fred, the older brother, albeit only by a year, being almost fatherly towards William throughout his life. Fred and William, though, stayed in contact with their father, sisters, step family and half-brothers and sisters.[9]

On his lack of memories of his early life, Hazell later wondered whether it was that his memory was sadly deficient, or 'did it simply refuse to register surroundings, sights and sounds repugnant even then to a sensitive one?' Perhaps those early years had been so unpleasant that they had been blotted out. He seemed to suggest it when he continued: 'I wonder! In adult life I was soon heard to say I could remember only what I *wished* to remember.'[10]

The valley and the village

Hazell wrote that he came to South Wales as a 'stripling' to make a new life, leaving behind his earlier life almost completely. He came to the coalfield because there was work available,[11] and was working in the pit by 16 years of age. With the coal industry at its peak people were sucked in by the attraction of high wages. William worked as a collier in Lady Windsor Colliery, which had been sunk in 1884, and around which the village of Ynysybwl had grown. By 1911, Ynysybwl had a population of 5,149 and the booming economy of the community meant there was multiple-occupation of houses and overcrowding. It appears that he pretended he was older than he really was, so that by the time he was 19 years of age he was receiving a man's wage,[12] usually paid only at 21.

It is not known why Hazell chose Ynysybwl and whether it was due to a personal contact or through a chance occurrence. Hazell's first lodgings were in Charlie Gates's terraced house amongst rows of terraced houses, which Hazell referred to as 'brick boxes with slate lids'.[13] Hazell became related to Gates through marriage and it is likely that Hazell met his wife Deborah Elizabeth through Gates.[14] Gates's family home was described as typical of valleys terrace domesticity and respectability, with black and white china dogs either side of a set of brass candlesticks, graduated in size, and a flagstone-floored kitchen. Demonstrating an awareness of gender issues that he was to display throughout his life, Hazell observed and later detailed the daily chores of 'Mrs G' and her daughter, recognising the burden they had to bear. He referred to the dignity of the kitchen floor, which was swept and scrubbed daily and well sanded until no cracks could be seen. He described it as holy ground, yet was aware of the price that had to be paid, 'for it was the daily result of a woman's sacrificial, yea sacramental toil'. He likened it to 'pure slavery', although he said women did not regard it as such as they took 'pride to toil and fight the daily dirt demon'.[15]

Whatever the circumstances of his arrival in Ynysybwl, the village and what he came to refer to as 'my valley' became his home for the rest of his life. Hazell said that people came to the valleys 'to improve their status and secure... a higher standard of living', while some also brought with them their rural habits including cultivating land, whether allotments or gardens, and rearing pigs and chickens.[16] He remembered 'going down the main street, [where] one could hear all the dialects and accents of the British Isles.'[17]

In spite of the cosmopolitan picture painted by Hazell,

Ynysybwl, once formed, was noted for its insularity and closeness, suggested Chris Baggs. Between 1907 and 1925, only 186 of 3,274 workers (8%) registered in the local pit travelled in from outside the village.[18] Ynysybwl was 'an independent and self-contained community',[19] which was accentuated by not being in a valley with other towns and villages. Instead it was on its own, neither in the Aberdare Valley nor a part of Pontypridd. However, with Pontypridd nearby it was not remote.

Looking back from 1953 Hazell pointed out that, as only a few dozen families were original inhabitants and people had come from a dozen counties in England and Wales, there was 'something amusing about the attitude of the old[er] inhabitants to the newcomers, [as] nine-tenths of the population had settled [there] within the last 50 years.'. Hazell wrote warmly of his new home on many occasions and 'to love and be loved in return by a place and its people' was a precondition to being accepted:

into the holy fellowship[,] and the valley is slow to accept. Time and circumstances must show whether one can safely be initiated… It seems to be accepted that the good family man is the most likely to make a good citizen. The valley is no exception to this rule. To marry a girl of the valley [which he did] is halfway towards acceptance and adoption. In the days of which I speak, even the neighbouring valleys were, more or less "foreign" [with] our isolation. "Is she an Ynysybwl girl?" Just as in over-the-hill Rhondda, only Rhondda-girls could be accepted without question.

He went on:

One could say then (although one never did, you just vaguely felt it) that five to ten years residence, at least, was a probationary period in the valley. You were "on trial"…' However 'If you had the 'Hen Iaith' [ie spoke Welsh] it was different! To speak Welsh was of course an "open sesame" to the Capel Mawr [which was] the influential centres [sic] of the valley then.[20]

Hazell came to a community where the Welsh language was strong. In Ynysybwl the Welsh language held sway in those early years, and would have been used around him daily in all aspects of life, sufficiently so that the 1901 rules of the Ynysybwl Co-operative Society were in Welsh. However, while all discussions of the Society were in Welsh, the minutes of the meetings were recorded in English.[21] Elsewhere, he described the speech of Welsh people as having 'a lilt, a singing quality about it; something that makes music of plain words and poetry of everyday things.'[22]

Family man

William Hazell married Deborah Elizabeth Pask on 21 December 1910. He said on his marriage certificate that he was a collier aged 22, although he was only 20. Deborah Elizabeth was three years older than him and the daughter of a local greengrocer, William Pask, of Robert Street, Ynysybwl. Deborah Elizabeth was not recorded as having a rank or profession, although presumably she would have worked in her father's shop. After marriage they lived at 27 Thompson Street, then moved to 8A Clive Terrace, before, in 1929, moving up the street to 24 Clive Terrace, which they bought, and where Hazell was to live for the rest of his life. Clive Terrace was an ordinary valleys terrace and number 24 sat on the hill, looked directly down on Lady Windsor Colliery. The Pasks were original inhabitants, although Deborah Elizabeth was not a Welsh speaker.[23]

William and Deborah Elizabeth had six children in 11 years between 1911 and 1922. Lilian Maud was the eldest followed in quick succession by William George; Ivy Doreen; Leslie Frederick, Austen Cyril and Roy Glandred in 1922. Hazell referred little to his early married life in his writings, except to say that he saw the South Wales coast for the first time in 1911, and he played with his boys on the Roman road, near the village, laying an ambush for the Centurion and his legion.[24]

It is not known when he joined the Ynysybwl Co-operative Society. As a lodger, it is unlikely that he would have been a member, as that status was usually reserved for heads of household. In 1909 there were 730 members in the Society of whom 350 were in Ynysybwl, 335 in Abercynon and 45 in Cilfynydd.[25] It is probable that he joined them as a member the following year, on marriage.

Getting involved: Hazell's 'Cocksure Twenties'

Hazell arrived in the South Wales valleys at a time when class consciousness was taking hold. The mid-Edwardian period saw a decisive shift from Liberal to Labour within the local labour movement. A branch of the Independent Labour Party (ILP) was established in Ynysybwl in February 1906. By 1907, the Lady Windsor lodge minute books indicate an increasingly class-conscious outlook with a substantial level of activity invested in building labour institutions in the area, achieving labour representation on local bodies and undertaking propaganda work on behalf of those standing for office. John E Morgan said that, while in the early decades of the colliery's life, the Ocean Colliery Company attitudes had been paternal, relations with the lodge committee became 'one of constant friction' from the early 20th Century until the 1930s.[26]

There was a continual stream of speakers in the village, including John McLean and Sylvia Pankhurst, either through the lodge or the ILP. Morgan recounts that during the period of political transition from Liberal to Labour, public meetings were very lively with relentless heckling. That transition was also evident in the lodge committee where '[n]aturally and inevitably there was friction... and a considerable amount of acrimony, until the socialist element finally became predominant.'[27]

A leading local figure in the labour movement, Morgan Walters, had helped form the lodge, the workmen's institute and

29

the ILP, and brought 'the fiery zeal of an ardent social reformer and the vision of a seer and true pioneer' to the local co-operative society. Before being victimised and forced to leave Ynysybwl in 1913, Walters played a key role in inspiring and guiding the 'young band of enthusiasts' who became 'Labour' and changed the nature and scope of movements that affected the community. J E Morgan described the flowering of that generation on the lodge committee between 1900 and 1920 who 'vied honourably with each other in projects for improvements in conditions at the colliery or in the social environment'. Three quarters of them were members of economics classes, co-operative bookkeeping classes or in the ILP, and Morgan said they were a 'splendid team' whose record of achievement [in coming decades] was [to be] amazing.[28] Hazell became a key member of that group.

Two others in the group with whom Hazell worked closely over decades were the brothers Abel and John E Morgan. Abel started work in Lady Windsor in 1892 aged 14, joined the lodge committee in 1904, and remained on it until 1929. He was lodge delegate to the Pontypridd District, and a delegate to South Wales Miners' Federation and Miners' Federation of Great Britain (MFGB) conferences. When the Ocean Combine Committee was formed in 1914, Abel Morgan was its first secretary, while his brother John was later its secretary for 10 years. Abel had been associated with the Social Democratic Federation but, in 1898, became influenced by the ILP and was one of those involved in establishing its branch in Ynysybwl. He supported the new socialist leaders and in 1926 was described as 'a stalwart in that movement when it was not considered respectable to stand and listen to the gospel proclaimed by ever so few.' Abel was also a key figure in the Ynysybwl Co-operative Society, joining its Education Committee in 1907 and becoming the Committee's secretary in 1908. Abel was committed to adult education, particularly through the co-operative movement and became a strong supporter of the Workers' Education Association (WEA). John E was a founder member of the Lady Windsor lodge and also one of the founders of the local ILP branch. He became lodge secretary in 1901 (a post which he held for decades). He was associated with the Unofficial Reform Committee, which had written *The Miners' Next Step*, an influential pamphlet in South Wales and he seems to have been one of its major distributors, presumably amongst the workers of Lady Windsor and nearby collieries.[29] For Hazell, a left-leaning man of huge intellectual curiosity, the pamphlet's industrial unionist outlook is bound to have engaged him. Unfortunately there is no evidence of the extent to which he was influenced by it or on his views of industrial unionism.

Although the Lady Windsor lodge maintained a steady approach in its own policies and politics, Hazell and the lodge were affected by the increasing industrial strife in the central coalfield. Matters came to a head in 1910 with the Cambrian miners' lockout and the Aberdare block strike. Keir Hardie wrote at the time: 'The Rhondda and Aberdare valleys are thronged with police, mounted and otherwise; detachments of soldiers are billeted... The entire district looks like a besieged area in war time.'[30] For Hazell the memory of troops quartered in the Park Hotel, Pontypridd, lorries filled with blankets for troops and imported police, lived with him and a half a century later he could record that 'Even my usually calm self was stirred and excited by the struggle.'[31] When, during the railwaymen's strike of 1911, two men were shot dead by troops in Llanelli, an open air meeting was held in Ynysybwl, and a resolution presented condemning the Government's actions.[32] It was during this ferment of ideas and action that Hazell came of age.

Hazell was a voracious reader, reading Gray's *Elegy* at 13 and Gibbon's *Decline and Fall* and Macaulay's *Essays* at the age of 16 'and **enjoying them**, mark you!'[33] As a youth, Hazell had an inquisitive nature, which he retained throughout his life. He had an insatiable interest in learning, and attended mining classes at Trerobart School to become a colliery official, which was a popular path at that time for young men looking for self-improvement and advancement. Like many others he then turned his attention to other subjects of learning, particularly political economy. He recorded 'In my own youth, industry allowed little time for leisure, yet I found, for 15 years, evenings precious and fruitful, for study, under county council, WEA and NCLC auspices' as well as through the co-operative movement classes in industrial history, economics and other subjects. Hazell's catholic approach to study reflected the wider approaches to the consumption of learning that prevailed in Ynysybwl. While a strong tradition of worker's education developed in the village, porous borders existed between ideologically competing providers, with students apparently moving easily between the WEA classes of John Thomas and the Plebs and Labour College classes of A J Cook.[34]

Richard Lewis identified co-operative societies as providing a base for the WEA, otherwise largely denied it in the coalfield. Lewis said that the co-operative movement, 'in some ways most closely embodied the ideals of radical progressivism: collective but voluntary, commercial but not aggressively competitive, socially conscious but imbued with "self-help", non-capitalist but not anti-capitalist'.[35] These also became the values of William Hazell although through his experience, Hazell was at times profoundly anti-capitalist.

The Co-operative Movement in South Wales

The co-operative movement was slow to develop in Wales. Early ventures in the 1840s and 1850s were followed by the opening of the Cwmbach Society in 1860 which, because it was the first society that endured, has been considered to be 'the beginning' of co-operation in Wales. From 1860 the setting up of retail co-operatives became a common feature across South Wales. However, the attrition rate of these early societies was high. It was later perceived that co-operation had made a 'false start' in South Wales and it was said that the process had to start all over again in the 1880s,[36] although such an analysis overlooked the small number of exceptional societies, such as Blaina and Cwmbach, which made good progress from the 1860s.

Co-operative historians correctly identified that the early co-operative movement was weak in South Wales and Beatrice Potter (later Webb) in her 1891 study referred to the 'incapacity or indifference of the South Wales miners' compared with the co-operative development that had taken place in English and Scottish coalfields. However, she also acknowledged that co-operation had made a 'fresh start' in South Wales. A second wave of co-operative societies was established in South Wales in a burst of development which lasted from the 1880s until the early 20th Century. Ynysybwl was one of 34 societies established in South Wales in the four years 1888-1891. Even so, the movement was still nascent in South Wales, as is evident from the 1900 Newport Co-operative Congress Report (the first to be held in South Wales) which recorded that in the previous year, the 65 societies between Pembroke Dock and Chepstow had a total membership of only 22,714.[37]

The Ynysybwl Co-operative Society

In *The Gleaming Vision*, Hazell carefully reconstructed the cautious early years of the YCS, and its slow but steady progress. The Society was established in 1889 and was inspired by Edward Jones, a mining engineer with the Ocean Colliery Company, who became its first chairman. As happened in other steam coal villages at the end of the 19th Century, the co-operative society in Ynysybwl became an early part of the new community, being formed three years after the first coal was extracted from the Lady

Windsor Colliery. At that time within the colliery, miners had only loosely formed workmen's committees and checkweighers' committees, and had not yet created a union organisation.[38]

Understandably, Hazell applauded the achievements of earlier generations of co-operators and identified the pioneers, nearly all colliery workmen, who sought self-improvement for themselves and their families. *The Gleaming Vision* located the creation of the Ynysybwl Society in a time when the men felt the need to organise themselves to come to grips with economic and social forces. Using J E Morgan's description of people developing 'new ways of *saving themselves* by intelligent social organisation',[39] Hazell emphasised that co-operation was based in practical idealism, which contributed to the building of a Co-operative Commonwealth as an alternative to capitalism.

Such practical idealism, based in collective self-help, was not well received by local traders. While at this stage co-operation did not have sufficient strength anywhere in South Wales to be considered a threat to the shopocracy, private traders would have been aware of the strength that the movement had gained in Lancashire, Durham and elsewhere. In 1891 local traders passed a resolution that stated:

> We shopkeepers have decided that this co-operative system must be broken down and is not going to live in Ynysybwl. We have decided to break it down in six months time.[40]

Although they failed in their intention, the then infant Society would have to contend with private traders' opposition for decades.

The social and economic strength of collective entrepreneurship as a way of doing business was reflected in the remarkable growth that was achieved. The Society extended beyond its original Ynysybwl shop and during the Edwardian period opened branches in Abercynon, Cilfynydd and Coedpenmaen Road, Pontypridd, and a substantial bakery was built off Glyn Street,

Ynysybwl, from which a profitable daily bread delivery service grew. After what was described as the period of pioneering and foundation stone-laying had ended,[41] the business continued to grow and diversify. By the Great War, it had an abattoir and provided collective life insurance for members, who were also offered dentistry in Pontypridd.

The growth of co-operation in South Wales from the 1890s to the Great War was helped by the increased prosperity of the valleys. However, Hazell saw co-operative expansion as being about much more than opening shops and providing services, describing it as 'the genesis of a new social order' which was 'in the hearts and minds of the people'.[42] This expansion of the Society also occurred at a time when the population was assuming an increasing class consciousness. Co-operation both benefited from, and became a manifestation of, how people saw and expressed themselves. This applied equally to Welsh speakers who referred to their societies as 'siop ni' (our shop) rather than 'the co-op'.[43]

Hazell became involved in the co-operative movement in 1913-4 through the education programme of the Ynysybwl Society, of which Abel Morgan was the 'energetic education committee secretary' and D J Edwards, a checkweigher, the Chairman. The young students 'swotted' at various subjects concerning social progress 'for the pure love of learning', and Hazell gained Co-operative Union certificates in a range of subjects including 'that not-so-dismal science of economics', citizenship, co-operation, co-operative book-keeping and co-operative problems. He became immersed in the culture of co-operation, and attended a YCS conference in Pontypridd, where Amos Mann of the Labour Partnership Association gave a paper on the topical subject of 'The Remedy for the Labour Unrest'. Hazell took the movement's pioneering evening classes and correspondence courses, studying under Fred Hall, who helped lay the foundations of the national education programme. Hazell contrasted himself with others who became specialists in co-operative book-keeping 'who soon knew, "more and more about less and less"', recognising that his role was to know less and less about more and more. While foundations were laid poring over economics and citizenship in the family parlour on winter evenings, his perspectives were broadened by attending summer schools and weekend events, where 'we came together from mill, mine, factory, and counter.' However, he would later suggest that events, persons and circumstances had been, possibly, his greatest teacher.[44] Convinced of the value of learning, he became a committed educationalist for the rest of his life, whether through the co-operative movement, chapel, miners' union or local authority.

Co-operation had a considerable social presence which extended far beyond the sales in its stores. YCS was much more than an economic entity, having its own co-operative culture with roots deep in its communities. In its promulgation of co-operative values and in presenting an alternative to capitalism, it provided a strong and extensive philosophical basis for life and for the running of society. The Society regularly organized conferences, music events and lectures, as well as product exhibitions and annual excursions. In the winter months, 'numerous propaganda and concert-meetings' were arranged. Prior to the Great War, the Education Committee organised two children's choirs and arranged co-operative educational classes for children, young people and adults, all of which it continued to undertake for decades. As many as 1,000 children and youths attended the classes each year. YCS was a major social, ethical and cultural influencer of children, young people and adults about how society should run.[45]

Most of the cultural activity organised by the Education Committee of YCS was linked to the semi-autonomous local branches of the Women's Co-operative Guild (WCG), a radical, overtly campaigning, national organisation. The Guild was also significant in providing women with a forum through which to engage actively in the movement and the Society. Although a woman did not become a member of the Management Board of YCS until 1921, the WCG, which had six branches in the area covered by the Society,[46] provided an alternative route for women's involvement.

The work of the Ynysybwl Society was underpinned by the circulation of 5,000 monthly copies of the *Local Pages* of the *Wheatsheaf* magazine. This publication was a regular locally-based news service of co-operative life, edited by Abel Morgan in 1926, and later by Hazell.[47] The *Local Pages*, along with YCS's education classes, provided an impressive outreach which gave solid grounding in co-operative principles to much of the local adult and child population.

The direct relationship between the co-operative movement and the mining industry is an obvious one. The economic fortunes of the coal industry, whether boom or bust, were reflected in the balance sheets of the Society. However, the relationship took many forms. The role of YCS during industrial disputes was an important and enduring one throughout its history. By the time of the publication of its 21st anniversary souvenir in July 1910, which set out the achievements of the Society, YCS said it had already proved its value in three industrial disputes. It was reported that the miners' lockout of 1898 failed to shake the stability of YCS and in the 1912 national coal strike the Society consolidated its relationship with the population by selling provisions at practically cost price, even though it reduced profits. Just as the mining industry and co-operation were intertwined, so there was a clear overlap between those who were local miners' leaders and members of boards of co-operative societies. These complementary roles were epitomised in Ynysybwl by Morgan

Walters, who exercised such influence on the rising generation of young activists. A powerfully persuasive Welsh speaker, Walters believed that 'trade unionism was to undermine the capitalists' industrial power while 'socialism, with co-operation, was to achieve economic emancipation'. Another local leader, W H May, who later became a miners' agent, did 'great work for the miners' cause', was an URC activist, lodge chairman in 1911-12, involved in the ILP and a member of the Board of YCS.[48]

While the co-operative movement was formally non-political, the transition from Liberal to Labour, evident in politics and in the miners' lodge, also took place in the Ynysybwl Society and the movement more generally in South Wales. In the early years of the 20th Century the YCS Board was predominantly Liberal, although some like Abel Morgan were socialists. When chapel-going Liberal William Watkins, who was Chair of the Brecon, Glamorgan and Monmouth Board of Education of the Co-operative Union, found out that the nascent ILP, with perhaps a dozen members, was seeking to bring co-operation and socialism closer together by affiliating the ILP and co-operative movement, he condemned the move at one of its meetings in Merthyr and the proposition stalled. However, opposition to the advance of socialism had its limits and by 1911, Watkins was chair and Morgan secretary of that Education Board.[49] It is unknown whether this relationship was based in co-existence, collaboration or was contested. However, as the labour movement gathered strength in the first quarter of the 20th Century, the co-operative movement increasingly became an integral part of it.

Hazell's inclination to omit controversy or scandal from *The Gleaming Vision* is evident in his intriguing reference to a complete change of officers and manager of the Society which occurred at this time. Although Hazell would have known the circumstances behind such dramatic events, he did not elaborate on them except to say that the manager 'did not fit in too well to the newer ideas of democracy in co-operative circles and left in 1912.'[50] Whether this might have related to other moves towards democratic accountability evident in the labour movement, such as was evident in the pamphlet *The Miners' Next Step*, is open to conjecture.

The Great War

In *The Gleaming Vision*, Hazell wove the major threads of the Great War as they affected the Ynysybwl Society. He described YCS trading under exceptional circumstances as food supplies became a source of anxiety and shops crowded with people looking for scarce food items. Hazell referred to the local population's rising horror at the slaughter in the trenches and the increasing difficulties experienced by the Society and its members. These, he suggested, reinforced the attraction of the 'peaceful revolution' which co-operation represented, with people revolted by war-time profiteering and, from 1916-17, 'nauseated by the war, with its bloodshed and lying propaganda'.[51]

Internally the introduction of conscription had 'an instant and ever-increasing impact on the Society's manpower', as it was difficult to staff shops and satisfy customers.[52] The loss of experienced male employees who went to the forces resulted in their being replaced by young inexperienced girls and medically unfit men. The most significant change was on the Society's leadership, when Owen Jones and Sam Davies, who were both under military age, were appointed as the new General Manager and General Secretary respectively. Such a leap of generations was against the traditions of the movement. However, it proved valuable in providing an important infusion of 'new blood' into the Society's leadership.

Hazell was first elected to the YCS Management Committee in 1915 when he was 24 years old and by then a father of three. Hazell said that his 'first avowed intent' was to be a co-operative pilgrim which 'was my chosen path, come wind, come weather.'[53] He fulfilled the role with conviction and without wavering for the rest of his life. He served on the Board continuously from 1915 until his death in 1964, apart from a period of nine months. The strong and stable relationship that Hazell developed with Sam Davies and Owen Jones later provided the Society with a powerful organisational backbone.

Hazell quickly began to assume roles and responsibilities within the Society, attending his first Co-operative Wholesale Society (CWS) meeting as a YCS delegate at the Bute Terrace Depot, in Cardiff, in 1915. These quarterly CWS business meetings were important dates in the co-operative calendar. Members from South Wales societies were joined by colleagues from Gloucestershire and Herefordshire and considered the reports on the wide range of CWS businesses, both in Britain and overseas. At these profoundly democratic events, national CWS Directors were asked questions on any subject by representatives of co-operative societies that held shares in the wholesale businesses. Frequently there were complaints about the range and quality of the products provided by the CWS to local societies.

A new headquarters built by the CWS was opened in St Mary Street, Cardiff, in December 1916 and Hazell attended the first quarterly meeting held there, recording members' pride at their imposing new building in the heart of the city.[54] The iconic building (more recently known as the Hodge Building) was a symbol of the growing significance of the co-operative movement in South Wales, and the economic power it represented would have been a source of considerable concern to private traders.

The opening of the new CWS headquarters was a positive event against a much more negative backdrop. During the Great War there was much dissatisfaction felt across the co-operative movement at the way co-operatives were treated by the Government, not least through the policies of the Ministry of Food, including the 'datum line' allocations of foodstuffs. Co-operative frustrations came to a head in 1917. In May, an historic Co-operative Congress was held in the Albert Hall, Swansea. At that Congress, which Hazell probably attended as an observer, the accumulated grievances determined the movement to directly enter politics to protect its own interests, leading to the formation of the Co-operative Party. That autumn Hazell and others from the Ynysybwl Society attended a special emergency co-operative conference in London to air grievances, following which all 900 delegates went to the House of Commons to lobby their MPs.[55]

The extension of co-operative activity into the political sphere was reflected in Ynysybwl. YCS affiliated to the newly-established Co-operative Party and sent delegates to annual Party conferences. However, it did not establish the Co-operative Party separately at constituency level although in 1917 it did decide to affiliate to the four Trades & Labour Councils in its geographical area – Pontypridd, Mountain Ash, Caerphilly and Llantrisant – with co-operative delegates appointed to attend their meetings.[56] This significant change meant that the Society formally became a structural part of the local labour movement and no longer relied on informal relationships, overlapping individual memberships and any shared aspirations. It also reflected a deepening class consciousness within the co-operative movement.

Little is known of Hazell's views on or activities related to the Great War. The war completely divided the co-operative movement, with many taking a pacifist position, although a few of the Society's staff volunteered for the military at the outbreak of war. Hazell's name was not mentioned in John Morgan's accessible papers as being for or against the war. Nor was Hazell's position made clear in his statement decades later in *The Gleaming Vision* where he spoke of some people being 'pure pacifist', many being in intermediate positions, 'to the equally sincere stand taken by the majority' to support the declaration of war.[57] The only solid evidence of Hazell's views is of August 1917, when he moved the notice of motion at the Ynysybwl Society Quarterly Meeting which stated:

> That this meeting is of [the] opinion that the time has arrived when the International Co-operative Alliance should join with other democratic organisations in considering a basis of a people's peace based upon international co-operation; the ending of all secret diplomacy, and the control of foreign policy by the people.[58]

The motion was supported by many, and it was carried by a huge majority.

Some of Hazell's closest collaborators, such as Abel and John E Morgan, resolutely opposed the war. Abel opposed it from the start, giving strong support to anti-war movements such as the No Conscription Fellowship and the National Council for Civil Liberties. Ynysybwl was identified for its stance against the war. Abel's home in Thompson Street was described as a haven for those opposed to the war. He and his brother John were responsible for bringing a stream of anti-war speakers, including John McLean, to Ynysybwl, and for putting them up.[59] When conscription became law and many pacifists became conscientious objectors to military service Hazell said that they 'paid dearly for their principles in many ways'.[60] His words convey understanding and sympathy. However, it is not clear whether he gave them his support at the time, and whether he opposed the war. Hazell would have been close to some conscientious objectors. Bethuel Morgan, the younger brother of Abel and John, became an objector, receiving harsh treatment for his beliefs, which embittered Abel. Bethuel, along with Emrys Hughes, was one of four local boys who were subjected to court martial in Cardiff Barracks and marched through the streets of Cardiff under military escort. The joint Mynachdy, Darranddu and Lady Windsor lodges protested against their treatment. A well-attended meeting of the Lady Windsor Lodge unanimously passed a resolution against conscription, and a year later, it opposed the disenfranchisement of conscientious objectors. Lady Windsor lodge did not support the war, nor did it take part in recruiting.[61]

Although it is not known when Hazell became active in the Lodge, it is clear that he was prominent in lodge affairs in 1916, when a major dispute occurred over the men taking control of the Institute from the Ocean Colliery Company. This experience caused bad feelings between lodge officials and the management. The assertion of independence by the men saw the lodge secretary, John E Morgan, become the new Institute Chairman, a position he held for the next 19 years. Hazell became the Institute's vice-chairman, a position he occupied until 1923, when he became Secretary, a post he then held for 11 years. Morgan recorded that the men, most of them trades unionists, with little preparation (although some had attended co-operative education evening classes in book-keeping) took responsibility for running the Institute and made it into a much more substantial and successful venture, including opening it up for labour propaganda meetings.[62]

CHAPTER 2

Life Between the Wars
– Years of Endurance

The Lodge After The War

By 1918, Hazell was at the centre of lodge activities, accumulating roles and posts. His growing influence is evident. He was lodge delegate to the SWMF Annual Conference, undertook essential daily tasks such as being part of delegations to management and taking 'show cards'. He chaired lodge meetings and general meetings of the joint lodges, including one which decided to support the anti-war candidate T E Nicholas as Labour Party candidate for Aberdare Division against the jingoist C B Stanton. In late 1919, when the vice-chairman of the lodge resigned, Hazell was chosen to replace him. Exceptionally, at one annual lodge meeting the Conservative Party supporters took a majority of seats on the committee and the young Labour men were relegated to lesser positions. Hazell was given the role of lodge auditor,[1] although power quickly swung back in favour of the young labourites.

The post-war political shift in support towards the Labour Party was reflected in Ynysybwl. Labour established itself when it won seats on the Board of Guardians and District Council in 1919, which Morgan identified as the period when the tide had definitely turned. Lieven noted the strength of the opposition that was overcome in that, Labour's first, local victory. Hazell later wrote of Woosnam, the successful Labour candidate: 'Ynysybwl had returned him in the confidence that he would represent his own class.'[2] Hazell later described this period of his life as his 'cocksure twenties'.[3] His levels of hyper-activism permitted little time for home life as Deborah Elizabeth carried the burden of four children at home while her husband was working in the pit or at Federation or co-operative meetings. Although Hazell might shortly argue for equality for women in the co-operative movement, and there was no doubting his commitment to and love of his wife, in practice William was able to fully engage with his labour movement activities because Deborah Elizabeth assumed full domestic responsibilities in a way that was then the norm in valleys households.

In the pit the period from September 1920 was a trying one for Hazell as twice in a few weeks his actions did not find favour in the lodge committee. A resolution was passed at a General Meeting deprecating his actions in assisting a haulier who was working overtime against lodge instructions.[4] Hazell acknowledged he had done it, but unknowingly. Hazell blundered on this issue, which was already a cause of disunity within the lodge. Less than a month later, he was reported by a fellow worker, W P Breeze, who claimed that Hazell had destroyed his work, having hit out a pair of timber put up by him. Hazell said that on many previous occasions Breeze had used Hazell's dressed timber (timber already prepared for use by Hazell) and which had Hazell's initials chalked on them. Breeze admitted that the timber had been notched. Lacking the willingness to grasp the issue, the lodge committee decided that such circumstances were caused by a lack of timber in the colliery, and sent a delegation to the management, including both Breeze and Hazell. A week later, a letter from Hazell was read to the lodge committee which said:

> On two recent occasions my actions as a workman have called for condemnation by the… committee[;] the comments on the last case I resent, as I still desire and intend to defend the product of my labour, it seems to me the right course now to resign, this I do and thank you for all your past kindness.

John E Morgan and Richard Woosnam, the Secretary and Chairman of the lodge, were sent by the committee to see Hazell 'stating that the committee desires him to reconsider his decision to resign.' Hazell, displaying his usual tact, said that he would give it further thought, but he did not return to the lodge committee. However, his general standing in the colliery remained high and the day after his resignation the General Meeting selected him to attend a coalfield conference.[5]

In this period of acute class conflict at the end of the Great War, the national and international policy positions adopted by the Lady Windsor lodge reflected the profound class divide that existed in British society. Mirroring the position of much of the labour movement, the lodge resolved that it was ready to take action protesting against the British Government intervening in Russia when the MFGB called for it. The lodge also opposed the Polish attack on Russia, calling for the TUC to declare a national strike to force the British Government to insist that Poland made peace. A general meeting supported the nationalisation of the mines in February 1920, and instructed the conference delegate to support a policy of direct action to achieve it if necessary. The lodge also supported the police union after the 1919 police strike. However, even at a time of considerable antagonism between men and the Ocean Coal Company at Lady Windsor, the lodge committee conducted itself in a responsible way in matters related to the colliery. When the lodge took strike action locally, it was for issues such as getting the management to undertake necessary repairs in the colliery. Lady Windsor was a highly democratic lodge with all policy and political issues decided by the general meeting of the workmen, rather than just the lodge committee, although attendance at general meetings could be low. A series of lectures organised by the lodge committee reflected its mainstream labourist view, rather than a highly radical one.[6] This mixture of both radical and responsible, exemplified by the Lady Windsor lodge, were also characteristics of Hazell throughout his life.

YCS After The War

In spite of the difficulties of wartime, the Ynysybwl Society experienced a period of phenomenal growth and it emerged stronger and with its boundaries greatly enlarged. During the war, a butchery and new branches were opened in Pwllgwaun and the Graig in Pontypridd. Between 1914 and 1918, membership nearly trebled from 1,665 to 4,757, trade increased nearly 12 times from £19,631 to £232,000 and capital almost trebled from £15,487 to £45,585.[7]

The remarkable growth rates continued after the war. Further branches were opened in Old Ynysybwl, Glancynon, Taffs Well and Trehafod in 1919 and 1920. Acquisitions and takeovers also occurred, such as in Llantwit Fardre where the local society was in difficulties. By 1920, the Society's membership had increased to 6,474, trade reached nearly £500,000 and capital was £115,064.[8] This remarkable surge in activity was reflected in the Society's capital, which represented savings of nearly £20 per member, indicating both the level of affluence in coalfield society and the confidence the members felt in YCS.

The growth of the Society as measured by all yardsticks – increase in the number of shops, membership, turnover, surplus and members' capital – required Board members to be a highly entrepreneurial group. In their direct challenge to private sector business interests they displayed business acumen, skills in negotiation and could collectively take risks.

The accumulation of members' capital provided the funding

for a marked shift in retail power from private to collective entrepreneurship. The 'great assault' on Pontypridd in 1919-1920 when the Society obtained premises in Market Square, outflanked those private traders who sought to keep the co-operative from the town centre by keeping sites or shops off the market.[9] The Society's move from backstreet branches and surrounding villages to the centre of Pontypridd was significant. Hazell saw it as an assault on the private profit system in the town. At a time of much debate over private ownership in the mining industry, the co-operative movement's incremental tackling of private enterprise in the retail sector achieved considerable success.

A major undertaking, such as obtaining premises in Pontypridd town centre, needed the Board to take its membership with them. The democratic process ran the risk that the details of the transaction and the property concerned might be 'leaked' to a private trader. That the Ynysybwl Society was able to successfully complete the deals suggests that members maintained discipline in keeping the operation confidential. The unanimous decision of members to support the proposal was an endorsement of the leadership shown by the Society's Board.

Hazell was always conscious of the risks involved in using members' capital.

> A co-operative committee always realises it is handling and investing capital belonging to its thousands of small shareholders. It has to be cautious. A certain proportion of the Society's assets has to be liquid.[10]

Yet Hazell said that YCS had 'proved themselves worthy to receive and hold funds for their members' and provided a haven for members' savings. The way in which co-operative societies' Boards provided collectivist business leadership, exercised financial skill and retained the long-term confidence of their memberships, whose savings were risked to fund business development, is an under-remarked feature of working class organisation in South Wales. Such collective entrepreneurship deserves a place in both labour and business histories of South Wales. The reconciling of separate issues – the development of an entrepreneurial undertaking, the ability to compete against other traders, looking after individual members capital, while building of 'the co-operative commonwealth' which looked to meet the needs of its membership 'from the cradle to the grave'[11] was not easy – not least the never to be resolved conundrum of fundamentally transforming from within the market in which they were competing.

The miners lockout of 1921 and its aftermath

In 1921, post-war economic growth, which helped increase the Ynysybwl Society's turnover, ended. As economic difficulties in the South Wales coalfield began to take hold, the management at Lady Windsor Colliery laid off workers on 'stop days' through lack of demand for coal.[12] Matters came to a head when the coal industry, which had been under government control since the war, was deregulated. The coalowners announced a considerable reduction in wages, which the miners resisted, resulting in them being locked out of the collieries.

Hazell had not been on the lodge committee for five months since the criticism of him in October 1920 and was not involved in the first week of organising the lockout. However, at the General Meeting on 7 April the 'strike committee' was increased to include Abel Morgan and William Hazell, with others whose identities were disguised by John E Morgan's use of shorthand.[13]

The early stage of the lockout was one of ferment. Two days after Hazell joined the strike committee, a joint general meeting of Lady Windsor and Mynachdy lodges on 9 April at 10am heard from D L Davies, the Miners' Agent, that the Triple Alliance of unions had decided to strike in support of the miners. The meeting resolved to support the SWMF decision to withdraw safetymen from the pits. Those men, such as fanmen and pumpmen, were usually allowed to continue during disputes to keep the colliery in a working condition. A deputation went to the management at 1pm and management agreed to withdraw them. The Union's action was a very serious step and John E Morgan recounted that 'Never in the long experience of the writer had there been such a tense moment' in the relations between men and management.[14]

There was a bustle of activity with daily – sometimes twice daily – meetings of the strike committee. Strike bulletins were posted in the windows of co-operative shops. Hazell was chosen to be one of a small number of speakers chosen to travel to other areas. Contact was made with the Director of Education about feeding children in school, although it was decided to not yet set up a communal kitchen, although the lodge asked for the use of the Institute in readiness, as well as the churches for tables. Following the 'defection' of the Triple Alliance, the Joint General Meeting enforced the tightest controls over the colliery, with Hazell a key leader. Within days the mood changed. The Joint Strike Committee learned that a Distress Committee was being established by 'outsiders' and as that committee developed a wide social base with tradesmen and teachers being supportive, it was agreed that henceforth funds be paid into the Distress Fund rather than to each member individually. A communal soup kitchen was established at the Institute, which served 52,000 meals during the lockout.[15]

Throughout the three months of the dispute, the YCS played a prominent part in helping sustain the miners' struggle, although to its own economic cost. Early in the lockout, lodge members, who were also co-operative members, were urged to attend the Society's General Meeting to press it to reduce the price of milk because, as the largest milk retailer in the town, it could set a lead in reducing the price charged by others. It was estimated that during the lockout, with the support of the CWS, co-operative societies in South Wales provided £1 million of goods to members, and sometimes to the miners' union via miners' lodges, often without guarantees in return.[16] With its resources focussed exclusively on the miners' struggle, YCS did not send a delegate to the Scarborough Co-operative Congress in May 1921, the first time they had not done so for five years.

In acknowledging the role of the YCS during the 1921 lockout Tom Watkins said: 'Well thank the Co-operative... It kept the people sane here... they had their money there do you see.' He continued:

> The Co-operative was the salvation of the working class here. All this dividend, interest they were getting; dividend at two and nine and never lower than two and six, it was accumulating you see. It kept them through the strike, the majority of them. Of course there was a lot that didn't belong to the Co-op and they were the worst off do you see. So you've got to thank the Co-operative Society for a lot haven't you.'[17]

While no adequate account has yet been written of the 1921 three-month lockout, Hazell described it as 'a hideous nightmare', which had a profound impact on the people of the valleys and was disastrous for the co-operative movement in South Wales. Stocks slumped in value; the debts of members accumulated, (only a proportion of them being repaid), members' capital dwindled and their purchasing power declined. As a result of the lockout, sales reduced to £243,312 in 1922 – less than half the 1920 turnover of £494,073 – and decreased trade meant overheads increased proportionately. While membership and members' shareholdings remained remarkably resilient, profits, which had been £40,871 in 1920, collapsed to £840.[18] The consequences were felt by the Ynysybwl Society for years afterwards. Cursed by bad timing, Hazell was elected President of the YCS for the first time in 1921 but was deselected after a year as he had to face the members and tell them that, due to the lockout, there was no surplus to pay a dividend on nine months' purchases.[19]

It is possible that before the 1921 conflict the co-operative movement had become heady at the prospect of a miners' strike. Although it had previously argued against one, in October 1920 an editorial in the *Co-operative News* entitled 'The Movement's Bit in the Battle' argued that

> Precedents, customs, traditions must all go by the board in a great national emergency like that which now confronts us. If necessary, our trade accounts must show a loss for the coming quarter, but the miners and the other workers affected by the strike must be fed...

The editorial commended to societies everywhere that 'dividend must be sacrificed in order that prices in co-operative stores in distressed areas may be kept down to the lowest minimum.' Evoking 'the great coal strike' of 1912 when the co-operative movement was 'the people's bulwark', it said the upcoming struggle was likely to be more bitter than that previous one. It argued not to worry about possible losses for if the workers stuck together they could not lose. The editorial continued that if 'the strike should be a prolonged one... it must be the function of the co-operative movement to use all its resources and all its energy as the *commissariat department of the people*.'[20] Here was the movement's official voice, no doubt inflamed during a period of heightened class consciousness, using Bolshevist language to call for self-sacrifice in order to give full support to the miners. Even when the other unions abandoned the cause, which might have given the co-operative movement pause for thought, it chose to remain steadfast and place its resources at the miners' disposal.

Reflecting on the lockout a year after the stoppage, Hazell said that at the time it had not been possible to see things in their true perspective but 'to-day the lessons of the calamitous stoppage in the coal industry are more apparent'. With a biting phrase, he described the situation during 1921 as 'the trade unions having called the fight and left the co-operators to finance it'. He compared the experience of South Wales where the co-operative societies took all the risk with the situation in Northumberland where societies had a lien on miners' future earnings or where institutes and halls had been mortgaged to raise funds to purchase goods from the societies. Relations with trades unions were strained by the lockout and Hazell thought that the unions were not concerned as to whether the thousands of pounds outstanding were ever repaid. He said that: 'Recriminations are useless. Too much mutual fault-finding has been done'. Hazell foresaw further industrial disputes in the coal industry and said that the past should guide co-operative societies in preparing for future troubles. While hoping for the best, it was necessary for the co-operative movement to prepare for the worst and 'put the consumers' movement on a sound and sensible cash basis…'[21] The 1921 lockout proved terminal for some societies and grievously damaged others, providing a salutary lesson for co-operators not to prejudice the economic base of their societies for the broader interests of the labour movement.

The years leading to 1921 had seen national discussions about bringing the different wings of the labour movement, including co-operatives, closer together in what was described as a 'fusion of forces'. When a conference was held on the issue in Swansea in January 1923 Hazell, perhaps somewhat soured by the lockout, wrote a letter saying there was more fusion of forces in Ynysybwl than 'any amount of theoretical fusion on paper'. He pointed out that the Lady Windsor Institute and Library, which catered for over 1,000 workmen, was a member of the YCS, and that the Lady Windsor Lodge, the Mynachdy Lodge, the Lady Windsor Library and Institute, the Lady Windsor Nursing Fund, the Band and the YCS all banked with the Co-operative Bank. The Ynysybwl Institute, 'an institution second to none in the conduct of its affairs on business lines', banked with the CWS and most of its library books were purchased through the CWS book-selling department in Newcastle. All other purchases were done through YCS. With Abel Morgan as Secretary of the Institute and Hazell as Secretary of the Library Committee it is hard to imagine any other arrangement. Hazell did not point out, although he could have, that the YCS had been affiliated to, and sent delegates to, meetings of the Pontypridd; Mountain Ash, Caerphilly and Llantrisant Trades and Labour Councils.[22] Such inter-relationships were germane to labour in valleys society where 'the co-op' was an integral part of the labour movement. As Hazell said, the fusion of forces to which others aspired elsewhere in Britain was already a practical reality in this part of the coalfield. However, the experience of 1921 meant relations could be strained.

One of the key internal issues highlighted by the lockout was the co-operative movement's use of credit. Hazell argued that a cash system was needed to replace 'the wasteful, uneconomic, demoralising, and anti-co-operative credit system'. He described how during the dispute 'practically every society situated in the coal basin of South Wales found itself called upon to allow the necessities of life – to a percentage of their members – on credit for an indefinite period without (a) any security as to repayment, or (b) any provision for interest on overdue accounts.' He pointed out that credit policy varied, with discretion resting at times with the general manager, the finance sub-committee, sometimes completely with the branch manager, or between the branch manager and branch committee members. He said that in such circumstances, management committees of societies had to take responsibility for 'allowing *credit to workers out of other workers' savings*'.[23] Hazell said that as a committee-man previously, the fear of loss of trade had weighed on him when considering introducing a cash system into YCS, but now all lingering doubts had been removed. He urged an adoption of cash trading by individual societies, adding that uniformity across South Wales was essential.

After 1922, the Society's trading situation improved. By 1925, financial stability returned and sales and capital increased. Debts were reduced and a bank overdraft of £450 was converted to a balance of nearly £15,000.[24] Although the dividend paid was low by historic standards it rose to 1/2d, which was considered encouraging, taking into account the depressed state of the coal trade. In what was to prove a forlorn hope, the *Co-operative News* said that 'provided there are no more industrial disputes in the area, and no more closing of collieries, the Society should soon be doing as much trade as at the height of the boom period of 1919 and 1920.'[25] Hazell's foresight about needing to prepare for the worst was to prove more accurate.

Hazell and the CWS

Hazell was an inveterate attender of co-operative events, conferences and district meetings. There he met and studied delegates from other retail societies in South Wales to learn from them, as he had members of the Ynysybwl Society Board of Management in his early years. Hazell attended the Co-operative Congress for the first time as a YCS delegate in Liverpool in 1918, but he did not speak in the debates. He regularly attended the CWS South Wales Division meetings in Cardiff, where Blaina and Cwmbach were amongst the 'big noises'. He listened to and learned from an older generation of CWS Directors including Hazell's hero (Sir) Thomas Allen of Blaina and later Aneurin Davies of Aberdare. He said that he became a 'good listener', and occasionally took part in discussion. However reports of the meetings indicate that Hazell quickly gained the necessary confidence to ask questions and made interjections where his keen sense of humour was often apparent.[26] Around a hundred delegates from over 50 societies regularly questioned

CWS Directors which could last for an hour and seem closer to an interrogation.

Hazell's early relationship with the CWS was neatly captured in an article called 'A Democratic Romance'. He recalled encountering 'a friend in another democratic movement' en route to the CWS quarterly meeting, and was 'twitted' about spending a lovely spring day considering the CWS report and balance sheet. Overly eloquently, he described how '66 years [of CWS] democracy in action has made romance into history and history into romance' during which period CWS trade had risen from £50,000 in 1864 to over £59 million. Hazell explained that in eight regional centres across the country, the operation and working of co-operative factories (amongst them shirts made in Cardiff), mills, mines, convalescent homes, health insurance, banks and exports, tea estates and international supply chains, amongst others, were considered. Trades that were experiencing economic difficulty were monitored closely and reports received on co-operative publishing ventures, including the *Wheatsheaf*, which went to 900,000 homes each month. The provision of health insurance – a sphere 'previously so exclusively capitalist in ownership and outlook' – sat alongside the Bank whose £725 million turnover made them all collective millionaires. As Hazell analysed the work of the CWS he observed 'All aspects of your new social order come under one or other of these headings.'[27] As the YCS had shares in the CWS, held its money in the CWS bank and used products produced by CWS businesses, such meetings were central to the Society's interest. In this overly positive account Hazell did not address the tensions that were inherent in the relationship between local independent societies and the CWS with its national agenda, which would become far more evident during the coming years.[28]

This was a movement with a consciously internationalist perspective. In October 1925, delegates asked questions on what was, for the labour movement, the politically significant issue of wheat imports from revolutionary Russia. Questions were also asked about labour conditions in the tea plantations of Ceylon and India, including hours of labour, weekly or monthly wages per man, woman and child and the age limits for children leaving education to work. A year earlier, Hazell's question about flour supply was answered by a CWS Director, in terms of monitoring the grain markets of the United States and Canada. As the Ynysybwl Society owned shares in the co-operative businesses about which questions were being asked, there was a direct link between the consumers of Ynysybwl and the producers of North America, Asia and Soviet Union. It was unavoidable to feel part of an international movement, as well as realising they were subject to the vagaries of international markets. These complementary local, national and international activities were seen by Hazell as essential to the building of the Co-operative Commonwealth. It is interesting that in his 'hardening thirties' and 'dogmatic forties' he could acknowledge that his relationship with the CWS was a romantic one. In spite of a series of battles, looking back in November 1940, after 25 years of involvement, he would still say that his favourite co-operative meetings were those of the CWS.[29]

Other co-operative meetings could be less rewarding. Hazell attended the 1926 Belfast Congress and was unenamoured with the way Congress functioned. In a critique addressing what he described as 'the taboo' of the organisation of the Co-operative Congress itself, he wondered 'whether the crowded Congress was really conducive to good business or not'? His harshly-worded article described the conference as unwieldy, with more than twice the numbers of the national parliament. As a result only the first two or three rows of delegates were able to hear what was being said by some speakers. He called for smaller delegations from each society and for the rules to be revised accordingly.

Some delegates, he suggested, were more interested in attending the next conference than in the co-operative mission and taking an ever wider swipe he wrote that 'personal ambitions, ideas of Congress as a joy-ride, a seaside trip, or a cheap means of annual holidays, must be put aside in the interest of national co-operative well-being.'[30] Such criticisms were untypical of Hazell's writing and displayed the impatience of a young man wanting radical change quickly. He also anticipated a 'degeneracy' of Congress, coinciding with the rise of what he called 'disruptive and subversive sections within our commonwealth' although he did not make clear whether that meant members of the Communist Party. While Hazell supported Russia after the revolution, he did not subsequently respond to its magnetic pull, much less that of its Party. As with the co-operative movement more generally, in relation to political economy Hazell's compass pointed towards Rochdale, not Moscow. As he said, 'Singing the "Internationale" is all right, friend, but here is practical work, even to hands in pockets'.[31]

Hazell the Writer

In 1917, during convalescence from pneumonia, Hazell wrote his first contribution for the *Co-operative News*.[32] His earliest traced attributed articles appear in 1922 in the *Co-operative News*, *The Producer* and the *Colliery Workers Magazine*. From the beginning, his writing addressed large contemporary themes and displayed capacity and confidence. His published pieces were tightly argued, punchy, and showed clarity and sharpness.

In May 1922 he wrote the first of countless articles over decades on the principles and practice, strengths and weaknesses of co-operation. He identified co-operation as a counter to 'generations of unrestricted individualism' and 'insidious persuasions of the private trader and profit seeker'. He argued that, as well as trade, the movement must meet to share conversations, music and song and he suggested a national co-operative calendar with festivals throughout the year to include dates to commemorate Robert Owen, Holyoake and Mitchell, as the Labour Party did with Keir Hardie. The calendar would include the commemoration of May Day with the rest of the labour movement, a women's co-operative day, an international co-operative day, as well as an annual educational rally.[33] He called for an intense missionary spirit to build the 'State within a State' as the movement was sometimes described. Finally, he called for a breaking down of the divisions between committees and officials on one hand and employees and members on the other 'all duly partitioned off and labelled accordingly'. He described 'these artificial barriers which almost amount to a caste system in our midst', and called for them to be ended.

Hazell wrote about the environment as early as April 1923 in *The Colliery Workers' Magazine*. Referring to one of Robert Owen's favourite themes 'environment' being 'the lesson of the hour', he wrote:

> Down in the valley, the Collieries dominate with an overpowering oppressiveness, everything and everybody. Their dusts smother, their noises deafen, their clouds of smoke and steam pollute; they bring home vividly a symbol of that industrialism that Owen tried in vain to curb; monsters whom humanising legislation in the shape of the Mines Act has failed to tame: so much for the environment of the valley.[34]

He contrasted this with the hillsides.

> But 15 minutes walk has taken us out of the pits; chimney stacks have disappeared; smoke and steam is passed. Eargate no longer records the hoot of locomotive and rumble of wagons, and we leave the last of the miners' cottages behind us.
>
> Nature now dominates all – the rough grazing fields around us, heather, fern, rock, and spring above us, hill and dale, with an occasional farmhouse in the distance.

However, Hazell understood environment both in its physical dimension and in the way that it shaped circumstances. The hilltops, he said, put 'industrialism in true proportions' and that from there 'the narrow outlook of the valley' could be seen in perspective. From that viewpoint, steel and coal no longer overawed, but were, instead, servants. He also gained an agricultural perspective from the hilltops: 'we no longer see sense in men growing flowers and vegetables on ashtips and quarry heaps.' He said while various remedies, including communism, guild socialism, co-operation, Whitley Councils, and industrial courts, fired the imagination, he thought it was necessary to look at the disease rather than possible remedies and wondered whether the relationship between "master and man" could ever succeed in the narrowness of the valley. He pointed to the environment itself as shaping attitudes and relations for 'shadows are there, [in the narrowness of the valley] and suspicion points to shadows as hiding places for those lurking things that distort our judgement and prevent frankness and sincerity between us'. Minds were, he said, more open on the tops of the hills.[35] These were remarkable insights for a comparatively young man who, while immersed in the daily arm-wrestle with colliery managers and company over pay and conditions, had the capacity to detach himself from the immediate and adopt a panoramic view. He maintained an awareness of his environment throughout his life, returning to the theme regularly until the late 1950s.

Another early telling article of Hazell was published in September 1923 entitled 'No Afterthought: No Side Show. Women's Representation Must Be Increased'. Acknowledging pride in the Ynysybwl Board having two women members, he argued for equality for women in the co-operative movement saying:

> ...a Co-operative Society managed entirely by men, lacking
> the woman's point of view and the feminine outlook, will be a

one-sided, ill-balanced affair; and where co-operation between the sexes is lacking there cannot be fullness of purpose in our co-operation for trade and commerce.

...co-operators have always vaunted the "equal citizenship" to obtain in our movement, i.e. one vote for each member regardless of sex, and a voice to influence other votes, with all other privileges and responsibilities of membership... if we wish to keep the lead we had in the early days we must increase women's representation on all our co-operative bodies.[36]

Although Hazell's language would now appear archaic, he had a gender perspective, which recognised that a woman's view was different from that of men, was of value in itself and needed to be incorporated more fully across the movement. Even so, the representation of women within the Ynysybwl Society was far from ideal and equality within the movement would be difficult while male heads of household could hold the family's vote.

The following year, Hazell wrote a powerful essay against war to coincide with Anti-War Sunday in which he said that he had heard the comment used from a Sunday afternoon pulpit: 'Suppose another war should break out'. He cautioned against the way that such thoughts could unconsciously enter into people's thought and speech 'in a slipshod[,] careless, fatalistic fashion'. In an outpouring quite unlike his other writings he referred to the 'horrible, tremendous, appalling power of mob hatred, ultra-nationalism, and imperialistic exploitation, the unthinking jingoism of the war crowd. What a motive power! Yes a veritable power-house of monstrous ill-will!'[37]

In May 1925 Hazell questioned where the Co-operative Movement should stand in relation to the Empire, arguing that in the spirit of internationalism 'Co-operators today can brush aside the old theories of Empire... and co-operators can affirm their faith in[,] and adherence to, a Co-operative Commonwealth of Nations.' He said that the 20th Century had to be built through great movements which were 'international in scope and character'. Internationalism, he said, was the only means of securing the unity of mankind, and, of course, that should be built through the co-operative movement. He contrasted what he described as military and trading supermen who 'control and shape, the destinies of Empire' with the ordinary men and women who were building the co-operative movement. In a world still seared by war, the imaginary lines drawn on maps that represented national boundaries stood in the way of social progress 'keeping the peoples apart, making all nations potential enemies...'.[38] Hazell would return regularly to the issues of environment, gender, the threat of war and the barriers created by national boundaries for a further three decades.

Hazell wrote as he lived, as co-operator, miner or trades unionist, though at this stage he confined his subjects to his public life. In 1923, following the resignation of W R John, Hazell was unanimously selected as the Labour candidate, and was elected subsequently as Councillor for Ynysybwl on the Mountain Ash Urban District Council. He attended his first meeting on 6 November 1923 and took his place on various committees including some of the most important: Housing, Education, Sanitary and Public Health, and Finance and General Purposes. A year after being elected he was writing articles on his role as a local councillor. In order to improve his writing, Hazell sought the views of others, such as local government officers, on what to publish and they mentored him in the intricacies of council and educational matters. Hazell said that in order to write he read and re-read to gain knowledge, and then he thought and thought hard. During this early period, W S Collins of Cardiff – a 'journalist with ideals'[39] – became an 'unpaid tutor' to Hazell. As Collins was the *Co-operative News'* correspondent in South Wales, Hazell did not write about South Wales matters for the paper.

At the time of Hazell's election control of the Council was contested: Labour was far from being the dominant party.

Other councillors included two local tradesmen, who were very suspicious of any active co-operator (although Hazell said they could tolerate trades unionists for they did not threaten their establishments as did co-operative societies), two colliery officials and the land-agent of Lord Aberdare's estate, as well as a miners' agent, a few checkweighers, including George Hall, who was a councillor, and recently elected MP. In 1924, 26-year-old Jack Bailey, from Miskin, Mountain Ash, who would later rise to national prominence as Secretary of the Co-operative Party, was also elected as a Labour Councillor to the Mountain Ash UDC.[40]

In *The Colliery Workers' Magazine*, the journal of the SWMF, Hazell wrote a series of articles about his daily experience as a Labour councillor and as a miner. There he used his everyday experience to write down his own credo, criticise the failure of capitalism, whether through public health, educational provision or meat regulations to build up a body of evidence on the conditions in the valleys. In October 1924, he wrote a powerful, at times bitter, piece based on the School Medical Officer's Report for 1923, which had been considered by the Council's Education Committee, relating it to broader discussions of capital punishment that were being considered. Looking at the conditions within which people lived, he referred to 'sentences of death that are passed on a wholesale scale every day, by reason of the system under which they live', while highly respectable members of society did not give it a passing thought. He argued that it was just as wrong to take away 20 or 30 years of life as to take away life itself. He questioned why a miner's life expectancy should be 45 years. He said that the Miners' Federation should have as a basic principle of its objects that 'the miner, his wife, and his children' should be able to live as long and as happy and useful a life as the 'rest of the human family''. This would be achieved through exorcising 'that cruelest demon in modern history "Economic Circumstances"'. For Hazell:

Infants, as yet unborn, that through bad housing, malnutrition, want of sufficient or suitable clothing, are doomed to a few brief months of existence. Mothers, who by the overwork of a Miner's home, and the never-ending struggle to make ends meet, are condemned to an early grave without any formalities, such as trial by jury, and judge in black cap.[41]

He noted that 1500 of 1594 children attended by the school dentist suffered disease, which he described as 'a worse indictment of Capitalism than can be found in any Socialist literature' and said, more generally, that the Geddes public expenditure cuts were resulting in 'massacres of the innocent.' He said councillors' work on committees needed more time to deal with important work, like School Medical Officer's Reports rather than 'the continual rush from mine, railway and checkweigher's cabin'.[42]

In November 1925, in an article on meat regulations, he argued for improved public health, saying that 'the hundreds of thousands of pounds that have been spent in building sanatoriums, hospitals, etc., and in training nurses and doctors, should have been spent in the prevention of these diseases that threaten to decimate and ultimately exterminate the white races of the world.' He saw tuberculosis and cancer as being a 'retribution which has overtaken us as a result of the enthronement of private enterprise and production or profit.' He described bread being produced and cattle slaughtered in insanitary conditions and food prepared and packed 'in factories whose circumstances absolutely invite contamination and filth.' He said those things had been allowed by the current and previous generation 'in the name of private enterprise and individual gain; and we are reaping a terrible harvest.' He pointed out that co-operative slaughter houses were better structures with better sanitation than private ones but there was not one operated by the state. Hazell continued 'God speed' the time when the community would insist on public abattoirs in every town. Finally, he saw such conditions as a reason for achieving increased Labour representation in Parliament and on local bodies as they would sustain efforts towards 'Healthy Homes, Healthy People, and Healthy Minds.'[43]

Hazell believed that all Labour councillors felt that the most interesting and inspiring part of their role was their work in the Education Committee. He wrote that, in spite of economic circumstances, they were seeking to make available the best educational opportunities 'that we remember with a sigh were never placed within our reach when we attended school'. He spelled out the benefits of children coming to school fed instead of hungry and receiving medical attention, justifying educational and other expenditure on moral, economic and social grounds. He wrote of the 'universally detested' Circular 1371 which proposed to cut the national grant to local education authorities, as a betrayal of pupils, teachers and education authorities. Children's future prospects would be 'irreparably injured'. The burden would shift to local ratepayers of the already necessitous areas, instead of being borne by national taxation. 'Of course, the wealthy classes will still be able to send their boys and girls to the best private schools and colleges, with the usual travel-tour round the world to complete their "polish."'[44]

Hazell wrote for the *Colliery Workers Magazine* from 1923 to 1927, appearing alongside Mark Starr who worked in nearby Mynachdy Colliery and who rose to prominence as an adult educator. Hazell's writings showed an early interest in history and the lessons that the past could hold for the present and future. In July 1924, his article 'A Page of Mining History' looked back on the state of slavery or bondage of Scottish miners in the late 18th Century. He praised the 'rebels, agitators, stirrers up of strife' who had achieved 'the freedom of the coal slaves', in whose memory no statues had been erected, while 'orthodox historians' had 'passed them by in silence'. He continued

We can keep alive the spirit of rebellion so long as there is a slave to set free; let us be proud of the name of agitator while there is yet a single oppression to agitate against. Our Cenotaph, our Memorial, to the Pioneers of Progress, must consist of a living, growing army of men and women determined to further social justice.'

He finished by referring to the contemporary situation arguing: 'It is but a small thing after all, to ask of the Miners of South Wales, to be true to their Federation, and in so doing, to be true to themselves.'[45] Hazell's commitment to the Miners' Federation was demonstrated in an article where he saw obtaining 100 per cent union membership as part of 'attaining industrial justice under a new social system' and achieving a full life. Accomplishments gained as a musician, a 'fine amateur gardener', or as a Christian were insufficient on their own and needed to be complemented by 'our movements' – trades union, labour and co-operative.'[46]

In the summer of 1925, Hazell suffered ill health and a vote of sympathy was passed by the lodge. A week later the lodge granted him £5, saying that 'owing to his serious illness' he was likely to be out of work for a long period. Six weeks later lodge officers supported Hazell's application for admittance to Talygarn Convalescent Home, an action approved at the next general meeting, although possibly not without some dissent. While the nature of his illness is unknown, he is likely to have been suffering from tuberculosis. It is almost certain that he was later admitted to Cefn Mably sanatorium, as he recalled resting in a convalescent home in St Mellons, just outside Newport, after a distressing illness.[47] One of these two periods of convalescence was probably the nine months when he was not on the YCS Board, which was the only period he was not a member between 1915 and 1964.

The General Strike and Miners' Lockout
In May 1926, for the second time in five years, the miners were locked out of the pits as colliery companies sought to reduce

wages and increase hours of work. However, unlike in 1921, other unions supported the miners in a General Strike which was solid. A joint strike committee was set up in Ynysybwl comprising representatives of Lady Windsor Lodge, Mynachdy Lodge and local representatives of the National Union of Railwaymen. The Committee, which met every morning and controlled transport locally, was linked to the Pontypridd Central [Strike] Committee, which granted permits to YCS to deliver food. A protest meeting of miners' wives was held. As the situation intensified, on 7 May all members of the Mountain Ash UDC, including Hazell, were appointed to the Local Coal Emergency Special Committee and to the Food Committee. However, after nine days the TUC General Council lost its nerve and ended the General Strike. The authority which had been assumed by trades unionists locally was not easily relinquished and in mid-May the Lady Windsor Lodge was still controlling some traffic to Pontypridd.[48]

The collapse of the General Strike changed the nature of the dispute as the miners were left to fight alone. Lodge business focussed on relief for distress and strike pay. With a long struggle in prospect YCS directors could not afford to imperil the Society during the prolonged industrial struggle that was evidently ahead. The generous credit policy adopted towards the miners in the 1921 lockout could not be repeated in 1926. The Society therefore operated a limited credit system dependent upon members bringing to the stores food vouchers issued by the Board of Guardians; in total £20,000 of support was provided.[49]

The YCS also took the central role in organising 14 communal food centres under the direct supervision of O R Jones, the Society's General Manager, supported by the staff of the Society with voluntary assistance from miners. Funded by the MFGB and other organisations set up to assist the struggle, the food centres were so successful that the YCS and Jones were publicly thanked by the Pontypridd District of Miners for the excellent arrangements.[50]

Surprisingly, the titanic industrial conflicts of 1921 and 1926 received comparatively little attention in *The Gleaming Vision*. Even though the General Strike was the biggest industrial conflict in British history, and YCS played a significant role in both lockouts, Hazell chose not to elaborate in the Society's history. However, he picked up aspects elsewhere.

Hazell described the 1926 lockout as 'seven lean, bitter, months'[51] and various measures were taken in the community to help with distress. A fish market was established and an entertainment committee held free concerts at the Hall. The Ynysybwl co-operative boot repair centre was set up in the Institute, with Hazell serving on its committee and a School Children's Boot Fund Committee was established by the Council. Over 1000 pairs of children's and adults' boots and shoes were repaired, with leather provided by the Society of Friends. The Institute was asked in May to use their funds for relief and in October the lodge sent a delegation asking the Institute to loan £200. Numerous meetings took place with 'a galaxy of speakers from all over the coalfield'.[52] When the Board of Guardians stopped relief for children of the unemployed in Ynysybwl, Hazell addressed a mass meeting protesting against the Guardians' action. When the Prime Minister told the United States that there was no distress amongst the miners in Britain, Mountain Ash UDC passed a resolution condemning him; this showed the extent to which the Council had changed in a few years – only two councillors voted against.[53]

As the dispute dragged on, according to Hazell, 'men tightened their belts and cursed inwardly – but were loyal to their cause.'[54] While this was mainly true at Lady Windsor Colliery, it was not so in Mynachdy drift mine, at the top of the village, where some men returned to work in July. Picketing had little effect, so a joint lodge meeting was held on 16 August under police supervision. When the police banned a second meeting, it was held anyway at short notice on the Welfare Ground. A crowd of people then went to the Old Village, near the Mynachdy Level, where some Mynachdy workers lived and an altercation took place. With tensions rising as more men returned, Hazell was one of 18 men asked by the Lady Windsor Lodge to picket Mynachdy. The first man returned to work in Lady Windsor in August. As late as mid-November the resistance of the Ynysybwl men was clear when, after being locked out for over six months, approximately 600 rejected the terms offered against 14 who voted to accept.[55] When the dispute ended on 31 November only 40 men had returned to work.

Overall, the extent of disturbances was limited compared with other places. One 'scab' was assaulted on his way to work, resulting in one man being sent to prison for three months' hard labour. The disturbance in the Old Village resulted in five men appearing in Swansea Assizes in February 1927. When extra police were sent to the area towards the end of the lockout, Hazell moved a resolution at the Council meeting, protesting that extra police were 'quite uncalled for and unnecessary', and letters were sent to the Prime Minister, Home Secretary, local MP and Chief Constable of Glamorgan. An amendment that no action be taken, moved by John Christopher and seconded by Col Morgan Morgan, two councillors who traditionally represented the interests of capital, received only their votes, all others including Hazell voting for the resolution.[56] A reply from Lt Col Sir Rhys Williams, Chairman of the Standing Joint Committee of Glamorgan, referred to recent occurrences at Abercwmboi, whereupon councillors instructed the Clerk to reply that 'Abercwmboi is not within this Council's urban area, and that there have been no riots in this area nor are there likely to be any.'[57] The six-month lockout ended with the defeat of the miners – the second in five years – and there was enduring bitterness on both sides.

Ideological divisions on the Council, which were evident during the lockout, became increasingly stark. Overturning the traditional basis of seniority for electing chairs of committees, they now became determined along class lines. When the War Office sought permission to show films to Territorial soldiers, only the two interests of 'capital' voted in favour. Likewise, Aberdare & District Chamber of Trade's call for the Council to support the continuation of the post of High Constable was defeated by nine votes to three, while the Authority agreed to close its schools to celebrate May Day.[58]

After the end of the lockout Hazell returned to the lodge committee[59] and months later wrote 'Strictly Non-Political' which addressed the shallowness of the argument of separating trades union activity from politics and, specifically, keeping politics out of the South Wales Miners' Federation. Written in response to the founding of a breakaway Industrial or 'Non-Political' union, he parodied the situation of how a metaphorical non-pol 'Dai', working a non-pol shift, found himself unable to use safety lamps, scowled at the pitman who had just inspected the shaft, and objected to being searched for matches. Dai found himself unable to function with non-pol purity, as he looked for roof support and needed medical attention and a host of other provisions, which all came through Acts of Parliament. Dai realised that it was impossible to live a non-political life, and so paid his Federation political levy, and requested of the writer that his story be dedicated to the new Non-Political Industrial Union of South Wales. Hazell's humour ended on a serious note, though, with a call to 'Let us have more and more political and industrial action in order to make life more liveable for the workers of our land.'[60] Two decades later, during the Second World War, when industrial action was seen as unpatriotic, Hazell would defend unofficial strikes, highlighting the importance of strikes in bringing emancipation and progress.

The 1921 and 1926 lockouts caused a deep reflection by Hazell and within YCS. Hazell believed that the co-operative societies in South Wales gave all they had in the lockouts and even mortgaged their future prospects to see it through.[61] He recounted the difficulties of running a co-operative business. Such were the strains that, after 1926, YCS:

> felt itself unable to withstand the pressure for credit by those whose capital had been exhausted. After all, many of these people had been regular customers all their lives, and the Society had the benefit of their trading. [62]

From 1920 to 1930, while membership and capital stood still, the Society's overall trade fell. Therefore, following the success of its hire purchase scheme for furniture in 1928, YCS set up a Mutuality Club, which allowed repayment over 20 weeks.[63] While such credit schemes went against the basic co-operative principles established by the Rochdale Pioneers, and had previously been opposed by Hazell, YCS felt it had no other option because of 'the methods adopted by our competitors, the continuously rising standard of living, with the luxury of yesteryear tending to become the necessity of today, modern furnishing methods and the increasing realisation by the masses of the possibilities of the use of credit.'[64] As well as credit-based schemes, YCS operated a number of clubs which were not credit based for purchasers of limited means. Ynysybwl Society also deferred members' debts, allowing them to repay the thousands of pounds they owed when better times returned. Hazell said it was not until the rearmament programme of 1938[65] that economic recovery allowed people individually and collectively to get back onto their feet and pay off the burden of debt built up over more than a decade.

Hazell saw it thus:

without the co-operative societies of the area – the help and credit they gave to countless families, and the dividends accumulated for decades, together with the habits of thrift which co-operation had inculcated – black despair would have descended upon many homes and families before the 1920s were out.'[66]

Although under economic pressure, YCS continued to deliver its extensive educational and cultural activities. The extent of the provision can be gauged from a report in 1926 which said that, for the previous 12 years, as many as 1,000 children and youths attended the classes in any one session and, for that year, 10 junior and eight intermediate classes were organised. Several adult classes were run every winter and many students gained scholarships to the Co-operative Union Summer School. The Junior Choir had more members than could be accommodated and some had to wait for vacancies to occur before they could be absorbed. A series of public meetings organised by the Education Committee including Mrs Bedhall, National President of WCG, as well as a weekend school held at YMCA Pontypridd at which Professor Hall spoke. Hazell chaired the Saturday evening session on 'Trusts, Combines and Cartels'. Such events were regular, and the Rt Hon A V Alexander, First Lord of the Admiralty in the Labour Government, and the foremost protagonist for co-operation in Parliament, spoke on 'Co-operation' at a crowded meeting in the Workmen's Hall.[67] A Co-operative Men's Guild existed and in 1929 it was reported that 'another' branch of the Guild had been formed in Treforest.[68] The Society's educational and cultural roles and its publication of the local edition of the *Wheatsheaf*, which was produced monthly for decades, received scant mention in the *Gleaming Vision*, where Hazell focused on the business aspects of the Society. Such absences are surprising, particularly as Hazell was so actively involved in their delivery and made statements at various times about co-operative life and culture being as important as trading.

Family Affairs

When Hazell's niece Marjorie (Fred's daughter) visited the family around 1928, she considered the family situation to be 'grim'. Marjorie was aware that Deborah Elizabeth – 'a lovely, lovely person' – who worked hard for her family and husband exerted herself to boil water for when Hazell came home and bathed in the kitchen. It was also obvious that Hazell loved his wife very much. Although the physical demands of a woman's life who had already borne six children were taking their toll, at the time of Marjorie's visit it had not yet become apparent that Deborah Elizabeth was ill.[69] Later, with Deborah Elizabeth ailing and Lilian away training as a nurse, much of the domestic burden fell to Ivy.

The demands of household chores eased somewhat when, in January 1931, one of the earliest pithead baths in South Wales was opened at Lady Windsor Colliery. At least preparing Hazell's bath was one burden that the women of the household were now spared. The pithead baths opened more than a decade after Hazell had moved the resolution proposing them in 1920. The 'hostile feeling' against them, which existed amongst the men when he first made the proposal, was gradually overcome and Hazell marked the opening of the baths with an article in the *Ocean and National Magazine*, the house journal of the Ocean Colliery Company.

> For once unanimity had been reached at Ynysybwl. This much-to-be desired state – rare as rubies and fine gold – has been actually and positively achieved at Lady Windsor.[70]

Pointing to the consensus achieved, he wondered if it might be possible to also reach 'unanimity and harmony' in other matters connected with the coal industry?[71]

Humorously, Hazell listed the impact of the baths, such as at YCS where sales of scrubbing brushes were down by 75%, although padlocks sales had gone up by 500%. More sharply, he mixed humour and bitterness, saying that the hardest hit would be the local undertakers 'For their most lucrative trade has been for... "donkey's years" the providing of funerals for those prematurely worn out women who used to lift those heavy tubs, carry those murderous boilers, full of water, and build those big fires to boil water for, perhaps, four or five men.'[72] Shortly afterwards his wife, Deborah Elizabeth, would become another of those prematurely worn-out women.

Into The Dark Years: Relieving Distress

The 1926 lockout was followed by a marked economic downturn resulting in unemployment and short time working. Hazell described the post-1926 experience in the South Wales valleys as an industrial revolution in reverse gear.

The coalfield's difficult economic circumstances seeped through to every institution in the community. In 1929, Hazell presented the annual report and balance sheet of the Institute to its AGM, regretting that 'poundage' continued to be disappointing, due to low wages. However, he said there was still a good working balance in the bank and cinema and billiard tables were working well. There was a lack of support for the lecture series, and a fear that lectures in Welsh would have to be abandoned due to 'a lack of appreciation'. By 1933, the Institute's economic position had deteriorated and Hazell reported that poundage was not covering the expenses of running the Hall, although a recent innovation whereby the unemployed were given all the privileges of the Institute for 1d per week was a great success. Furthermore, Hazell secured a large number of valuable books from Manchester City Libraries (presumably through co-operative movement connections) and nearly 11,000 books were issued in the year. With the Institute struggling, committee members had not claimed any fees in the last year. Increasingly novel ways were sought to raise money for struggling voluntary organisations. At a time when fundraising was essential but difficult, in 1932 Hazell played the role of counsel for the claimants in a Dunmow Flitch trial, in Ynysybwl, organised to support the Cardiff Infirmary and Pontypridd Hospital.[73]

Hazell was involved in various arrangements to relieve distress. In 1928, he joined the Pontypridd Committee of the Lord Mayor's Distress Fund for Miners. A few months later, on 4 December 1928, a special meeting of the Council was called on how to respond to the closure of Nixon's Collieries in Mountain Ash. As the Church of St Martin's-in-the-Fields was supporting certain parishes in the valley, but not other areas including Abercynon, Penrhiwceiber or Ynysybwl, the Society of Friends was approached about assuming responsibility for a part of the valley and a Central Fund was established to act as an 'umbrella' and cover the whole of the district. The Friends were given use of the Council Chamber for work with those with allotments and free use of schools to distribute seeds to allotment holders. William Noble, the Quaker, spoke to the Council's Sanitary and Public Health Committee on a scheme in Miskin Recreation Grounds for single unemployed men who otherwise received no form of assistance. While such arrangements were aimed at ameliorating problems rather than addressing root causes, they earned Hazell's enduring respect.[74]

While Hazell was involved through local government in relieving distress, early on the co-operative movement was excluded from national structures. This was surprising for, as the *Co-operative News* pointed out, no-one had done as much to support the miners via loans or grants in the previous eight years as the co-operative movement.[75] Conditions in the coalfield meant that Hazell's involvement in organising relief was long-term. When a new Coalfields Distress Committee (including the Lord Mayor's Fund) was set up Hazell was chosen to serve on it as one of the UDC's representatives.

In a community almost literally on its uppers, a boot fund provided by the Coalfields Distress Committee was administered by the Director of Education. Lists were produced of those insufficiently clad or had 'bad footgear' and 240 children were provided with new boots. Such were levels of deprivation that in December 1936, when Lord Portal gave £2,500 for new boots of children in distressed areas, the Education Committee asked if its share of over £100 could be used to repair boots rather than buy new ones to make it stretch further.[76]

Local economic circumstances can be measured by the number of working days lost at the pit. Over 60 days were lost at Lady Windsor Colliery in 1930 and 1931. In 1932, 132 working days, including 16 full weeks, were lost and in 1933 and 1934 over 100 days, including 12 full weeks. In 1935, 61 days were lost, including 10 full weeks.[77] The population of Ynysybwl, down to 4,849 in 1931 from 5,133 in 1921, continued to fall throughout the 1930s as short-time working and unemployment took their toll. *The Gleaming Vision* did not give extensive consideration to the years of worst privation from 1927 to the Second World War, though Hazell's observations were biting. Describing them as 'orphans of a pitiless economic blizzard', Hazell recounted how thousands of good YCS members were 'torn by the roots from their life-long environment and friends; their savings long ago exhausted, and their resources of clothing down to the barest minimum'.[78] In 1953 he described the inter-war years as a period of 'social hell, public distress and domestic agony' for a population 'bowed down by hopelessness, despair and let it now be said real demoralisation'.[79]

In November 1932 Hazell wrote to Lilian:

> There has been no work for a fortnight, and no prospects at present. It will be a very poor Xmas for Ynysybwl this year I am afraid. The Ocean Co. are dismissing hundreds of men at most of their pits now but so far, nothing has transpired at Lady Windsor, only rumours.[80]

The Hazells were short of money. Hazell commented that, with the cold weather, they had to have a fire in the kitchen 'and we have a coal and wood problem, among other problems'. Hazell kept a garden in his '"spare" time' of which he 'planted every inch' as a means of helping make ends meet.[81]

Hazell the Councillor

When Hazell was elected chair of the Mountain Ash UDC in 1930, a biographical profile was published in the *Ocean and National Magazine* which described Hazell as

> One of the level-headed type of democratic representatives [whose] honesty and integrity command the respect of those holding different views. His desire to improve the lot of his fellow-men is unquestioned, and he has laboured consistently to secure the end in view.[82]

It said that as the Labour candidate he had been returned unopposed in local council elections since 1923. On an earlier occasion, a fellow miner had written that 'the general feeling is that it would be difficult to find a better representative throughout the whole area.'[83] He was described as 'bringing into all spheres of his activity a rare and conspicuous saneness of judgement,'[84] qualities which he would also have brought to his role as a magistrate.[85]

During his first 15 years as a councillor, Hazell and the Council were largely on the defensive, trying to ameliorate the difficulties that befell them. The suffering of the community was evident in multiple ways and the scale and immediacy of issues confronted by the local authority was enormous.

The Council was responsible for the work of the Medical Officer for Health. One smallpox epidemic was so extensive that the Cefnpennar smallpox hospital was full to overflowing and a former school building had to be brought into service.[86] A report from the School Medical Officer (SMO) on malnutrition among schoolchildren said 'many of our people are nearing the poverty line and are fast becoming unable to purchase the necessary quantity and quality of food to ward off malnutrition.' The SMO said it was his duty to 'prevent our children reaching this stage of semistarvation…' and 'the only way I can suggest of preventing such a catastrophe' is by giving a hot meal to all children identified as necessitous. The Education Committee agreed and Hazell, as its Chairman, oversaw the machinery for delivering relief, with schools used for relief distribution meetings. In October 1929, 195 scholars were determined to be suffering from malnutrition. The following year, 450 were considered necessitous cases and 589 were provided with milk at school. Quarterly reports confirmed that the great majority showed considerable improvement as a result of the Council's intervention. When a stoppage in the coal industry occurred in 1931, the Council looked to provide milk and meals to necessitous children on Saturdays and Sundays.[87]

There was no doubting the value of Hazell's role of local councillor – it allowed him to serve those in greatest need. Hazell chaired Council meetings on constructing a new trunk sewer as a major scheme to provide work for the unemployed and the Council sought to relieve unemployment by building a bathing pool for Ynysybwl and repairing or building local roads. He regularly appeared on the platform at the Workmen's Hall giving public feedback on his work. In one meeting there was a protest against the Surveyor appointing one person permanently rather than using unemployed men in relays as was agreed by the Council. The challenge of housing was always a daunting one for Hazell. In 1931, he repeated his call for a housing policy within the district, as his first appeal had not been taken up. He complemented his argument by writing an article on slum clearance.[88] Council business was often a rearguard action to offset economic and social decline and try and maintain elements of social justice in a community increasingly under siege.

The respect in which Hazell was held could allow him to

make reasoned argument for progressive positions. Hazell often led or supported campaigns through the committee structure of the Council to seek to make incremental – but potentially far-reaching – social improvements. Two maternal and child health issues exemplified what might be achieved by pushing at social boundaries. When a letter was received from the Women's Section of the Mountain Ash Labour Party arguing against the rule about non-admittance of unmarried women as patients to the Maternity Ward of the Authority's hospital, (as their care was provided through Poor Law institutions) Hazell was one of the majority who voted for it be rescinded. A year later, Hazell moved the resolution that the Council establish birth control clinics. Within a month the Welsh Board of Health reacted, saying that the Authority had no power to establish birth control clinics, that maternity clinics were to be used for their intended purpose, the health of nursing or expectant mothers, that birth control clinics could only be 'strictly incidental' to the work of the maternity clinics, and that such birth control clinics had to be and could only be for married women or nursing or expectant mothers.[89] While not all campaigns were won, under Labour control the Council explored ways of improving people's lives, or at least offsetting their worsening.

Co-operation

As the Labour Government prepared a Bill to reorganise the coal industry, Hazell wrote an important article in October 1929 entitled 'Is There a Co-operative Solution to the Problems of the Coal Industry?' Looking at the lived experience of miners through their co-operative societies, whether in South Wales, Scotland or Kent, he contrasted what he called 'co-operative democracy in trade and commerce before their very eyes' – with the 'archaic, feudal, and brutal capitalist-owned coal combines which have made and are still busy making, millionaires and paupers…' He was not surprised that there had been a country-wide revolt of miners against coal capitalism and said that the miners' union, which had nurtured and supported the Labour Party, now looked to it 'to do something for their prostrate members'. He argued that the cooperative movement could not afford to ignore this national problem which affected such an important body of consumers as miners and their families. Hazell wrote that in spite of the reference in the Sankey Commission Report of 1919 to 'miners having an effective voice in the direction of the mine' and the Samuel Commission of 1926 referring to reorganisation including co-operative selling, he said that up to then:

> these words have only been abused in connection with King Coal.
> There has been a spurious ring about them. '"Co-operation in
> industry" has only been a deceitful cloak of dictatorship (and not
> "of the proletariat")! ...'"Industrial peace" meant the peace of a
> stricken and carnage-strewn battlefield!'

He continued: 'There is not an industry extant which calls more loudly and insistently for the application of co-operative methods' and the movement was capable of adding one more industry to those it operated. With bitter and powerful words Hazell said more efficiency and output could be attained with fewer officials if 'co-operation and mutual confidence' were substituted for 'suspicion and slave driving'. He ended with a clarion call:

> Co-operators! You have heard of societies for the prevention of
> cruelty to children – and animals! Will you become a society for
> the prevention of cruelty to miners?[90]

When the Board of the Co-operative Union created a national Co-operative Coal Trade Association (CCTA), in 1931, Hazell was one of the eight men elected to be on its Western Section, on which he stayed throughout the 1930s. As its chair in 1932-3 Hazell joined the national executive of the CCTA.[91]

This allowed him to use his experience of working in the coal industry within the structures of the co-operative movement. He saw how the coal industry and coal sales operated across the country, the processes by which prices were set and the wariness and friction that existed between the co-operative movement and private traders. Membership of the national executive also gave Hazell access to discussions with the Government's Mines Department as well as meeting regularly with the highest people in the co-operative movement. Hazell's experience of working in the pit for 20 years, plus his views on how co-operation could be introduced to the mining industry, made these valuable fora to make practical, informed contributions.

Perhaps one of the more surprising issues addressed by Hazell in the inter-war years was the despoiling of the natural environment. At a time when unemployment, short time and the means test weighed heavily, Hazell could still raise his eyes to other issues.

> From where I am sitting I can see half a mile of ugly colliery
> rubbish tips – on common land. This land belonged to the people
> of these valleys, but not a 1d piece has come to them as rent
> for the use of this land as tipping ground. Shame on the people
> responsible for this spoliation![92]

This he attributed in part to a previous generation of councillors who had facilitated the defiling of the landscape. It was in contrast to the period before the Great War when, unlike in the Rhondda or Aberdare valleys, the Ynysybwl valley was unspoilt by coal tips. Hazell lauded the Ocean colliery's mining engineer, Edward Jones, who would have regarded it as a personal disgrace to have dumped rubbish on the hillsides when it could be carefully put back 'in the recesses underground from whence the coal had been extracted.'[93] Over decades from 1923 to the late 1950s, Hazell commented on the industrial landscape in the valley where 'the ugly rubbish-tip seemed to dominate all' contrasting it with the view from the mountain top where it was nothing more than 'a spot on this panorama of hill and vale'.[94]

Throughout his life, Hazell attended events of all sorts and at every level within the co-operative movement. For example he would go to a Cardiff Woodcraft Folk meeting to get children interested in a love of the open air and international peace, or preside over the YCS Juvenile Choir's performance of the operetta 'Concordia'. Equally, as an executive member, he would attend the Monmouthshire, Brecon and East Glamorgan District Association of retail societies.[95]

Hazell was also actively engaged in the Western Section's educational activities.[96] He was interested in the process of learning, including content and methodology, suggesting that the pages of the co-operative journal *The Producer* could be used to develop educational tools. Co-operative educationalists could then equip themselves to develop presentations on (for example) business trends and productive and distributive co-operative trading, adding that a well prepared address 'lightened with a few homely illustrations and local references always gets home at a guild meeting.'[97] Indeed, his commitment to educational work through the lodge, institute, chapel and local authority (as well as the co-operative movement) was seemingly without limit. He accepted invitations indiscriminately on all subjects: one talk called 'Echoes of Long Ago', covered local history from the Ice Age! Many of these would later become subjects for his articles. He reported one that did not go down well: having read Henry Ford's book *My Philosophy of Industry* when it was published in 1929, Hazell gave a talk to a Guild on 'Henry Ford the Philosopher', which was frostily received and never repeated.[98]

Thinking, speaking, writing and doing for Hazell were indivisible. In December 1929, he addressed the subject of amalgamation of co-operative societies to which he would return at various points in the coming decades. Hazell opined that moves towards a national society, with a bureaucracy in Manchester or London, would undermine self-reliance and initiative of local officials – 'the locally appointed and controlled man of the Movement' whose contact with the local members and customers were indispensable in 'the domestic economy of Co-operation'.[99] Amalgamation, argued Hazell, was presented as the cure for all difficulties that societies experienced, adding 'there is a danger that the Movement may be stampeded into accepting a policy which is not altogether in its best interests, but is, at the moment, fashionable, and whose opponents are not always so vocal as its supporters.' Hazell felt there was not opposition to amalgamations *per se*, for local amalgamations of societies took place continually. However, that was quite different from 'nationalising' local societies into one large body.

Hazell revisited the subject in 1930, cautioning against amalgamations involving the acquisition of private businesses with 'huge buildings and swollen totals of customers', which would not produce convinced and loyal co-operators. Eighteen months previously he had visited a large society 'a giant compared to any South Wales society' where 'the advantages of large-scale co-operation were strikingly absent'. Comparing it to South Wales he said individual members' purchases were low and in a street of 50 houses there were only three co-operative calls, compared with 25 to 35 calls by the co-operative van of a typical South Wales valley society.[100] Welsh co-operators, he suggested, were far too modest about their achievements, and that South Wales had many 'sound, well managed and financially stable societies, large and small' and the few that could not be included had difficulties dating from 1921 and 1926.[101] He had already opined that in many societies of over 2,000 members the 'spirit of oneness, association and fellowship has almost reached the breaking point'.[102] He argued that 'the type of member' in South Wales was second to none. While he did not elaborate, elsewhere he referred to sales per member in South Wales and the Western Section being only second to Scotland – which he described as 'the acid test of loyalty'.[103]

While Hazell expressed disgruntlement in CWS meetings that its factories only supplied a third of the goods sold by retail societies,[104] he recognised that the CWS was key to the future of co-operation. Quoting Percy Redfern, the historian of the CWS, he agreed that success had been achieved through the support the CWS had given to local societies *without weakening local control and self reliance*.[105] Indeed the support being provided by CWS was sustaining societies in economic difficulty.

Hazell presented a co-operative development programme for South Wales, proposing that CWS and retail societies work together in four co-operative centres of furniture and allied trades, three or fewer pasteurising plants supplying the valleys, and co-ordination in the meat trade. He argued 'if the retail societies and their federated expression – the CWS' moved together then both could benefit. He added: 'True, the process may be, apparently, slower, but it will be surer, financially sounder, and will also leave that local element of democratic control and interest, which is indispensable to co-operation.'[106] However, Hazell was equally clear that small retail societies should not enter the field of production as this was the job of the CWS.[107] Local democracy versus centralised national control was a theme to which Hazell returned both in relation to the nationalised coal industry and in the great co-operative debates of the 1950s.

Involvement in the co-operative movement at a national level required Hazell to make regular trips to Manchester, for which he received an allowance to cover his day job, as well as subsistence for attending meetings.[108] With irregular working in the pit, the extra income helped the strained domestic budget. He found the travelling taxing: 'I have to be in Manchester on Thurs and Fri next – a most weary journey for one with no company,'[109] but such journeys did 'bring in a little grist for the mill'[110] – albeit at personal sacrifice. In May 1933, he reported having attended a meeting in Manchester and he:

> travelled on the night train from Cardiff Thursday night[,] went to a meeting on Friday and travelled back by the midnight train from M/c [Manchester], so losing two nights sleep. The money so saved on hotel etc, came in to help at home. Happily, I do not feel much the worse for these things…

However, there are indications that his conscience may not have been entirely comfortable with the arrangements, as conveyed in his additional, cryptic, statement: 'it is a little relief to think & hope that someone will know & understand these things.'[111] This may relate to negative comments made within his wife's family about his having various sources of money. Compared with other miners Hazell was in a slightly advantageous position in receiving the occasional small amount of expenses for attending meetings of the Council and co-operative movement, as well as the small sums received for articles published in the *Co-operative News*.[112] While this money would have helped ease the immediacy of hardship, particularly during periods of acute adversity, the family was still living in straitened circumstances.

Home Sweet Home?

Reports of Hazell and his family appeared in the *Ocean and National Magazine* over several years. The magazine, which was an official company publication, was a strange combination of technical articles on coal mining mixed with local news from the Company's villages reported by miner-journalists. Hazell was invited to write a Christmas greeting in the magazine in December 1928. His sons' school exams, Lilian's advancement in the nursing profession when she went to train in the Radcliffe Hospital, Oxford in 1929 and family weddings were all recorded in its pages.[113]

Hazell was aspirational for his children and none of his four sons followed their father 'down the pit'. William George, his oldest son (commonly known in his early years as 'Willie' and henceforth described as such to avoid confusion) was successful in his terminal examinations at Pontypridd County School, when it was observed 'for the son of English [speaking] parents to do so well in Welsh is an achievement of which Councillor and Mrs Hazell are naturally proud.'[114] Willie attended the sixth form but did not gain his Higher Certificate. Hazell explained to Lilian:

> The standard is being put very high, and only the very smartest with an "examination temperament" can hope to be successful. However, it is only a temporary check, and there is nothing to worry about, although it is useless to deny that it would have meant a great deal to Willie and us if he had been successful. [115]

This sense of disappointment would not have been lost on Willie. Throughout his life Willie combined a personal sense of failure with a wish not to let his father down. This critical combination undermined Willie, whatever his achievements, until after his father's death decades later. The sacrifices made in the Hazell household to pay for the children's education added a further burden of which Willie would have been aware. When he went to Carmarthen in 1933, apparently to undergo some form of further education or training, Hazell wrote to Lilian 'I trust Providence that we shall be able to get him all the really essential things by the appointed time' and asked Lilian to send Willie a little pocket money 'now and again'.[116]

The lack of work in the pit required Hazell to transfer to the night shift. In November 1932, he had said to Lilian, who was working as a staff nurse: 'I cannot quite understand why you should do quite so much night work, although someone has to do the night duty of course'.[117] However, in May 1933 he wrote:

> I shall be on the night shift every alternate week for some time now. I have not said so at home yet, but they will have to put up

with it as I cannot help it. I have to obey orders as you have to do. I shall not leave home until 10.30 p.m. and will be home in the mornings at 6.45 or thereabouts. Colliery work is slavery – undiluted slavery. I had for 3 days work last week – hard work too & honest service 21/- after stoppages for Dr. etc, etc. At 19 years of age I was earning 7/6 a shift & sometimes more! The people that talk of Bolshevism ought to come to the mines & do a spot of work & then talk.[118]

At this stage Hazell's letters to family were headed 'Home Sweet Home' or 'H.S.H.' His closeness to Lilian and his love and affection for her are obvious in his letters. Hazell's pride for his daughter was evident when he expressed hope that he could visit her in Oxford where she was working as a nurse and see 'the lioness in her den.'[119] However, the boys may not have felt that he had invested in them to the same extent.

For Lilian's 21st birthday on 13 September 1932 Hazell wrote: 'I send my extra special love & kisses on this occasion', adding 'the 13th – not an unlucky day by any means – see the 13th Chapter of Corinthians and its 13 splendid verses that will never die'. He noted that he was exactly double her age, as on 27 August he had become 42 years of age. His birthday congratulations, though, were qualified, saying 'From now on you are – for better or worse – a woman.' For a man who dealt in words and their meaning, this deliberate comment would have been influenced by the early death of his mother, the harshness of the life of his wife, Deborah Elizabeth, Lilian's mother, who was seriously ill and taking to her bed to rest during the day, as well reflecting his awareness of the general hardships of women. Hazell told Lilian 'Mother has not changed a great deal since you were here. At any rate she seems no worse.'[120]

Two months later Hazell reported 'Mother is… not quite so well, Doctor came last evening and injected & after some little excitement she seems to have got over it again'. Hazell despaired at the treatment his wife was receiving – much of it based in self-medication. When Deborah Elizabeth was in hospital, again, in early 1933, Hazell wrote telling his wife not to think of the others on the ward, just to lay quiet and get better. He said that he had not gone to the Council that evening, but had instead spoken at a meeting of the Abercynon Women's Guild adding: 'tell [Ivy] if there is anything else you want as I have the money to get it', having worked five shifts the previous week. He sent Deborah Elizabeth his love and kisses adding 'The boys are good and there is nothing special to complain of.'[121]

In May 1933, Hazell told Lilian that Deborah Elizabeth, by now out of hospital, had pains in the head. His wife also thought that her face had been twisted by some attack, but Hazell put that down to her imagination. He said that Lilian must try and impress on her mother 'the need to battle with these "feelings" which trouble her so much at times.' Deborah Elizabeth's heart was better and she had been out walking and in the big chair four times that week. Hazell updated Lilian on the family in London, with whom they had close links. The visit of Uncle Jim, apparently a man of some means, had been a disappointment, as some of his actions could be seen as ungenerous. Hazell sought to explain Jim's attitude, putting it down to someone in Mother's family telling Jim that Hazell had 'pots of money rolling in from various sources – which of course is not true. Other silly things may have been said.' Hazell's sense of decency comes through in his comment: 'We must assume that Uncle Jim was not intentionally unkind'. Hazell, though, did allow himself one regret: 'The only thing I thought was that he might have taken Mother for a run in the car.'[122]

In the same letter Hazell opened his heart to his daughter:

I look back and see that life in spite of all its difficulties has been worth while. Vinegar there has been it is true but the honey has not been always absent.

There was an unspoken sense of foreboding in that letter to

Lilian of 13 May 1933. He expressed his disappointment that she had postponed her holidays, saying that August seemed a long way off and she 'had better take some opportunity of coming home before then', and offered to help her with the fare.

Deborah Elizabeth died on Thursday 6 July 1933, aged 46 years, from acute heart problems. Willie wrote to Lilian saying that her father wished her to come home immediately by the first train 'Friday morning without fail. Please do not hesitate.'[123] Deborah Elizabeth was buried in the local cemetery on Monday 10 July in late afternoon, with the cortège leaving the house at 4.30pm. The service had three hymns, and her memorial card read "She hath done what she could" (Mark xiv. 8).[124]

The impact of Deborah Elizabeth's long-term illness and her premature death took a heavy toll on Hazell. It would appear that after her death he suffered some form of emotional collapse, which may well have been prolonged. Over a decade later, in 1948, he wrote an article which almost certainly referred to his reaction to the suffering of Deborah Elizabeth:

> Permit the recital of an intimate personal experience. For five years the shadow of domestic tragedy hung heavy and dark. For five years I could not, I must not, dare not forget. When all was over, I found myself in a hospital bed in a city infirmary. I had remembered too much and too long.[125]

Hazell's life had, indeed, had its share of 'vinegar', and experiences to forget. He had lost his mother as a child, and a sister while in his teens. He had been mistreated by his step-mother, had suffered at least one serious illness, and had lived through the 1921 and 1926 lockouts, as well as suffering the economic hardship of the first years of the Depression. Then his wife of more than 20 years, and mother of his six children, died.

It seems to have been too much for the man. The year after his wife's death, Hazell was still ailing, losing 'three weeks of life as a convalescent at Roden in 1934'.[126] He therefore spent at least three periods in convalescent homes – at Talygarn in 1925; once near Newport, probably in Cefn Mably, and at the CWS Roden home in 1934.

In his essay on the importance of blocking out painful memories, he later commented:

> Tribulations will come. But I can and will forget. To hope that everything – domestic, financial and physical – will go permanently right with me is ludicrously optimistic; there are long odds, very long, against it happening; but at least, some of the daily slings and arrows of outrageous fortune I can, and will, forget.'[127]

At the time of Deborah Elizabeth's death, Lilian was 21 years old, had left home and was training to be a nurse; Willie, who was aged around 20, was undertaking some form of education or training in Carmarthen, and Ivy, aged 18, was, it appears, still at home, having looked after her mother. Austen was a 14-year-old pupil in Pontypridd County School, and Roy was 11. It is not known whether Leslie, then aged 17, was still in school. With Deborah Elizabeth's death and Lilian's absence the Hazell household was one predominantly of young males. Possibly as a result of the death of her mother and to support the family, Lilian returned to South Wales, working for a short while as a night sister at Pontypridd Cottage Hospital before undertaking midwifery training, as well as working in a Nursing Home and private houses in the Cardiff area.[128]

Immersion

The period after Deborah Elizabeth's death shows no indication of Hazell seeking to lighten his load. Indeed he may have taken the opportunity to immerse himself in activity to escape his grief. In January 1934, he chaired a day school in the Institute on modern social problems. In September 1934 he participated in a Western Sectional Board conference on 'Towards Co-operative Civilisation', attended by over 130 people, which became a discussion on co-operation under fascism in Italy and Germany. At that stage, before the nature of Nazism became clear, he agreed with Sir Thomas Allen who counterposed co-operation as an alternative to both communism and fascism. In addition to his labour, co-operative and Council involvement Hazell continued as 'an energetic worker in the religious and social life of the village',[129] including being active in the Glyn Street Presbyterian Church, Ynysybwl, where he was a staunch member.[130]

In the two years after Deborah Elizabeth's death Hazell made considerable changes in the positions he held, though it is not known if these were connected to the personal impact of her death on him. Hazell was elected Chairman of Mountain Ash UDC which required considerable personal commitment as the Council's main ceremonial representative. In 1935, he gave up being the longest-serving Secretary to the Institute, a post he had held for 12 years. At the height of the Ocean Combine Committee's battle against the Industrial or 'scab' union, he was elected Chairman of the Lady Windsor Lodge, an office he occupied until 1937. After the death in 1935 of William Brown (who had replaced Hazell as President of YCS in 1922), Hazell once again became President of the Ynysybwl Society, the largest business in Pontypridd.[131] These positions involved responsibilities that required Hazell to operate in quite different ways. Being lodge chairman unavoidably involved antagonistic class relations, in contrast to secretary of the institute or President of YCS, the latter of which combined ambassador and diplomat with collective entrepreneur. Whatever the motivations it would have impacted on his family as the combination of roles would have required enormous amounts of time, reducing that time available for his children.

Despite difficult circumstances Hazell kept writing. When the Co-operative Congress came to Cardiff, in 1935, the *Co-operative Review* published his long piece on the experience of the valleys over the previous 30 years. Looking at the plight of people still suffering from the Depression, Hazell described Merthyr as 'the mortuary of shameful capitalist exploitation', referred to the coal industry as 'the sport of soulless combines and the banks' and accused Cardiff of having an almost parasitic relationship with the coal-producing valleys of South Wales.[132] Later Hazell wrote of thousands of miners' daughters 'miserably under-clothed and ill-nourished, yet cheerful withal' who had to go to domestic service in London and other cities (including his daughter Ivy in Bristol) and of the postal orders they sent home to help families survive. He lamented that men – no doubt including himself – did everything they could to save a penny or bring in a few coppers to the household exchequer. His highest regard was reserved for wives and mothers. Always conscious of gender roles, he described them as:

> real heroines all the way through. Their struggle has been and still is, an epic one! They have mended and patched; begged and borrowed; and economised in a hundred and one ways.

He added:

> When another word of discouragement would have sent husband and father to the reservoir or gas-oven, that word has never been spoken, but a kiss and a misty-eyed smile have shown the way to another day's hope, and trust in a problematic future.[133]

Yet, in the traumatic times of the 1920s and 1930s, when economic circumstances were at their most desperate, and political polarisation was acute, Hazell retained his perspective and gradualist vision of how to build a better society. He identified with earlier generations of co-operators who had seen co-operation as a way of avoiding 'extreme accumulations of wealth and poverty'.[134] He wrote that his philosophy of life was not based in kingdom, republic or commune, as only co-operation could regenerate man. Hazell was an idealist who considered his vision an attainable one through co-operation. He never lost that vision, however utopian, based in his faith in the human spirit.[135] However, Hazell's utopian vision was grounded in cold reality. He did not just believe in the moral economy of co-operation, he believed it to be a more efficient system than other capitalist forms of retail/commercial enterprise.[136] In the *Co-operative Official* he wrote that he had given up asking for loyalty at his Society's business meetings years before as co-operation had to be based on service and efficiency, rather than appeals to loyalty.

> It cuts no ice. It sells no goods. It gets no trade. We must give such services and offer such value as will command – aye, *command*, our members' trade. This is the only way we shall get and keep trade and keep co-operative counters and factories busy. Appeals for loyalty are worse than useless. They give the impression that your goods are so poor or high-priced that they cannot be sold without a sentimental, almost pathetic, appeal to your members' belief in a theoretic system of shopkeeping.

He continued: 'The finest practical propaganda… is a bright, modern, co-operative shop, efficiently stocked and staffed, and serving goods at right prices.'[137]

YCS

On taking up the role of President of YCS, the *South Wales Supplement* included a biography of Hazell which described his top quality as 'his staunch conviction that the co-operative movement and its principles will bring his fellow workers out of the slough of despond into which capitalism has pitched them, and in which it ruthlessly holds them down.' W S Collins described Hazell as a working miner who studied the problems of the working class.

> When others have hesitated or sought to temporise, Hazell has gone plodding along without haste and without rest, confident in the belief that men and women have only to will progress and it will be so.[138]

Through his writings, Hazell gained a prominence for the Ynysybwl Society which stretched beyond South Wales, as well as gaining a personal national profile. In the late 1930s, the *Co-operative News* ran a series about prominent British co-operators called 'Men of Mark' in which Hazell was the 40th co-operator profiled.

Being President of the Ynysybwl Society was Hazell's first love, though a demanding one. Years later he wrote an extended essay in what was almost a job description and personal specification for the role. He said that being President of a Society meant often heading the largest business organisation in a town. The post, he argued, was equivalent to the chair of the council or mayor of a city, and was the local representative of a worldwide commonwealth who should be honoured by the society for 'in honouring him or her they will be honouring themselves and the… movement.' He said co-operators should place their President in such public esteem that they could not be overlooked, and local civic functions would not be complete without them.[139]

At various times over four decades Hazell addressed different aspects of the organisational (as well as philosophical, economic or cultural aspects) of the movement. Hazell recognised that much of its success was due to the 'energy, self-sacrifice and devotion to duty' of society officials and their high level of business acumen and management. While he did not wish to take anything away from the elected co-operative committees, he said it was 'quite apparent that spare-time supervision by committees, meeting largely in the evenings after shops and places of business had closed, could not be sufficient to account for the efficiency of co-operative business service throughout the country. Overall, he praised the high traditions of the co-operative civil service whose conscientious abilities were put at the disposal of the elected committees. Hazell said that chief officers' views should not be lightly disregarded, although the President must retain his own mind, while equally the chief officers should value the President's co-operative, business and social acumen.[140]

Of the functioning of societies' boards of directors, also known as management committees, Hazell said that much of the success of the movement was due to the 'democractically elected, spare time, unpaid, and to some extent, unsung, services of committees of co-operative societies. He likened the attributes of members of co-operative boards with the 12 Apostles (optimists, pessimists, a denier, a betrayer, a doubter).[141] While relations between full-time officials and elected members could be a source of tension in the movement, it would appear that in Ynysybwl the relationship remained positive over decades, reflecting the way that Hazell managed it.

Hazell contrasted members of the Ynysybwl Board with directors in private enterprises. He pointed out that as President he was entitled to receive 1/6d for each meeting attended while directors were entitled to 1/-. However, no-one drew the money, which accumulated to pay for the annual May Day visit to co-operative factories, which were a combination of business, education and pleasure. For example, in 1932, over a period of two days, they visited a cabinet and furniture factory, a clothes factory, and then the CWS depot at Bristol, before visiting the Avonmouth flour mills which supplied all South Wales societies. Hazell considered it unimaginable that private sector directors would not draw fees – even during the Depression YCS Directors did not draw fees, although for some to have done so would have eased domestic financial pressures.[142] The rate paid was still the same in 1954 as in 1920.

When, ten years later, Ben Bowen Thomas, late Warden of Coleg Harlech, and Permanent Secretary to the Board of Education, deplored the fact that "Wales is fast becoming a Committee-nation", Hazell sprang to their defence, saying 'These committees, of mainly working men, command our respect for their voluntary work for the movement.'[143] He described YCS committee membership as representing a fair cross section of the community.

> They should know what people in every walk of life are saying and thinking about their society! They are able to act as a living link between the official management and the members right through the districts.[144]

However, Hazell pointed out that co-operative societies still lacked a gender balance. He noted that in most Welsh co-operative societies, Boards of between nine and 12 Directors featured only one or two women, commenting:

> With the growing strength of the women's guild movement, it is more than surprising that our business meetings, consisting of men and women, do not elect more of the female sex to our committees. Evidently, women's emancipation is not yet complete![145]

While gender balance on the YCS Board may not have changed greatly, its occupational composition had diversified considerably by the late 1930s. The Board was no longer dominated by miners and its 15 members included a locomotive driver, an electrical engineer and manager for the district council, a colliery timber drawer, a co-operative grocery assistant, two teachers, a retired miner, an unemployed miner, a working miner, a pithead baths superintendent, a railway goods clerk, a cinema manager, a married woman, a female health visitor and district nurse, and a widow. Hazell, it would appear, was the only working miner on the committee.[146]

Ynysybwl was advanced in employee representation on the Board. In 1920 YCS became the first society in Wales to allow an employee to serve on the Board in what was considered, even decades later, to be a revolutionary step. Miss Annie Hughes represented the staff for 17 years, before retiring in 1938, being the longest serving woman on the committee as well as the employee representative. The policy was still controversial nearly two decades later when H J Twigg of the Co-operative Union's Labour Department strongly disagreed with the policy. Hazell countered that YCS employee representatives helped employees become more responsible.[147]

Hazell analysed the minutiae of the functioning of the co-operative movement and illuminated what could appear mundane, giving it life and meaning. An article written on a meeting agenda drew on Edward Carpenter's book on civilisation, Schweitzer's contribution to the human race, and the thoughts of St Paul.[148] Minute taking at meetings became an analysis of power relations within an organisation: 'Where minutes are constantly "taken as read" an official obviously has great power in his hands'. He broadened this into an analysis of the role of a society's secretary, whose verbal contributions can either be 'useful, diplomatic evasions, coaxing blandishments, or even autocratic pronouncements, according [to whether] the committee can be treated with frank confidence, cajoled or frightened.'[149] John E Morgan described Hazell as an 'excellent chairman of meetings and committees, presiding with dignity and competence, and capable at all times of keeping the discussion at a level temperature,' while Hazell pointed out that the capable and efficient chairman 'can make or mar, inspire or depress, retard or carry forward, the meeting or committee' as well as demonstrating an understanding of Machiavelli.[150]

New YCS premises were opened in Church Street, Pontypridd, in June 1932. A photograph catches Hazell against a sea of people thronging outside and capturing the excitement and significance of the day. After 43 years, the Society's headquarters transferred from Ynysybwl, where it had been located since its foundation, to Pontypridd. The new building had offices and a boardroom on the third floor. Hazell visited daily, undertaking routine but necessary tasks, such as signing a multiplicity of documents including cheques, new loan books, 'traders' credits' and renewals of leases.[151] Such duties Hazell would carry out diligently and with dignity for nearly 30 years.

An 'Exhibition of Co-operative Productions' was put on in the Palais de Dance as part of the celebrations of the new premises. Over 500 invitees, including 64 representatives of neighbouring societies, were present including David Evans JP, of the Tredegar Society who was also the General Manager of Tredegar Iron & Coal Company. Taking into account that the event took place when class antagonisms in the coalfield were at their most acute, Evans' contribution casts an interesting light on relations between capital and labour. In a remarkable identification with labour for the head of a coal company, he said that they were 'making great headway in this people's movement. He added 'to the gibe that "Labour cannot govern," he would retort: come to our co-operative societies and see for yourselves.'[152] While polarisation between capital and labour was acute in the coal industry, apparently it did not necessarily extend to those same people in their co-operative movement roles.

Overall Ynysybwl suffered less than many other societies. In *The Gleaming Vision*, Hazell recognised that 'one of the incredible things in these incredible valleys during [the inter-war years] was the survival of the people's co-operative societies', adding with a typical turn of phrase, 'for, in the main, they were founded upon the fortunes of the working-classes – and misfortune now reigned supreme.'[153] YCS sales, which had collapsed after the 1921 lockout and dipped again after the 1926 lockout, increased after 1927 and stabilised at around one third lower than before the 1921 lockout. However neither YCS membership nor share capital collapsed after either lockout. While demand remained suppressed, YCS turnover did not collapse in the way experienced by some other societies where whole districts suffered colliery closures, such as Blaina.

During the most difficult years of the Depression YCS trade remained broadly stable at around £300,000 per year, before increasing from 1933, year on year, to £513,994 in 1940. By 1940 YCS membership had reached 9,131 from 6,618 in 1933 (and 7,141 in 1920). Profits too remained steady after 1926, before increasing markedly at the end of the 1930s. Members share capital had been £103,458 in 1920, declining to £74,435 in 1927, but then increased year-on-year to £161,692 in 1940.[154] This was a good performance, bearing in mind the general economic conditions. It confirmed the business acumen of the Society's leadership and the members' commitment to collective entrepreneurship.

YCS continued to develop during the Depression, in spite of – even seeing opportunities in – the negative economic conditions in the valleys. The co-operative branch in Caerphilly was taken over after the liquidation of the Aber Valley and Senghenydd Society due to the closure of the Universal Colliery, Senghenydd, in 1928. The development of new council estates continued to provide opportunities for new branches, such as in Rhydfelin where YCS constructed an attractive Art Deco building, as it did in its remodeling of the Taffs Well branch. At the end of the 1930s, the Aber and Senghenydd branches joined Caerphilly in YCS, so strengthening the Society further. Indeed the Caerphilly branch flourished so much after joining YCS that adjoining shops were purchased, but planned redevelopment was unable to proceed due to the Second World War.[155]

In spite of the difficulties, YCS strove to improve services to its customers. As early as 1930, it supplied members in Caerphilly with pasteurised milk from the Newport Society. It extended its services beyond individual members in being contracted with the Aberdare Society to provide pasteurised milk to schools across Mountain Ash UDC area. This was a major contribution to the health of the local population, made possible by the CWS

Creamery in Llanharan. By 1937 the Societies had won three of the four contracts to supply schools with groceries, bread, milk and meat.[156] YCS was therefore not reliant exclusively on members' demand but diversified its sales, so strengthening the business. Combining its ideological commitment with business decisions YCS showed its loyalty to the movement by obtaining all of its goods from the CWS, so living up to its aspiration of building the Co-operative Commonwealth though trade.

However, some areas covered by the Society suffered greatly. Hazell identified Taffs Well as having very high unemployment rates. When opening the new branch shop there, in order to try and give a broader view, Hazell reminded members that they were not an isolated group in a South Wales town, but an integral part of an international movement with millions of members. As YCS subscribed to all co-operative funds and causes, including the International Co-operative Alliance,[157] these were not just empty words; however they may have made a rather hollow sound to co-operators in Taffs Well.

Lady Windsor Colliery experienced its most difficult year in 1936 when 211 working days were lost. As a result it was reported that 40 per cent of YCS's membership had been compelled to seek work elsewhere, and that 30 per cent of its membership were unemployed. However, at the end of 1936 it was considered that the economic tide had turned and that prospects in Pontypridd and District were better than they had been for some time as more regular work became available and closed collieries reopened. As confirmation, YCS did its best Christmas trade for 10 years. By early 1937, Hazell reported, societies were beginning to recover from the difficult period that had started in 1921. Such hope, though, was premature. A mass meeting of the unemployed was still being held in September 1938 as unemployment and underemployment reduced YCS sales and capital.[158]

The 1935 Co-operative Congress provided an opportunity to

demonstrate the influence of co-operation in the South Wales valleys. YCS arranged six special trains to take 8,000 school children from Caerphilly and Pontypridd to the CWS exhibition in Cardiff, showing its capacity for mass mobilisation. Mountain Ash Education Committee's decision to close the schools for an afternoon to allow children to go to the exhibition courtesy of Aberdare Co-operative Society also demonstrated the place of co-operation in mainstream valleys society. In contrast Cardiff Education Committee refused permission for its schoolchildren to attend the exhibition for which it was said to have received much criticism. A close supportive relationship existed between valleys local authorities and co-operative societies and the way the culture of co-operation permeated valleys life was seen, each year, when the Education Committee agreed free use of rooms for evening classes for ten to 18-year-olds on 'Principles of Co-operation'.[159]

Two of Hazell's major interests were brought together in 'Co-operators on Local Authorities' in which Hazell challenged those who doubted that co-operators should be elected to local authorities, or that societies 'should become "mixed up in politics"' instead positing them as complimentary roles. As ever, Hazell gave an historical perspective, looking back to the turn of the century when Councils and Boards of Guardians were comprised of 'tradesmen, a few ministers and clergymen, a sprinkling of professional men and the local colliery magnates or their nominees.' He argued that while supposedly giving communal service, 'their private beliefs, their traditions, and their upbringing' were individualistic, with local authority contracts and agreements favouring private interests as local legislators worshipped the 'trinity [of] rent, interest and profit!' Co-operative society tenders for council services, he continued, were returned unopened, and the levels of co-operative rates were set by their competitors.[160] He did not point out, as he could have, that the situation was now reversed in valleys authorities controlled by Labour where co-operative societies were winning the contracts.

Looking back, Hazell reflected that everything in local government from 1923 to 1937-8 was over-shadowed by the slump in the coal trade and the Depression in the valleys. With good citizens failing to pay their rates, arrears built up, which were subsequently written off and consequently, local expenditure was 'cut to the bone'.[161] However, despite real difficulties the Council supported its population under siege. For example, in November 1935 Hazell moved the resolution to provide milk to pupils at Infants School whose parents were below the scale of income fixed by the Education Committee. The following year, possibly stretching its responsibilities to the limit, the Committee considered malnutrition amongst infants younger than school age as well as mothers. In December 1936, the Committee decided to provide meals and milk to children through school holidays. Two months earlier, in view of increased expenditure on meals for school children as a result of the Depression, Hazell was involved in the proposal that the Federation of Education Committees should meet to seek a 100 per cent grant from the Government to cover the costs of meals of children in necessitous areas.[162] While these were defensive, such actions helped consolidate the Labour Party's place in the community for decades to come.

Family Affairs

Hazell remarried on 10 November 1936 at St David's Presbyterian Chapel, Pontypridd. His bride, Gwladys Sarah Thomas, born 24 June 1889, was the head teacher of Clarence Street Special School in Mountain Ash, daughter of Henry Austin Thomas, Master Grocer in Mountain Ash. They would have met through Hazell's longstanding membership of the Council's Education Committee, which he chaired in 1934. Hazell was 46 years old, Gwlad was 47. Willie, who was by then a sergeant in the

Army Education Corps, was best man and Lilian and Ivy were bridesmaids.[163]

Gwlad gave up her comfortable professional life to become a miner's wife.[164] She left 'Northlands', in Mountain Ash, to live in a small terraced house in Ynysybwl. This was a considerable step, particularly as Hazell's work was erratic, and there was economic hardship in the household. While the domestic demands to serve the miners' needs had been eased by the opening of pit head baths for Lady Windsor Colliery in 1931, so it was now possible to arrive home showered and in clean clothes, there would still have been domestic work that needed attention, not least with children still at home. It is difficult to imagine Gwlad undertaking domestic tasks.

> She expected to be treated in a certain way. She expected men to stand up when she walked into the room. It was like having the Queen Mother there. She never mucked in with the washing up or anything like that.[165]

Gwlad was a deeply religious woman who before marriage had devoted much of her leisure time to religious work. She had been a Sunday School teacher at Ffrwd Baptist Chapel in Mountain Ash and later became the organist at Glyn Street Chapel in Ynysybwl. There were no children of the marriage, but they had a household cat.[166] They seem to have been a compatible couple. In his writings William referred to their making a short visit to London in late 1938, and while there seeing Emlyn Williams and Sybil Thorndike in the play 'The Corn is Green' at the Duchess Theatre. His comment 'as always in the Metropolis' indicates his familiarity with the capital and the cultural opportunities it offered. He later joked that he married a Welsh schoolmistress in order "to complete his education".[167]

The marriage had a considerable impact on and within the family. While his children had attended the wedding, they initially found it hard to accept.[168] While she was always known to Hazell's children and grandchildren as 'Auntie Gwlad', the relationship was formal, at least in the early years. Gwlad also made it clear that she did not want the boys to continue living at home, which caused a breech in the family.

Lilian left Pontypridd Cottage Hospital to take her midwifery qualification[169] before becoming a District Nurse in Box near Bath, and then Chippenham. Hazell gave away his second daughter, Ivy, at her wedding, in 1938, and Auntie Gwlad (exquisitely described as 'Mrs Councillor W Hazell') was one of the speakers at the wedding. However, when Lilian married in 1939 he did not attend the wedding. Family lore recalls it being for one of two reasons – or perhaps a combination of both. Possibly Hazell did not consider Lilian's husband, David (Davy) to be 'suitable' because although he was considered to be of a good Ynysybwl family he could not act as a breadwinner due to a car accident. Davy was described later by his brother-in-law, Willie, as having 'such sterling, sane and courageous qualities which I envy.'[170] However, it was also possible that Hazell's absence was over a spilt in the family due to the treatment of the boys after his second marriage.

As a result of the rift, the centre of family life for the siblings shifted from Ynysybwl and gravitated towards Lilian. Henceforth, Lilian assumed the role of the mother of the family and her home became the family home.[171] Such had been the closeness between Hazell and Lilian that his absence from the wedding, and the subsequent strained relations, must have been a source of enduring hurt for them both. The sense of his own early painful personal family history being repeated cannot have been lost on Hazell.

After his emotional collapse with the death of Deborah Elizabeth, came a gradual recovery.

> Then came slowly the mercy of, to some extent, forgetting, and looking forward to brighter days. I [had] remembered to forget.

He added:

When I forget the ought-not-to-be-remembered; when I allow my forgetting to exercise silently its healing power; I relax; I go faster in accomplishment; I do more, I am more, I have more; I am happier and healthier when I throw off the tyrannies of memory's relentless thrawl [sic]. Let me please, forget.[172]

Much of that forgetting would have been due to the companionship he found in his new relationship with Gwlad.

Over time it was apparent that Hazell was happy with the relationship with Gwlad and the children thought it good that he had someone of his own age with whom to be. Later the children got on with Auntie Gwlad, the grandchildren liked her and the family grew back together again, but that would take some years to be reached. Lilian, however, remained surrogate head of the family. In later years Auntie Gwlad complimented Lilian by

enumerat[ing] the things in which you excel – cooking, decorating, entertaining, etc, apart from your professional duties at the Hospital, and your literary tastes and your experience in driving. I feel sure Dad would be proud of you and Ivy.[173]

Gwlad, though, did not refer to the boys.

As with the death of Deborah Elizabeth, it is not possible to assess whether his new relationship with Gwlad caused him to change his responsibilities. However, in late 1937, upon the death of D L Davies, the former miners' agent and then MP for Pontypridd, who had long been associated with YCS, Hazell sought and received a nomination to replace him as the Labour candidate for Parliament but was unsuccessful in the selection process.[174]

Tackling 'The Establishment'

By the mid-1930s, Hazell was at times strongly oppositional in CWS meetings. Compared with his earlier relationship with the CWS, his comments were highly critical. He and others regularly raised with CWS Directors the need to bring new works to

South Wales. Constantly proposing ideas that would bring jobs to the region, in 1935, Hazell suggested establishing a car factory, although this was dismissed as unlikely. The following year, he suggested the production of light castings such as rainwater chutes and gutters, which CWS Directors promised to consider.[175]

Hazell questioned the focus and priorities of the CWS, arguing that with £3 million of trade passed through the CWS Cardiff depot from retail societies, South Wales had a disproportionately low number of CWS plant and that more should be established. He pointed out that of 200 CWS factories, works and mills, only three comparatively small factories and a milk depot existed there, adding 'we are not going to be satisfied until you do something for us'. These were strong words, both in the context of the quarterly Divisional meetings, and for the man making them. A few months later, O R Jones, the General Manager of YCS, proposed that the CWS could set up factories on the new Treforest Trading Estate although, again, the CWS Directors held out little hope of such action being taken.[176]

The lack of CWS commitment resulted in Hazell being central to South Wales societies taking concerted action to apply pressure on the CWS. In September 1937, he presided over an 'unofficial' conference, held at Cardiff City Hall, to launch a campaign for more CWS factories in South Wales and Monmouthshire. Forty-five societies were represented. It was extraordinary that the societies went outside the movement's formal organisational structures and highlighted that on this issue they had little faith in the movement's traditional ways of working. Hazell addressed the conference saying that all societies had certain rights as shareholders in the CWS and that South Wales did not have its fair share of UK works based on its membership and trade with the CWS. Delegates agreed to reconvene to consider the kinds of factories and works that could be introduced. Hazell was selected chairman and G H Davies of Penygraig as secretary with all arrangements left to them.[177]

At the reconvened October conference, Hazell said from the chair that because more colliers were working, people thought that the unemployment problem was solved; however, there were still 140,000 men out of work, which numbered 400,000 with dependents.[178] A committee was established and a group deputed to meet CWS Directors in London.

During this stand-off, relations with the CWS Board were further strained by proposals to change the method of electing its Directors, which would have potentially left South Wales without representation on the CWS Board. Hazell articulated members' opposition stating that 'the recommendation of the committee was a vote for the execution of South Wales and for its funeral'.[179]

The 'unofficial' meetings had an impact. At the subsequent Divisional meeting, the Chairman, J C Alston, a CWS Director, displaying a marked change in tone, saying that the Directors were 'very sympathetic' and 'extremely anxious to do all they possibly could' for South Wales.[180] At the next quarterly meeting Hazell again returned to the fray, analysing the location of proposed CWS business sites across Britain, including Greater London, Manchester, Newcastle and the Midlands, but that nothing was proposed for South Wales. The CWS congratulated the deputation on the presentation of their case, which had made an impression, and said that a report was being considered by the Board. However, the issue was raised again in the Divisional meeting of July 1938, suggesting that little progress had been made.[181]

The pressure exerted by Hazell and his colleagues achieved some success. By January 1939, the CWS had announced that it was planning to develop a provender mill (for animal feed) in Swansea, a creamery in Aberdare, and later a mineral water factory and a bedding factory employing 60-70 people on the Treforest Industrial Estate. However, this was insufficient to satisfy Hazell and a rare note of antagonism could be detected at the April 1939 CWS Divisional meeting, in his exchange with a CWS Director, J W Sutton. In response to Hazell's question: 'Are you now prepared to do something more for South Wales and Monmouthshire in regard to productive factories?' Sutton replied: 'We do not build productive works for the sake of doing it... they are built because they are likely to be a business proposition'.[182] Even so, Hazell's belligerence continued and he pursued the issue into the post-war period.

Hazell was also critical of the wider role of the CWS, describing its approach as 'timidity or worse'. He was scathing at the lack of practical action in the seven years since the 1928 Hartlepool Congress, when the movement overcame local rivalries to agree that the CWS should promote retail trading in areas where it was weak. However, wrote Hazell, the CWS had subsequently done nothing except for a proposal, agreed in January 1934, to establish a CWS Retail Society. Hazell lamented that the Co-operators' Year Book for 1935 'mournfully records that "at the time of going to press the CWS Retail Society had not yet commenced active operations"'.[183]

Therefore, when the CWS announced in 1936 that it was using its newly formed Co-operative Retail Services (CRS) to take over the Cardiff Co-operative Society, there was considerable questioning of the CWS role in the next Divisional meeting. The action by the CWS was revolutionary and controversial. Whereas the CWS was considered to have been authorized to support retail development in areas where no society existed, societies now felt it had exceeded its mandate in taking over an already existing society. This complete departure raised profound issues about roles and relationships between independent retail societies and the CWS. With Cardiff becoming what proved to be the first branch of the national CRS, this was not at all the sort of practical action for which Hazell had called.

Relations deteriorated further when the CWS proposed establishing and managing bazaar trading. At a special Divisional meeting, Hazell said he favoured developing bazaars, but he wanted retail societies involved in running them, not just the CWS. In a national referendum of member societies, the CWS proposal was defeated; when George Darling, who was employed by a co-operative journal, criticised the vote as 'a great blow to the movement', Hazell wrote a pointed letter to the *Co-operative News*, reminding Darling that the democratic voice of the movement had spoken, that the 'official view of the movement' was not that of CWS Directors or other organs, but rather that of 'the voice and decision of the societies', and that it was not for a salaried employee of the movement to question it.[184] A few days later the Second World War started, bringing hope of welcome peace and unity to the fraught relations that existed between South Wales societies and the CWS.

Normally a highly reasonable man, on issue after issue Hazell showed that when riled he could be a redoubtable adversary. Through his attendance at CWS Divisional meetings, his membership of committees of the Co-operative Union in Manchester, and his articles in the co-operative press, Hazell had a combination of outlets through which he was able to articulate his views. His criticisms, though, were not limited to issues within the co-operative movement.

In late 1938, Hazell strongly attacked the BBC for not providing radio air-time for co-operation in Britain. The movement had been in dispute with the BBC since a talk on the movement was cancelled in 1932. When Hazell attended a conference addressed by Hopkin Morris, the Welsh Regional Director of the BBC, he asked why there could not be a programme on co-operation on the BBC, to which Morris replied that he had no control over broadcasting as that was a matter for London, prompting Hazell to respond that the co-operative movement was 'an "outcast" of the air of Great Britain'. As the BBC reported on the rise and fall in the stock market and covered private business profits, Hazell asked all co-operators in Britain: 'Is the BBC's anti-co-operative bias justified? is it equitable? is it to continue? and, finally, what steps do we propose to take to alter it?'[185] Hazell returned to the issue, in 1944, on the centenary of the Rochdale Pioneers saying the broadcaster was prepared to promote the movement's story in its overseas programmes, but practically 'no mention' had been made on the Home Service. Hazell posed an open question to the Governors of the BBC: 'Is the co-operative ideal too controversial, too subversive, too revolutionary for the British public?' He declared that the BBC was prepared to treat co-operation 'as an export idea only – strictly not for home consumption'. Hazell considered it 'unutterable nonsense – if not hypocrisy' adding 'cooperation is revolutionary', but as it 'is a "peaceful revolution"' 'Of what, and of whom, then, is the BBC afraid?'[186] Twenty years after his original article of complaint, he had another jibe at the BBC when no-one from the co-operative movement in Wales was allowed to pay tribute to Robert Owen, on the centenary of his death, as a part of the Festival of Wales.[187]

Confronting Fascism

Hazell's attention continued to be taken by international affairs. In June 1936, he attended an International Peace Congress, with delegates from 21 countries, held at CWS Headquarters in Cardiff, with Lord Davies presiding. A month earlier, Mountain Ash UDC agreed to hold a town meeting on a plebiscite for peace.[188]

At that time, Hazell still saw communism as a distraction. In 1935 he wrote:

It is true that Communism raises its sinister head here and there. The wonder is that it has not attracted many more adherents in these days, with its promise of a short cut to economic emancipation and social justice. Alas for the deluded – there is no short cut to Utopia – the way is going to be long and hard. Canaan is yet a long way off! Co-operation still offers a safe path to the sincere seeker.[189]

However, the outbreak of the Spanish Civil War in July 1936 profoundly changed Hazell's perspective. It became clear that a peace thought possible only a month before could now not be attained and that the threat of European fascism had to be confronted. In November 1936 the *Co-operative News* published a truly remarkable article in which Hazell advocated that the co-operative movement should lead the popular front in Britain. Conscious of the destruction of independent co-operative movements in Italy and Germany, Hazell recognised the exceptional nature of the time in which they were living. He said that issues such as the Communist Party affiliation to the Labour Party or the overlapping of co-operative societies 'recede to [their] proper proportions' when faced with the proposition that the Labour Party would cease to exist if a totalitarian state were established in Britain. He said 'If democracy is to be saved from the furnace of Fascism and reaction…' why should it not be the Co-operative movement that led [a Popular Front] as it was the **most popular** movement in the country? He said there were seven-million members 'whom we have never **seriously** tried to organise politically'.[190]

He continued:

We have the nuclei, our stores, in every city, town and village, and hamlet in the land – and the co-operative store is a better 'cell' than any Communist mind ever invented! We have also a political machine already existing which could be quickly expanded in order to meet new situations.

Asking 'Would the people respond?' he answered with another question 'Why should they not respond?' He explained that the movement had 'the confidence of solid masses of the people' who:

> trust us with their savings… buy in our shops and stores… insure their lives with us; they feed their infants with our milk… and allow our funeral furnishing departments to bury their dead! Why, then should they not respond to our call?

Hazell went on that the movement had no dismal record of failure, of broken promises, 'of pious platitudes or pompous figureheads'. So why should not 'the people respond to the call of the rainbow banner-bearers?' He argued that

> the inherent stability of our membership; the soundness of our economics; the business training of our leadership; and our trained leadership will, in a Popular Front Party, secure for us the place in the progressive forces to which we have long been entitled.

Hazell said it was necessary to face up to the 'facts of the present situation – Democracy v. Reaction' and 'Make no Mistake!' He finished:

> The alternative? The only alternative for the co-operative movement of Britain to the 'Popular Front' with the salvage of democracy is… political extinction, and absorption in the Totalitarian State.[191]

It is not known if this powerful rallying call had been discussed with Jack Bailey – the national organiser of the Party and a former Mountain Ash district councillor with Hazell. In terms of 90 years of co-operative history, it really was a revolutionary call and showed how daring and inventive Hazell could be. It mixed trade with practical politics, adopting a strategy of using the economic and social trust built up with its membership base to mobilise them to political action. It was beyond anything he had previously written and was completely outwith the traditions of the co-operative movement.

This was a time of intense political activity for Hazell. Any suggestion of political neutrality in the co-operative movement was firmly cast off. YCS threw itself wholeheartedly into the Campaign against the Means Test and the proposed regulations of the Unemployment Assistance Board (UAB). With a commitment that such activity would continue until the regulations were withdrawn, Hazell addressed numerous demonstrations and meetings on behalf of the co-operative movement and the 7,000 members of the local society. Speaking at an open air event at Darren Park, Pontypridd, Hazell referred to the loyalty of the unemployed members of YCS, and to the support given by co-operators to the unemployed marchers to London. He recounted being asked were the trades unions, the Labour Party or co-operative movement the most important movement of the working class in Great Britain? He answered that all – co-operators, the trades unions, Labourites and Communists should forget their paltry differences, realise their oneness, and that which bound them together in the cause of progress.[192]

Hazell espoused Popular Front ideology, and linked the struggle against the UAB at home with the fight against fascism abroad. For him this duality had to be confronted head-on. When speaking he married the everyday work of co-operation with broader issues and ideals. For Hazell YCS was an integral part of the fight against fascism in Spain, Italy and Germany, and the Society's balance sheet was evidence of democratic resistance as well as the conquest over capitalism by collective effort – 'government of the people, for the people, and by the people'.[193] Interestingly, Hazell gives no account of such work in *The Gleaming Vision* and the political aspects of YCS's work are largely omitted from his account of the inter-war years.

In February 1938, he presided over a public meeting of the

Ynysybwl Labour Party which demanded the resignation of the Government over Britain's proposed alignment with Italy over Germany's *anschluss* with Austria. When a series of meetings by leading national co-operators took place across the valleys in 1938, Hazell appeared as a support speaker. YCS aided the Republican cause in Spain, making regular donations from 1936 to 1939. Equally, Mountain Ash UDC provided a lorry and driver to Mountain Ash Trades Council and Labour Party (TC&LP) for door to door collections for food for Spain. Mountain Ash UDC, again at the behest of the TC&LP, called on the Prime Minister and Foreign Secretary to set aside the non-intervention policy and to take immediate action to supply arms and munitions to the Spanish Government.[194] Hazell later criticised the 'the farcical intervention of non-intervention by British politicians, who have been intervening somewhere in the wide world for hundreds of years as a deliberate policy'.[195]

Hazell's consistent opposition to private enterprise was evident in all his activities and writings. In 'Co-operation Fights Capitalist Exploitation: Transforming Wage Slaves into Financiers and Employers' he considered that the co-operative movement had done much to replace the inferiority complex of the British working class and to convince members that they were everything as good as the Churchills or the Cecils. He linked his opposition to private business to international affairs and located co-operation in the context of the Great War and Franco's German bombers. He catalogued areas where the co-operative movement had led the transformation of working conditions for retail employees. In arguing that co-operation could surmount barriers of class, race and colour, as well as displace a 'spurious competitive system' and 'rout the profit motive', and suggesting that Rochdale might succeed where Geneva had failed in addressing the ills of the world, he showed an almost biblical faith in co-operation.[196]

Hazell would have attended Paul Robeson's concert in support of the International Brigade in the Pavilion, Mountain Ash, on 7 December 1938.[197] Hazell was a great admirer of Robeson and said of him:

> Take off your hat to a man of colour – a man every inch of him. He does not designate himself an artiste although he is one of Nature's artistes and gentlemen, and a champion of humanity. Salute the singer of 'Old Man River,' [sic] representative of a noble but oppressed race as he entitles his life story 'Paul Robeson, Negro.' No need for apology, Paul. Anyway, you would be the last man in the world to apologise for the colour of your skin. What did old Captain Fuller say, eh? 'God's image carved in ebony.'[198]

In May 1939, Hazell was still writing in the local press in support of the Popular Front as a way of facing down fascism and the Nazis.[199] The sporting, political and cultural were fused at a 'Basque Day' held at Ynysybwl in 1939, which was organised by the Lodge, the Institute and the Ynysybwl Labour Party. A large crowd attended a football match played between Basque Boys and Ynysybwl Boys and a new football presented by the Co-operative Society was autographed by Arthur Horner, President of the SWMF. A concert was held that evening, and a presentation was made to Morien Morgan, a local International Brigader and John E Morgan's son, 'in recognition of his services in Spain'.[200] As one war in Spain ended, preparations were already underway for another in which Hazell and YCS would be even more directly involved.

CHAPTER 3

Wartime

Preparing For War

Although local authorities were formally given responsibility for organising Air Raid Precautions (ARP) in 1937, ARP sprung to the top of the Council agenda in the second half of 1938. As the country prepared for war the regular cycle of monthly council meetings was overridden by war preparations, which gave a sense of urgency to the rhythm of Council life. Hazell was on the ARP committee which had responsibility for food, fuel, air raid precautions and evacuation arrangements. The Territorial Army was given permission to use school buildings, the police were granted use of Trerobart School for ARP and rooms in schools were converted into air raid wardens' posts. Teachers were trained in first aid and anti-gas precautions and children were to be prepared for respirator and air raid drills.[1]

The normal functions of the Authority were considerably added to by the demands of war, which became one of the main means of delivering extra services. The flurry of activity grew more intense as the Council's organisational machinery geared up in readiness. Some 38,400 gas masks were distributed to local civilians in the area, and rescue and decontamination equipment was arranged. The provision of bomb shelters, the digging of trenches and the feeding and education of evacuees were considered by the Council. In anticipation of bombing, the Mountain Ash district was scheduled to be a reception area for evacuees from Birmingham, and a census was taken by teachers in preparation.[2]

By May 1939, the ARP Committee was broadened to incorporate wide swathes of civil society. Many organisations were co-opted including the Women's Voluntary Service – set up just before the war to support the work of ARP – St John's Ambulance Society; the Mountain Ash branch of the National Union of Teachers, the Chamber of Trade and Aberdare and Ynysybwl Co-operative Societies, as well as the Glamorgan Constabulary. A special meeting of the Council in August 1939 established a Food Control Committee, on which Hazell served, which also had representatives of Aberdare and Ynysybwl Co-operative Societies, Grocers Association, Butchers Association, and the Association of Milk and Dairymen locally. The following month Hazell became a member of the newly formed Fuel Control Committee on which were the two co-operative societies, Coalowners Association and the local gas and electricity undertakings.[3]

War

The declaration of war on Germany on 3 September 1939 started a period of six years during which time lives were turned upside down, families were disrupted and unprecedented state controls were introduced over the minutiae of peoples' lives. Hazell heard Chamberlain's Sunday radio broadcast with 'an overwhelming sense of grief and a pre-vision of the crucifixion and martyrdom of humanity… none of the horrors which followed surprised me in any way.'[4]

The outbreak of war caused the cancellation of the YCS jubilee celebrations, which were to have included a series of concert-meetings and demonstrations. It was feared that the winter education programme for children and adults of YCS, though arranged, would also have to be called off.[5]

In spite of the cancellation of the festivities, Hazell said that there was still cause to celebrate as for the first time in the Society's history sales had reached over £200,000 for the half-year to 5 September 1939 and membership and capital has also grown. Taking a long term perspective, Hazell pointed out that membership had grown from 18 to 8,000 members over 50 years. He eulogised the Society as 'the result of generations of collective effort and self-sacrificing endeavour' which 'met all human needs between the cradle and the tombstone, and including both'. Combining romance with social enterprise he continued: 'its co-operative appeal has been broad-based on meeting all consumers' needs… with ample justice to its wage-earning employees; a stable financial policy, and a social and educational programme, which with feet firmly planted on the good earth of co-operative commerce yet reaches up to the ideals of the stars.'[6] However, had he looked back over the 20 year period to 1920, it would have revealed that while membership had grown by nearly 50 per cent, sales had hardly increased, demonstrating a successful spread of co-operation but a fall in families' acquisitive capacity.

The war required immediate changes in co-operative trading. Hazell was one of 80 delegates from 39 co-operative societies who discussed the introduction of rationing, and shop opening hours were reduced. A food control system was introduced, with each Food Control Committee, which was to be responsible for food rationing, having a local co-operative representative on it. This was markedly different from the experience of the First World War. The introduction of the 'black-out' impacted on the Society.[7]

The Second World War shook the village as never before. With the threat of invasion, all signage had to be removed that might aid the enemy, though whether the removal of the name 'Ynysybwl' from the shop fronts, or keeping the signs on display, particularly in places such as Senghenydd or Abercynon, would have assisted the invader or confused them, is open to question. By June 1940 price controls had been introduced by the Government. Men were called to the armed forces and women were employed in large numbers, many for the first time, in war industries on the Treforest Trading Estate and particularly in the Royal Ordnance Factories of Bridgend and Hirwaun. As many men and women left the village to join the armed or other services, other children and women came to the village as evacuees. As the *Co-operative News* reported: 'Britain is on the move', with the editor commenting 'never before in our history has the population been so fluid!'[8]

All four of Hazell's sons went to war. Willie was now a regular soldier, and in June 1940 was a staff sergeant/instructor (later promoted to Captain) in the Education Corps in Egypt – he commented 'education or what I do in war-time' is just like eating pie to a Hazell'.[9] Now an adult, he looked an eerily younger version of his father.[10] Austen and Leslie joined the army, and the youngest, Roy, went to the Merchant Navy. Gunner Austen Hazell, in France with the BEF, was captured by Germans but escaped while lined up for interrogation and got back to Britain.[11] Roy's period in the Merchant Marine was not long lasting and was bedevilled by ill-health. He wrote to his sister Lilian from the SS Marconi, 'somewhere at sea', heading back to Cardiff, saying his health was deteriorating. Roy acknowledged that Lilian had been right when she said he was too weak to stand sea life. He had been 'as weak as a dog' when they reached Sierra Leone, and so was paid off there, so had to return to Britain as a passenger. On his return it was apparent that his illness had taken a considerable toll, for Roy had until a short time previously 'enjoyed a splendid health and was of striking physique'.[12]

Lilian wrote to Willie saying Roy was being attended by a specialist, but expressing concerns about whether he would recover from his illness. Her brother replied:

only we can understand, because we know Roy and his life-story. The rotten part of it is that I was hoping he could get to the stage where he'd have money and health, and independence.

Willie said he was worried every night about Roy – a mere boy – in his pain, and was asking God's help. Lilian had said that she was determined that she or Ivy would be with Roy, and Willie emphasised that Lilian 'OUGHT' to be with him. Willie was going to try and get leave, but considered that it would be 'fairly useless'. He said that he was also concerned about their father, then 50 years old, to whom he had written encouragingly:

> but we can't hope that he will be the same as in the old days. He's not so young, and has weathered many mental and physical storms. Dad and Roy are my chief concern.

Of his other brothers Willie said 'As to Leslie and Austin [sic], anything can happen to them, as to other people's brothers, but one can just hope.'[13] The *Ocean and National Magazine* said:

> Joy and misgiving mingle strangely in the case of these four brothers... The happiness of safe emergence from the life and death struggle in France is chilled by the memory of their youngest brother's broken health, and their anxiety and regret find a widespread echo in the hearts of all friends.[14]

Due to the seriousness of Roy's condition, Leslie and Austen were given special leave to visit him. Two weeks after Willie's letter, as France fell on 16 June 1940, 'universally popular' Roy Glandred, aged 18, died. He was buried in Ynysybwl cemetery with his mother Deborah Elizabeth. Of the children, only Austen, Lilian and Ivy could be present.[15] With the death of his youngest son, the 'vinegar' in Hazell's life continued.

Following the first wave of evacuees from Birmingham in 1939 the risk of invasion after the evacuation of Dunkirk presented a new danger to Britain, causing a further, unanticipated, wave of evacuees to arrive from Sheerness in late May and early June 1940. A letter from the Ministry of Health, dated 6 June 1940, thanked the Council, officers, volunteers and householders who received the Kent children for the rapid and efficient preparations made for their arrival, as well as for the warm welcome they received. Ynysybwl Mixed School had windows wire-netted and doors sandbagged. A Welfare Committee was established in Ynysybwl to address any problems arising. It comprised Hazell and Abel Morgan, the evacuated headteacher and the billeting officer.[16] Swept up in constant Council meetings, Hazell may have welcomed such activity as a distraction, permitting him little time to grieve over Roy's death.

With the Luftwaffe's control of northern French airfields, South Wales was now within range of enemy bombers. By early July, the Mountain Ash district was subjected to constant raiding over 10 days. With the risk of invasion imminent, defence volunteers were organised to guard the Council's gasworks, while the electrical plant was protected by the men employed there. The Council planned to construct new air raid shelters, considered the location of mortuaries for air raid casualties and oversaw the provision of water tanks and emergency fire precautions. However, not all went smoothly. The air raid sirens were inaudible in Ynysybwl, and the Council looked, with little success, for undertakers to attend to the people who might be killed in air attacks.[17] The fall of France led once more to a collapse in the coal trade 'and our population simply fled from us', with able-bodied men and families going to seek work in Birmingham, Coventry and London.[18] Ironically it was precisely these areas that would soon become targets for bombing, and from which evacuees would flee, some to Ynysybwl. When the Battle of Britain was at its most intense Hazell looked ahead and wrote 'war work today, combined with domestic anxiety, and strain arising from air raids and consequent loss of sleep, demands more than a 100 per cent efficiency for month after month and, as far as we can see ahead, for year after year.'[19]

Hazell's work in the YCS, and the co-operative movement more widely, was part of his contribution to the war effort. The co-operative movement was called on by its leaders to 'stand calm and firm' and to play the utmost part in working for victory. CWS Divisional meetings were dominated by war issues. In one, no doubt informed by the experience of having three sons in the army, Hazell proposed a scheme to overcome the heavy costs of sending parcels, such as cigarettes, to troops in Britain; instead he proposed a scheme of co-operative vouchers which could be exchanged at the nearest co-operative shop to where they were stationed. CWS Directors said that the idea was intriguing, though not without its complications, but was worthy of consideration. Encouraged, Hazell quickly wrote up his proposal, explaining that those in the forces came from co-operative families, and were future home-builders. He said that the idea would serve both mothers and sons, while being a business proposition which maintained trading, and ensured future trade. When published in the *Co-operative News*, though, it carried the editorial postscript that a new Budget proposal of providing duty-free cigarettes or tobacco to troops could make such a voucher scheme superfluous. However, the topicality of the issue placed his practical thinking at the forefront of the movement.[20]

Food rationing, introduced by the Government in early 1940 and requiring people to register with a trader to receive goods, made a considerable impact. In January 1940, over 19,000 people registered with the Society for their butter, bacon and sugar rations. As the Society's membership at that time was 8,251, the figures included other family members, which reflected the reach of the Society. However this 'datum' basis of registrations was put under considerable pressure by the influx of refugees and the outflow of inhabitants with which the Society had to cope.

Although evacuees, often staying in Society's members' homes, brought their ration books with them, they increased demand for goods, which was not matched by supply.[21]

While the manner of the introduction of the rationing system was an improvement on the Great War, it still had anomalies. In September 1940 Hazell wrote an article on rationing. With the knowledge gained from his Presidency of the Ynysybwl Society and his membership of the Food Control Committee, as well as his personal experience of living – and working – on rations, Hazell railed against a situation where there was

> neither equality of treatment nor sacrifice under the present food rationing regulations. To put it positively and provocatively, the regulations render equality impossible of attainment.

Hazell then undertook a class-based analysis of how adult civilians were all 'lumped together in a spurious "equality"'. He pointed out that while the middle class could patronise hotels and restaurants and get food on top of their rations, with game and salmon available to rich patrons of poulterers, fishmongers and purveyors of other luxuries, artisans were restricted by their income and environment to meals at home and work. Idlers, office workers and industrial workers, he argued, all received the same rations, irrespective of the calories that they burned or the work they did – or did not do. He called for the special calorific needs of miners, steelworkers and other heavy workers to be recognised, and gave a compelling and detailed description of how the rationing of tea 'severely handicapped' miners underground, adversely affecting their efficiency. He said that he was normally averse to increasing the number of Government Departments but felt that a Ministry of Nutrition was needed to address these issues. These measures 'would not achieve equality' he said, 'but would do a great deal towards it by ironing out some of the grosser inequalities of a Rationing Scheme under a capitalist system.'[22] As usual, taking action as well as writing,

Hazell led a discussion on rationing at a meeting of the Brecon, Monmouth and East Glamorgan District Association, where all agreed that the rationing system should be overhauled.

The arrival of large numbers of evacuee children and women placed considerable pressure on services. Additional beds had to be provided at the maternity hospital and the Council requisitioned unoccupied premises, under Defence Regulations. Mountain Ash Boys Club had to accommodate a nursery and Ynysybwl school clinic doubled up as a food office. Schools and other social amenities became so full that Mountain Ash Council asked for air raid warden and first aid posts to be removed from school premises, and playgrounds were opened in the evenings for evacuated children. By October 1940, 2,266 billeting allowances were paid for people who had come to the district, including Ynysybwl, and there were also about 200 adults and children for whom no allowances were paid. People were still arriving independently from Sheerness, London and the east coast, but with government certificates. In December the Council considered communal feeding of the unemployed, old age pensioners and evacuees. Communal feeding, previously organised during industrial disputes by miners and their families on a voluntary basis, was now sponsored by the state because of the demands of wartime. Due to problems with mothers and children, the Council decided to focus on evacuees initially and the Council of Social Service set up two feeding centres for an experimental period with a canteen established in Ynysybwl Church Hall.[23]

During wartime, Hazell wrote, the Council struggled to maintain its local services, for 'Without them the people could not live.' Notwithstanding extra work generated by the risk of aerial bombardment and the needs of evacuees, the Council's daily work had to continue. A serious diphtheria outbreak gripped the district from the spring of 1940, when over 100 residents were admitted to the Authority's isolation hospital. In September, 87 new cases were reported and continued to be recorded for the rest of the year.[24] The strain on Council officers striving to sustain new and existing services was enormous.

During the war, Hazell seems to have been even more vigorous in holding CWS Directors to account. In April 1941, he critiqued a CWS report and balance sheet, saying he read it in the same way as he read war communiqués, looking not only at what was said, but also what was not said. He identified areas where the Directors had 'left them in the dark', which included restrictions on industries, and the probable closing of some CWS factories.[25]

Coal had been the first commodity brought under Government control in wartime but the premature introduction of regulations and early rationing brought chaos to the coal trade. Hazell was keenly aware of the local and national difficulties suffered by the coal trade in wartime. The setting up of coal supply machinery, difficulties arising such as the availability of wagons, the deferment of key workers, railway transport, hindrances caused by air raids, war damage, shortages of labour and fuel shortages and the distribution of coal during emergencies[26] were dealt with as a member of the Government's Emergency Coal Advisory Committee for East Glamorgan in 1940/41, as Chair of the Western Section of Co-operative Coal Trades Association and at the Association's National Executive.

Hazell attended emergency meetings in Manchester, in co-operative buildings protected by 10-feet high sandbag walls, to consider introducing controls due to the intensification of the war. During the dreary days and nights of wartime, train journeys to meetings could be long and dark, and travelling was a constant burden.[27] Hazell recounted one journey to a Coal Trade Association National Executive meeting which graphically conveyed his experiences in 1940 – which he considered the worst year of the war. He left Cardiff as the bombs were falling, and there was also 'enemy action' in Newport. He arrived in 'blackout Crewe' at 1am and the train, scheduled to have reached Manchester at 8.15pm, eventually arrived at 3am in the middle of an air raid. He then attempted to cross the city, 'wretchedly tired', feeling his way in pitch darkness. He had breakfast at 5am in the YMCA 'War-time Canteen – Open Day and Night' – before attending the meeting. He asked, 'was co-operative business of such importance that we had to risk injury, possibly life itself[,] on this journey? Was it really necessary?' before affirming his determination to see it through.[28] Business also took Hazell to London during the Blitz. He described being there at the time of 'a severe blitz' when ashes fell the following morning, several miles away, which 'were the pitiful remnants of the burning books – round the St Paul's area'.[29] When in July 1940, the Co-operative Union set up a Mutual Aid Scheme for societies that suffered war damage from bombing to help mitigate their losses and share the burden across the whole movement, YCS immediately pledged its quota of £1,670.[30]

The blitz quickly came closer to home. On 2 and 3 January 1941, the Council's Fire Brigade was called upon to help when Cardiff was bombed. The CWS headquarters in Cardiff, where Hazell attended Divisional meetings, was hit during the attack, including the Boardroom, which was destroyed, and the Assembly Hall. The following month, three firemen from Ynysybwl were injured in Swansea when fighting fires from enemy action during the 'three-night raid' from 19 to 23 February 1941.[31] During the Swansea blitz, the smart new premises of Swansea Co-operative Society, which had been built in 1926, were flattened. Hazell referred to the town's '1941 crucifixion' when 'the old Swansea disappeared in three nights, like Pompeii of old, though not through natural phenomena, but by the ghastly impact of total war.'[32] Call-outs to support other brigades such as Cardiff and Gloucester continued.[33]

Suddenly the arrangements being made for the Mountain Ash

district were very real. Fire watching was enhanced and business premises in Ynysybwl linked up with appropriate Street Fire Fighting Schemes. The personnel of the YCS Works Department formed a Civil Defence rescue team in Pontypridd and spotters and fire watchers were appointed at the gas works. Volunteers signed up for street fire watching, undertaking duties of not less than 48 hours per month. It was agreed to construct 15 purpose-built public surface shelters in Mountain Ash, Miskin, Penrhiwceiber, Abercynon and Ynysybwl, instead of relying on those in adapted buildings, and sandbags were provided for each house.[34]

Mountain Ash was bombed on 31 May 1941 and more than 1,000 houses were damaged and 100 made uninhabitable. The General Hospital was damaged by the blast and Duffryn Road School was completely destroyed. Rescue parties and decontamination squads were deployed.[35] A Richmal Crompton story of William Brown revealed 'bomb snobbery' displayed by some evacuees, with their tales of shelter life and how to deal with incendiaries, which had been told until '(t)he village was sick of such descriptions'. If local inhabitants of Mountain Ash were suffering any 'bomb inferiority complex', it would have quickly dissipated.[36] A Special Council meeting called to consider air raid damage agreed to hire over 60 slaters, carpenters and labourers. Perhaps a little belatedly the Council ordered 960 steel helmets for street fire volunteers, which represented approximately one in 30 of the district's population.[37] The raid was a small but immediate indication of the much greater suffering inflicted elsewhere. Although Ynysybwl itself was not bombed this air attack was sufficiently close for the population to know that no village, street or house was safe.

Parts of the community, often left shabby and tired after a decade of neglect, came into their own in a burst of improvisation to meet the demands placed on them by total war. An information centre was set up in Mountain Ash Workmen's Hall and Institute where the local Citizens Advice Bureau (CAB) provided support to those made homeless. Local activity to address demands thrown up by wartime continued apace. An appeal to residents was made through the press for help in billeting evacuees and a door-to-door collection took place for London's National Air Raid Distress Fund. The Council assumed new areas of responsibility, such as War Weapons Week and the War Charities Act, with seemingly each street setting up its own fund to welcome home people in the forces. The Maternity and Child Welfare Committee, of which Hazell was chair from May 1940, considered establishing wartime nurseries for children under five years old. The Public Health Committee, whose role seemed to grow ever wider, requisitioned all unnecessary iron or steel railings for the war effort. The Second World War provided the opportunity for Hazell to follow his chosen path in life, that of serving others, even more vigorously than before. With a willingness to address the most intractable of problems, Hazell became Chairman of Ynysybwl CAB and took charge of its panel dealing with ration book and food problems.[38]

Communal feeding, which had been established at the end of 1940, was superseded by a 'British restaurant' in Mountain Ash, while more were considered for Penrhiwceiber and Abercynon. Hazell, conscious that the middle and upper classes could eat unrationed food in restaurants, wrote supportively about these not-for-profit restaurants run by the Council, which offered cheap, nourishing meals for 'the hitherto unmet needs of the working and serving population and the poor'. He explained that by concentrating on one particular dish each day they applied mass production to catering, resulting in wholesome meals at economical prices. While criticising some for their poor location or other weaknesses Hazell said that after the war these communal restaurants should be taken over by the co-operative movement or municipal authorities. Hazell also identified the need for pit-head and factory canteens as 'urgent and self apparent', based, in part, on the experience that YCS was gaining in providing food for pit canteens locally. YCS considered that such catering for colliery workers was a 'national service' and, although the profit margin was small, the goodwill to the Society from the mining community was immense. As a *Co-operative News* editorial identified, although they had been set up to meet a need in abnormal circumstances, these new facilities had changed the habits and inclinations of the people. The co-operative movement, said the editorial, had to adapt to the changing habits of the people, and the provision of people's restaurants was a way of keeping the close link that was one of the movement's greatest assets.[39]

The expansion of the war industries and the need for new services slowly began to get some people back into work. There was, though, still a premium on jobs and a strict set of criteria was established for local authority employment with vacancies shared around the wards in succession, with each appointment lasting eight weeks. Councillors still had considerable scope for – indeed, power of – patronage. For example, it was for Hazell to recommend who should get the job of Ynysybwl Cemetery Clerk, and the appointment of labourers and of a 'Permanent Man' in Ynysybwl was left to the members of Ynysybwl ward to determine.[40]

Wartime gave the state – often through its local authority manifestation – unprecedented powers to regulate, organise and intervene in almost all aspects of life. The minutes of Mountain Ash UDC graphically depict its centrality to events locally, and demonstrate the important, dynamic and far-reaching role it played in an extraordinary period. The sense of shared purpose, change of pace and widening of focus during those years gave Hazell's work through local government, (as well as through the co-operative movement) added relevance as one of millions of unsung contributions to the war effort. Juliet Gardiner's observation that the war on the Home Front would be won by 'carrying on as usual, while making monumental changes, and "pretending that nothing untoward was happening"' captured perfectly Hazell's wartime experience.[41]

The growing of vegetables, which Hazell had done in the 1930s to help make domestic ends meet, was just as necessary a decade later as a response to the wartime 'Dig for Victory' campaign. His prodigious gardening efforts were rewarded in the quantity of food produced to supplement meagre rations and in winning the Cup at the Bristol Co-operative Society's Horticultural Association exhibition as the competitor who scored highest across all categories at the 1942 show. His obedience to the 'Grow More Food' dictum was captured in an article which, as well as giving thanks for produce which would help feed the family, also celebrated the feeding of his soul and spirit by mignonette flowers which grew unplanned in his onion patch. In his usual literary style, he held forth on the beauty of the mignonette as an alternative to 'brutality and war drunkenness'.[42]

There was occasional light relief from wartime duties. In 1940, Hazell went on holiday to North Wales, including Llanberis. Also, delegates of the Brecon, Monmouth and East Glamorgan District Association of the Co-operative Union, meeting at Pontypridd as guests of YCS, made a presentation to Hazell for having completed 25 years on the Society's Management Board.[43]

The increased employment and income levels of wartime transformed YCS's business. In his half-yearly report to September 1941, Hazell said that YCS's finances had never been more sound. In fact, the Society was drowning in cash. YCS invested in war bonds; contributed £2,500 to 'Pontypridd Warship Week' in 1942 and in 1943, gave £5,000 towards a fighter in the town's 'Wings for Victory' week, which carried the inscription 'Ynysybwl Co-operative' on it. These were on top of the Excess Profits Tax, Excess Profits Duty, and the National Defence

Contribution introduced for munitions and other industries, which the Society had to pay. YCS contributed liberally to the 'Help for Russia' fund, as well as providing support for China. While the Society would have liked to put more into its reserves, it could not as it would have incurred heavy taxation. The Society was also drowning in wartime controls. By September 1942, the *Co-operative News* reported that there were 8,000 regulations which applied to a co-operative society.[44]

Writing in Wartime

Throughout the war, whatever the circumstances, Hazell continued writing and his scope was as wide-ranging as ever. In April 1940 he wrote of a week spent visiting London. One morning he sat in the reading room of the British Museum 'thinking of a certain world's genius' who had sat there researching nearly 90 years earlier. His respect for Marx's intellect was obvious, not least in his description of him as 'this hero of thought'. Hazell paralleled Marx's drafting of the Communist Manifesto – 'his "Bible of the working classes"' – to the Rochdale Pioneers setting up their Society a year earlier. He urged co-operators to read *Capital*.

> Fellow-co-operators, read Charles Marks! If you fail to read or understand his earlier chapters, do not fail to read chapters 12 and 13. Here you find the finest history and indictment of the Industrial [*sic*] revolution I know of. Marx gives chapter and verse for everything.

Hazell's detailed comments on Marx, including the footnotes, showed that he studied his Marx as he studied his Bible or poetry. He regularly quoted Marx, though less frequently than the Bible. Hazell reported what he considered Marx's generally positive views of Robert Owen, as well as his comments in *Capital* that co-operation was 'being used as a cloak for reactionary humbug' and 'one of the isolated factors of transformation.'

Turning that comment on its head, Hazell wrote, 'Well, let us be proud of having taken some part, however small, in the work of transforming the world'. He only wished the co-operators in 1940 could be half as fearless as Marx had been when he wrote *Capital*. Writing with the war beginning to turn the world upside down, and conscious of Marx's time in London, he said 'May these islands ever provide refuge for the oppressed, regardless of their religion, race, politics, or economic beliefs.' He concluded 'the writer again puts forward the urgent plea: Read! Read right! Read left! But do not omit to read Marx...'[45]

Though he respected Marx, it was to Owen – whose words were 'social stilettos entering the atrophied social conscience of the early nineteenth century'[46] – that Hazell primarily looked for inspiration. Hazell readily acknowledged his indebtedness to Owen 'for his efforts, for his village system of co-operative trading, for the variety and enterprise of his educational work; [and] for his untiring pioneering in social welfare of his people.'[47] As with Marx, Hazell read Owen's writings, regularly drawing on his ideas or work. Hazell contrasted his own experience of 20 years membership of an education authority with Owen's educational policies and practice, saying that schools were still '"cramming" institutions, with obsolete examination methods, governed in part by punishments and threats, inadequately staffed by 'mass-production, two-year-course automatons and miscalled "teachers". He contrasted them with Owen's approach of opening children's minds and getting them to think without threat of punishment. His scathing comments were underlined by his view that educational opinion was 'still unready, and/or unwilling' to accept Owen's methods and teachings.[48]

In December 1941 he penned an article on the Welsh National Anthem, giving its words a radical interpretation. He wrote that the 'Land of my Fathers' must be returned to its people in a literal as well as spiritual sense, and that feudal land ownerships and land syndicates 'and leasehold abominations' should be swept away. He also gave it an environmental perspective, saying that 'defiled mining valleys must be cleansed, restored, and beautified.' He said how in 1940 he had seen 'heaps of slate quarry rubbish being tipped into the lake of lovely peace at Llanberis. "What a crime! What a sin! What an enormity against 'Gwlad! Gwlad!'"' Finally he evoked the anthem to counter German and Italian dictatorships.[49]

The co-operative movement began to discuss its post-war plans as early as February 1941. The next month, Hazell analysed different forms of peace, calling for a 'new Europe' in which co-operators had to be free to carry on their work for a new order of 'social security'.[50] The following year, he wrote of 'the urgency of our task in shaping the post-war policy of co-operation' in relation to the balance needed between 'stateism' [sic] and voluntary co-operation with few state fetters or controls. He identified the key issues as the reorganisation of the movement, and the attitude of the movement to the post-war state, as well as the interaction between them. On the movement's relations to the state, and its place within it, Hazell thought that a new government would 'have its hands full' with the post-war challenges of housing, demobilisation and the transition of the economy back to peacetime production, so 'any sensible post-war State should welcome the opportunity of having at hand a ready-made instrument of economic production and distribution – with limitless potentialities of expansion.' He said that such an opportunity '**may never come our way again**'. With its close links in every village, town and city, its basis in social justice, and by the 'sheer merit of its economic stability' the movement should '**compel**' the adoption of co-operation by any post-war central government.[51] Hazell believed that the movement had largely secured unity of purpose, but there was need for unity of action (although unity should not mean uniformity).[52] However, the clarity of Hazell's analysis was not matched by the movement's capacity or desire to address the issues he identified. Nor did the relationship between the co-operative movement and the post-war Labour Government meet Hazell's aspirations, with the differences between them becoming a key theme of his writing after 1945.

The publication of the Beveridge Report in late 1942 provided further evidence of Hazell's capacity for challenging thinking. At a time when the Beveridge Report was rapturously welcomed – *The Times* said it 'succeeded in crystallising the vague but keenly felt aspirations of millions of people'[53] – Hazell was unimpressed. In contrast to those who saw it as a 'second Magna Carta' or the 'People's Charter', Hazell wrote an article entitled 'Beveridge Report is Ambulance Work', saying that it envisaged no basic social or economic change. He argued that under Beveridge the 'Unholy Trinity' of Interest, Rent and Profit remained untouched and that it would not slay any of the five giants of Want, Disease, Ignorance, Squalor, and Idleness. It was, he concluded, what its title indicated, a report on social insurance on an actuarial basis, and gave 'Nothing for Nothing'. He continued that Beveridge's five giants were in fact 'One Giant with five heads, the giant being Competitive Capitalism'. He criticised Beveridge's comment that 'A revolutionary moment in the world's history is a time for revolutions, and not patching', saying that no revolution was proposed on any of the Report's 300 pages, adding that '[T]he worse than feudal land system; the financial octopus; the great industrial interests; the landlords – all can breathe again, for they remain untouched!' Analysing the Report from the perspective of nutrition levels or old age, he described it as 'ambulance work' and a 'patchwork', before concluding that 'every penny spent on co-operative business and so diverted from private enterprise, will in essence and reality, be more important in significance to our social future in the Commonwealth than every thousand pounds in the Beveridge Scheme'.[54] At a time when the Report had made

Beveridge a national hero, Hazell's independence of thought was confidently based in his own principles of what determined progress in social administration as well as a critical and forensic analysis of the 200,000-word report.

As a writer, Hazell could place co-operation within the scope of political philosophy or political economy. In arguing the movement's pathbreaking credentials, he pointed out that it accepted women's suffrage long before Mrs Pankhurst and the Women's Social and Political Union; that it introduced one person one vote early, and that it made capital the servant of industry and the community long before Marx wrote *Das Capital*, as well as adopting universalism (membership open to all). He said that co-operation made France's 1789 slogan 'Liberty, Equality, Fraternity' into a **workable and working formula**'.[55]

Writing in June 1942, before the victories in North Africa and Russia showed that the tide of war might turn in favour of the Allies, Hazell drew co-operators' attention to the old Welsh proverb *Bydd Ben – Bydd Bont*. He postulated co-operation as the bridge over which 'an agonised world' could pass to achieve 'a higher and peaceful plane of existence, a spiritual and material commonwealth'. He argued that 'If the co-operators of 1942 wish to achieve they must serve…'[56] and saw the unending quest of the co-operative ideal as 'essentially a commonwealth, a brotherhood, a classless society.'[57]

However, it was to a different brotherhood that Hazell looked when he wrote a powerful article entitled 'The Whole Nation is In Debt to "Strikers"'. His argument showed him as a man of principle, whose steady way of conducting his life sometimes masked innate radicalism. At a time when strikes were banned and, particularly unofficial strikes, considered by many to be unpatriotic, Hazell defended them saying: 'It is quite simple to state in undeniable terms the debt each and all owe to strikes'. He continued 'has not practically every reform and concession wrung from the employing classes through the years, been at some time or other, cause or subject matter of strike action?' He ranged wide, from the Dock Strike of 1889 to the Labour Party owing 'most of its motive-power and early dynamism to industrial disputes', arguing that many of the Labour MPs who voted in the House of Commons for the regulation against 'incitement' owed their early influence to participation in industrial disputes, strikes, or even 'incitement'. He reasoned that the origins of nine-tenths of voluntary movements, including friendly and co-operative societies could be traced to 'agitators'. He went on robustly:

> The nation is eternally in debt to the strike! What measures of emancipation for its masses, what means of progress for its workers, what organised expression of public opinion would have achieved so much without this now proscribed weapon?

before concluding:

> It is worth asking ourselves: Is coercion any real and solid remedy for social, economic and industrial evils? And again, if you illegalise open incitement to cease work, do you not drive agitation underground, and inevitably make it more dangerous to 'authority'?[58]

He later attributed the minimum wage, the eight-hour day, national agreements and the nationalisation of the coal industry to rank and file spontaneous action.[59] Hazell the trades unionist coexisted easily with Hazell the co-operator. Generally occupying different spheres, both were grounded in clear yet different principles which were not at odds.

Winding Down the War, Building for Peace

The challenges of wartime planning were exacerbated by social fluidity caused by inflows and outflows of population. In 1944, notification was received that 400 Bevin Boys would be allocated to Ynysybwl to work in Lady Windsor Colliery though finding billets for them was problematic.[60] Added to the mix were

American soldiers based in Pontypridd, Cilfynydd and Aberdare. To a valleys community that had become accustomed to losing its people in a constant outflow in the years up to the war, the population swirl experienced from 1939 to 1945 shook it upside down.

The attempts at planning the provision of services for evacuees exemplify the difficulties. In August 1943, a Council meeting on educational reorganisation discussed the considerable drop in the numbers of people accommodated locally under the Government's evacuation scheme, even though all community resources were still needed to support those remaining, including chapel vestries to feed schoolchildren. When V1 flying-bombs and V2 rockets were launched against London and the South East from mid-June 1944, the outflow from the district was reversed with 800 evacuees arriving in a week from Tunbridge Wells in Kent. Hazell chaired the Finance Committee which decided to send a loudspeaker van around the district asking householders to help, as well as getting churches to appeal to people. If insufficient billets were found compulsory billeting by the Council would be undertaken.[61]

In a CWS Divisional meeting in mid-July 1944, Hazell raised the influx of official and unofficial evacuees, who had been arriving daily for three weeks. 'What were societies to do to meet the requirements of these people?' he asked. CWS Directors reiterated what Hazell already knew, that the system by which goods were allocated was obsolete. Based on pre-war purchase levels, it did not take account of population flows. As a result, some parts of the country had surplus goods while others had shortages.[62] When in February 1945 Birmingham Council wrote a letter of appreciation for the support that had been given to its evacuees (most of whom had by then presumably returned to Birmingham), there were still 1,561 evacuees in the District of whom over 1,200 were children.[63]

This late burst of activity ran counter to the flow of most Council work, which was winding down the machinery of war. In September 1944 – five years after the blackout was imposed – the regulations eased to a 'dimout' before being lifted completely in April 1945. Mountain Ash UDC was also permitted a relaxation of fire guard duties before the fire service capacity was reduced, its equipment sold off and the Fire Guard Officer contract terminated. The emergency mortuary service was wound down and the British restaurant was to close.[64]

As war-related activity reduced, attention turned towards reconstruction. From 1943, increasing amounts of the Authority's time was spent planning post-war housing, education and other services. The mobilisation of the state during wartime had impacted on Hazell. It demonstrated what could be achieved when political will and state resources were harnessed and the speed at which it could be attained, offsetting to some extent the co-operative movement's traditional suspicion of the state. Local councils could be a motor for positive change: if nurseries could be established for women workers and increasing amenities and entertainments provided for workers during their summer holidays during wartime, why could such things not happen in peacetime?

During the last, vital, year of the war, Hazell was central to the Council's post-war planning, overseeing every aspect of its reconstruction plans. As he completed 21 years of service as a Councillor, he occupied a series of strategic posts, including Chair of both Housing and Finance Committees and was also elected Chairman of the Council,[65] giving him a unique vantage point.

In March 1944, Hazell chaired the Council committee that recommended building 120 houses in Ynysybwl. Three months later, he attended a meeting of all Glamorgan and Monmouthshire UDCs on post-war housing. Initially the Authority decided to concentrate on permanent housing but following a visit by Hazell and others to Northolt for a demonstration of pre-fabricated houses – prefabs – the decision was reversed. Two hundred factory made temporary houses were ordered although only 100 were allocated to them.[66]

Hazell was also actively engaged in post-war planning through the co-operative movement, becoming President of the Brecon, Monmouth and East Glamorgan District Association of the Western Section of the Co-operative Union in July 1943. He was involved in discussions on the future of the coal industry through the Western Section of the Coal Trade Association. In April 1945, Hazell called on the CWS to take over de-commissioned government factories, rather than allow private enterprise to get them. He also maintained pressure for more CWS factories for South Wales and raised questions about the roles of Wholesale Society Directors, and their manner of conducting business.[67]

Hazell was struck by the similarity of the problems faced by local authorities and the co-operative movement. Attending a conference of urban authorities in Westminster on the reorganisation of local government, with 1,047 urban and rural authorities in England and Wales and around 1,000 co-operative societies, he identified where each could complement the other. A key area was housing with Hazell convinced that only the state had the resources to address this national priority. As early as 1930, he had argued that the magnitude of the problem was too big for non-state resources,[68] recognising it as the only area beyond the capacity of the co-operative movement. As both sectors wondered what the future held for them, Hazell proposed how Council and co-operative activities could be woven seamlessly. Arguing that efforts should be focussed on the state to provide, he proposed: 'Co-operators, through their political party, should support national State action on housing, and not waste effort and fritter away energies on what must become merely trivial results through voluntary action.'[69] From a co-operative perspective he wrote that housing needs were 'so overwhelming that what we or any other voluntary movement may do can be only a drop in the bucket'. The co-operative movement, he stated, should therefore concentrate on furnishings needed for new housing, and possibly the provision of building materials.

Despite wartime difficulties, including queuing; rationing and shortages, the co-operative movement and the Ynysybwl Society flourished during the Second World War. YCS membership rose from 8,146 to 11,145, although its reach was much wider, with registration for rations rising to over 20,000 people. Paradoxically, though, the very growth of societies inhibited their capacity to deliver due to the movement being hamstrung by the 'Datum' limitations by which food was allocated according to pre-war trading patterns, which resulted in fewer goods to be shared amongst the membership. Even so, as the local population had better levels of income than in the previous decade and as people spent more and rebuilt their savings, the Society's economic base was strengthened. The Society's capital (i.e. individual members' savings with the Society) more than doubled from £202,764 to £429,538 and its trade for one half-year period rose from £200,352 to £352,021. The Society's reserves – albeit deliberately depressed to avoid disproportionate taxation – rose from £12,000 to £18,875. The Ynysybwl Society's Christmas trade for 1944 was a record. Moreover, the co-operative movement's policy of fair shares for all won it a good name for equitable distribution, which stood it in good stead after the war.[70]

Most significantly, a complete shift in the balance of retail power was demonstrated in 1944 when the Ynysybwl Society acquired the Pontypridd Shopping Arcade, which had 14 shops on each side. Private traders could no longer resist the economic power of YCS. Although government restrictions meant the development had to be deferred until after the war, it was intended to demolish the whole site to build a new emporium of several floors, possibly an assembly hall, a concert hall and a café on top.[71]

CHAPTER 4

Socialism in Our Time?

Post-War Reconstruction

Britain at the end of the Second World War was worn out, the population tired and their clothes were shabby. Those on the 'home front' with rationing, bombings, the blackout and shortages had endured the war just as much as members of the armed services. Alan Allport captured that period of 'weary faces' and 'grim purpose'. Retail had become 'synonymous with rudeness and petty tyranny' where choice and courtesy had become 'precious commodities' and it was 'not merely the absence of the goods they want, but of a frigid, half contemptuous manner... of the eternal 'No'.[1]

Hazell said that co-operators had been 'tried to the point of human endurance' and recorded:

> All of us connected with the administration of co-operative
> business during 1945 have been harassed almost to breaking point.
> Every day we anticipated that last straw under which we would
> finally collapse. ...Yet we have pulled ourselves together...[2]

While they had at times, lost perspective of the dreams of the movement, the worst had not happened, and they were 'still masters of our souls', with their co-operative ideals, although sorely tested, still intact.

As a lifelong Labour man, Hazell was delighted with the election of the Labour Government in July 1945, which he described as 'a people's government', with its strong mandate and large majority, and was proud that the Ynysybwl Society had four of its members elected to Parliament.[3] He welcomed the introduction of the National Health Service and the welfare state – with caveats – and saw the implications of taking over the Bank of England as 'possibly the most important and tangible foundations for national and social progress.'[4] However, he recognised that the Attlee Government had to travel a 'long and maybe hard road to a new Britain' and that unity was essential and called for a 'rock-like' support from informed co-operators.[5]

After six years of war, the economy was struggling, there were shortages of raw materials and austerity was debilitating. Without the strict personal discipline and shared sense of purpose of wartime, shortages of non-rationed goods resulted in the emergence of what Hazell referred to as the '1945 black market', which endured.[6]

A combination of factors meant that it was hard to meet the needs of co-operative members and other consumers. Industry, including co-operative capacity, needed to convert from wartime to peacetime production, while the Government emphasised producing for export rather than domestic consumption in order to address the balance of payments crisis. Hazell suggested that CWS factories had not been released from war work as freely as others and pressed for their conversion back to peacetime production, although CWS Directors disagreed, and co-operative society delegates at CWS Divisional meetings impatiently called for more production of consumer goods. However rationing of some foodstuffs tightened rather than eased and Hazell observed that queues were becoming more common and longer than during the war.[7] While the war had been won, it would prove more difficult to win the peace.

So difficult was the situation in 1946 and 1947 that Mountain Ash UDC received food gifts from the Dominions and Colonies for distribution to the aged and needy, with the British Red

Cross distributing food for the disabled. Canned fruits were sent from Australia 'to help to vary the British diet'. As there were considered to be fewer deserving cases in Ynysybwl than in other wards the village received less support. It fell to Hazell and Abel Morgan to decide who of those on public assistance in Ynysybwl were the most deserving to receive it.[8] While there would have been numbers of grateful recipients, in general distribution would have been a thankless task inevitably attracting criticism.

In 1946 the worrying spectre of unemployment returned to the valleys as Hazell reported its reappearance in Mountain Ash. In late 1944, Hazell had expressed concern over the White Paper on post-war employment policy and its acceptance of pockets of unemployment. With the Council still operating unemployment relief schemes and with memories of the difficult period after the Great War still fresh, a deputation was received from the Mountain Ash Unemployed Association. The hangover of the interwar years was evident in Mountain Ash with the Workmen's Institute still paying off part of accumulated rate arrears.[9]

The Ynysybwl Society's Management Board, too, was expecting difficult post-war years. Although its fears were not to be realised Hazell was one of several delegates who raised unemployment at a CWS meeting, returning to the familiar pre-war refrain for 'a clear cut and definitive statement' on CWS intentions in allocating factories and workshops to South Wales. Until the mid-1950s he pressed that South Wales had not got its share of productive works from the CWS. Unconvinced that the post-war boom was anything other than a passing phase, Hazell still believed that 'unemployment, poverty and insecurity were the peoples' enemies' just as they had been before the war.[10] For those of the South Wales valleys, the inter-war experience was too bitter and too recent to be quickly disregarded.

Despite the difficulties of the transition back to peacetime and post-war austerity there were clear signs of people's desire to make the most of peace. As ever Hazell was centrally involved, leading arrangements in Ynysybwl as Victory in Europe (VE) and Victory over Japan (VJ) Days were celebrated with street teas and bunting, and he was on the celebrations committee for the Victory Day national holiday on 8 June 1946.[11]

The major challenge facing Councillor Hazell was accommodation. Houses had deteriorated after ten years of neglect during the Depression, followed by six years of war when resources were prioritised towards the war effort. Although there had been some bomb damage in Mountain Ash the rest of the district was largely saved from the widespread destruction of housing stock suffered in Swansea and other urban centres. However, the demobilisation of the armed forces, with the return of men and women looking to set up new homes and start families, brought added demand. In January 1946, of the 493 people on the Authority's housing waiting list, 238 were in Ynysybwl, 145 in Abercynon and 110 in Mountain Ash and Penrhiwceiber. Ynysybwl therefore suffered the greatest housing pressure for, although it had only around 13 per cent of the Local Authority's population, it had nearly 50 per cent of the people on the housing list.[12]

The tight, centrally-controlled economy restricted the number of new houses that councils were allocated. Shortage of materials meant that only 124 houses were built in 1947. For 1949, the Authority's allocation for all houses, including the private sector, was 96. In a situation where demand so outstripped supply, housing allocation was fraught with difficulties. Hazell was one of two councillors from each ward brought onto the committee that determined their allocation. In March 1949, the Secretary of Lady Windsor Lodge wrote to the Council Houses Management Committee saying there had been an unfair allocation of 'prefabs' in Ynysybwl. The Committee replied that 'in spite of the difficulty of allocating a comparatively small number of houses amongst a very large number of applicants... after a careful consideration of all the circumstances of the applicants, the houses have been allocated to the most deserving cases.' The complaint by the Lodge may not have carried criticism of the local councillors, Hazell and Abel Morgan, implied at first sight: two months later council house management for the ward was revised and vested in a committee comprising the two men, plus the chairman of the Council,[13] giving them even greater influence over the allocation of council houses in Ynysybwl. As it was impossible to satisfy the competing demands of his electorate, housing was to remain a burden of office for Hazell.

Hazell's influence over prioritisation for council housing at a time of massive accommodation shortages highlights his considerable powers of patronage as a local councillor. Also, with unemployment and austerity still major problems, he had the power to determine who should get certain local authority jobs and who, of the most needy, should receive extra food. Such influence carried risks of corruption, favouritism or nepotism. All evidence suggests that Hazell was a man of rectitude. Indeed, he wrote that while most co-operative societies had rules against nepotism the President must guard against more insidious forms of favouritism, whether given or received, and had to avoid favours which would 'undermine his independence of soul and warp his keen sense of duty'. In local government he hinted at corrupt practices elsewhere, including the unhealthy canvassing of local councillors in the Rhondda around educational appointments, which had reached 'undesirable proportions' and which put great pressure on local education committees. He also referred to nepotism in local government in the Rhondda.[14] Although he did not explore the theme further, the fact that he was prepared to refer to such practices in print indicates his disapproval.

Despite difficult circumstances, including continued rationing, YCS made considerable progress in the early post-war years. The

Society undertook a development programme of renovations of buildings and branches from 1945 to 1952, despite government restrictions. As YCS took operational control of Abertridwr and Senghenydd, Caerphilly became increasingly important to the Society. Hazell's vision of co-operative societies furnishing new properties came to fruition and by 1947 YCS was providing furnishings for hundreds of houses and prefabs, including in Mountain Ash, Caerphilly and Ynysybwl.[15]

Hazell never lost sight of the importance of the grassroots co-operative member. In considering the role of the YCS in its society, he looked at the life of a notional member from the cradle to the grave, listing the services offered by the Society at each stage. His analysis included the changed use of the 'ever popular' dividend in the lives of its members over the 60 years of the Society's existence. He described its role in helping members through rainy days and sickness before the welfare state; as the emergency reserve of 'the divi' was made increasingly redundant by the welfare state, it was used to pay for holidays and 'quite a number' of members had used it to buy the house they lived in.[16]

The Diamond Jubilee of YCS in 1949 was both a celebration and an opportunity to promote the work of the Society, especially as the war had forced the cancellation of the 50th Anniversary celebrations. In May 1949 Hazell recorded that the Society's sales in the 12 months to March had exceeded £1 million for the first time. This was helped by the easing of rationing, such as on clothes and milk for domestic customers. External tributes came thick and fast. Robert Southern, Acting General Secretary of the Co-operative Union, referred to the Society's 'practical contribution in creating a sound social order based on freedom and enlightenment', sentiments with which Hazell would have concurred. A R Davies, Western Section secretary, said the achievements of YCS over 60 years were all the more remarkable bearing in mind the geographical area they operated in and the social and industrial conditions prevailing there.[17]

However, the Society's role was not necessarily appreciated in its own village. A survey on the extent and virility of voluntary association in Ynysybwl conducted by a local volunteer for Mass Observation in 1947[18] identified 19 local organisations. Pride of place was given to the miners' lodge, said to have been involved with all progressive agitations including extra bus services, ambulance car, miners' canteen, pit head baths, housing problems and recreation. The survey also identified the Institute Committee, which provided education and cultural activities including the cinema and library. The wide-ranging list covered everything from amateur dramatics to the Conservative Club 'almost entirely for drinking purposes' and showed the rich voluntary life of the village, particularly as it did not include the activities of the chapels. As a trustee of the Institute and member of the Canteen Committee, Hazell was involved in some of them.

Surprisingly, the survey, which even included the 'pretty passive' Unemployed Association, did not mention YCS. Apart from the WCG, the co-operative movement went unremarked. This was not through lack of effort for the Society still ran education classes, children's choirs and a range of other activities. Possibly the Society, although integral to everyday life, was so taken for granted that the correspondent failed to list it, regarding it as a shop and ignoring its non-retail activities and ideals. Equally, following the transfer of its headquarters to Pontypridd 15 years earlier, it may have been less visible in its original community, especially as the movement tended to focus on providing services for its own members. Another reason may have been that the co-operative movement sought to represent a sector – the consumer – which was still ahead of its time. Whatever the reason, or combination of reasons, the Society wore a cloak of invisibility to at least one person in its own village.

Such invisibility stood in contrast to the observations of one outsider, Raymond Fletcher, a journalist for the Labour newspaper *Tribune*, who visited in 1953. He described the village of Ynysybwl as 'a byword for progress' and noted that the co-operative shops in the sizeable town of Pontypridd were all branches of the Ynysybwl Co-operative Society, adding that it seemed strange that 'so large an organisation is based on so small a foundation'. He continued, 'but when you go to Ynysybwl and talk to the miners who run the Lady Windsor Library and Institute you begin to understand.' For Fletcher there were three key organisations in Ynysybwl – the co-op, the lodge and the institute.[19]

Hazell regularly attended Co-operative Congress in the 1940s, often combining it with related events, such as the Health Congress of the Royal Sanitary Institute. In 1946 he was elected to the eight-member Co-operative Congress Standing Orders Committee, representing the Western Section, where his high regard was reflected in the voting. Although he remained a member of Standing Orders for five years[20] Hazell was no apparatchik.

Hazell regularly addressed the theme of the human spirit. In 1945, he said that he was proud of the commercial success of the movement – with one in four of people of the country using its stores, but he posed the question: 'Shall commercialism, even co-operative commercialism, dominate our lives to the exclusion of spiritual values?' He suggested that the movement had become too focussed on profit at the cost of its larger social purpose, asking 'are we paying enough attention to the higher possibilities of co-operation, or is the balance sheet mentality over-developed?'[21] He answered his own question some years later in proposing that the co-operative shop was still an economic proposition from the social perspective which satisfied all ethical standards and the new social consciousness; it eliminated private profit, and returned the surplus to those who created it – the customer.[22]

When Alfred Barnes, MP, the Chairman of the Co-operative Party wrote of functionalism in his 1941 pamphlet *Plan Now*, Hazell challenged him with an essay which displayed considerable intellectual prowess. Hazell expressed concern that Italian and German fascism had used the functionalist model of 'institutionalising voluntary associations', emphasising 'it is very important for co-operators to work out the implications of that telling phrase!' As would become regularly apparent in the 1950s, the root of Hazell's concern was the relationship between the individual and the organisations supposedly working on his or her behalf, whether co-operative or state. As ever, Hazell argued that the organisation should be subordinate to the individual, not the reverse. While not a theoretician, Hazell was certainly a thinker. So strong were his opinions on Barnes' ideas that, exceptionally, the *Co-operative Official* felt obliged to distance itself from the author, saying that Hazell's views were not necessarily its own.[23]

However, any concerns that Hazell may have had about the principles and values of co-operation were as nothing compared with the criticisms he would develop in relation to the activities of the state.

Hazell and the Labour Government

Hazell took an early position on the Labour Government that displayed a maturity based on a lifetime's experience of the importance of unity and the need to build common ground, while not losing sight of the objectives to be achieved. He celebrated May Day 1947 by writing:

> The workers have their destinies in their own hands; they have liberty and freedom from past foul bondage. What May Day demonstrations demanded for 50 years is theirs. A Labour and Co-operative Government is in power at Westminster.[24]

He warned that it was necessary to support the Labour Government with discipline, to remain united, and avoid disintegration 'into warring, snarling sections melting into chaos, and once again give reaction its chance and opportunity! And reaction is waiting – and watching!'[25] He advised:

> Let our minor complaints not destroy our unity in purpose. The one ideology we should support is a co-operative and collectively planned Britain working for a world at peace.[26]

When asked by a comrade whether he was a left or right winger he answered: 'My friend, I think more of the bird than the wings.'[27] In the rich confines of lodge meetings, institute debates and valleys political discussions, Hazell, while a reasonable man, could be an implacable intellectual adversary. He appreciated the roles and relationships between worker and co-operator and his own economic understanding told him that: 'Marxian theories of surplus labour values get us nowhere when increases of wages for miners, electricians, gasworkers and railwaymen are placed fairly and squarely on the backs of the same people, as consumers, the day following.[28] He also argued:

> The thinking man to-day realises there is no bottomless Christmas stocking of undistributed surpluses in enterprises run by the people. And more! He knows that any factor in industry tending to inefficiency, whether it be redundancy on the railways or an over-staffed shop, or department, will have to be dealt with if Britain of the social services is to survive, pay her way, and prosper.[29]

Hazell welcomed the benefits of state planning. Comparing the periods after the two world wars he argued, in January 1947:

> Let those who object to a *planned* town consider the *planless*, sunless, life-destroying towns and cities of the past. Let those who object to *planned* industry ponder the lessons, grim and tragic, of a century and a half of *planless* uncontrolled capitalist enterprise. Let those who scoff at *planned* finance, think deeply over the

dominance of cruelly *planless* £.s.d. and man's crucifixion on a cross of gold in modern times. There can be only one answer![30]

However, Hazell held considerable reservations about some aspects of the Government's programme. The movement's vision of creating a 'Co-operative Commonwealth' was based on a markedly different approach to how industries and services should be collectively organised and delivered from that adopted by the Labour Government. In 1946, before the mines were nationalised, Hazell published the first of a number of articles that criticised the Government's method of nationalising the industry. He proposed that only co-operative principles could produce the results desired for the industry.[31] He consistently argued that control of industries and sectors of the economy would be better managed if they were based in, or at least included, co-operative principles and people, rather than using state structures, saying co-operation should be more than '"a plank in post-war reconstruction" – make it the very platform.'[32]

The form of nationalisation raised larger issues about the role of the co-operative movement in a socialist society and the nature of the relationship between the co-operative movement and a Labour Government during a period of social transformation. It also raised issues about the relationship between the individual citizen and the state, and the position of the individual in a collectivist society. In an essay to mark international co-operators day in July 1947 he considered the fifth object of the Rochdale Pioneers of 1844, which was 'we shall proceed to arrange the powers of production, distribution, education and government.' When this was written, he said, it had been idealistic and 'entirely impracticable'. A century later the labour movement had 'for better or worse… captured Britain's central Government and the destinies of "production and distribution" are largely in its hands'. He asked:

[W]hat part in 'arranging the powers' did the Socialist Government propose to allot to co-operation? Is co-operation to be merely a 'tool of the state', as under Communist rule, or is it to be in the role and place of an equal partner?

The response of the Government was neither: frustratingly for Hazell, the co-operative movement was largely ignored.[33] Whether the new Cabinet Ministers had trades union backgrounds whose previous focus had been on the point of production rather than consumption, municipal socialists who were used to the local state delivering services, or were state socialists, the new Government was not rooted in, driven by, or inclined towards co-operative approaches to the delivery of socialised industries or services.

As the first wave of industries were nationalised Hazell wrote that some felt that the co-operative movement, with 103 years of pioneering achievement, and in sight of triumph, was being forestalled by state socialism, which was taking a short cut to the goal.[34] He engaged in discussions of the day in considering whether the food supply system, including milk and bread, as well as furniture and coal distribution – all areas of co-operative activity – would be taken over and delivered by local municipal authorities. With the nationalisation of the Bank of England and uncertainty around the future of iron and steel Hazell wondered what would happen to the CWS bank and co-operative foundries and metal industries? He asked how should the co-operative movement respond in this situation? Should it wait and see what the Labour Government wished to do, or should it seek an early agreement? Indeed would 'a Socialist State Cabinet' be willing to commit itself to a long term agreement? Observing that the movement was 'a fairly efficient operative unit, equipped for its task in no small measure' he stated that any government that failed to recognise this would make the outcome much the worse for the citizens of Britain. He argued that the Soviet government had reintroduced co-operation, not because of its love for Rochdale principles but through facing up to past lessons learned from non-effective State distribution. 'Perhaps', he concluded ironically, 'Britain can learn from [the Soviet experience]'.[35]

By 1949, he questioned whether 'State Socialism' was opening too many doors for parasites who were 'formerly too respectable to touch it with a twenty-foot pole!', and who could ruin any national industry or enterprise. He contrasted it with the co-operative movement which he said did not have a history of parasites.[36] For Hazell, co-operation was the brightest example of public ownership and democracy in the country. He pointed out that the movement had never been subsidised out of the rates (as municipal enterprises had to be), had not been supported by taxes (as state enterprises were), and had not sought government subsidies to keep operating. The movement was fully and democratically open and could not avoid awkward questions, unlike state corporations like the Coal Board. He believed, therefore, that a fair operating environment had been denied them.[37]

Hazell grew increasingly critical of the tentacles of state planning and organisation. He also expressed his reservations about some of Labour's actions affecting the co-operative movement, such as shop sites on local authority housing estates and the maximum capital holding of individual members in their Society. These concerns were exacerbated by conjecture over discussions within the Labour Party and Government about the state taking over retail distribution and insurance, including the Co-operative Insurance Society.[38]

As the next General Election grew closer, and voices within the Labour Party considered what should be the next wave of development towards building a socialist society, tensions emerged. With state intervention in the ascendant, there was considerable discussion around whether the distributive trade and/or the retail sector, including co-operative shops, should be nationalised. Hazell continued to express his concerns that the state accretion of roles which people themselves had until then undertaken could undermine the voluntary action that was key to people actively engaging in the delivery of services on their own behalf.

When Lord Beveridge published his lesser known 'Voluntary Action' just before Christmas 1948 and 'The Evidence of Voluntary Action' in 1949, Hazell welcomed them warmly. Describing Beveridge as 'one of the chief architects of State Action in social improvements', Hazell said that Beveridge had recognised that 'fields still lie open, outside the realm of compulsory State acts, for associations of voluntary, non-conscripted, Rochdale-minded men and women!' He continued 'The greatest mistake any State can make is to ignore or neglect the possibilities and potentialities of Consumers and Producers Co-operation...'[39]

A friend asked what had become of the Co-operative Commonwealth – that 'State within a State!' which had:

'Co-operation for all purposes of life.' All! No exceptions, no reservations, no hesitations. Co-operation was to embrace all departments of life...[40]

His friend, he said, blamed the situation on politicians who, decades earlier, had stolen the co-operative movement's thunder, 'picked our brains' and 'substituted for our beloved Commonwealth a Socialist State run by Fabians and Ruskin College students, plus retired trade union officials.' His friend said it required acts of men, not Acts of Parliament. Hazell, though, urged his friend not to waste time bemoaning lost opportunities for the 'live dynamic of voluntary mutual aid will outlast and outshine many schemes of static coercion by State or commune'.

Jack Bailey, now General Secretary of the Co-operative Party (and an old collaborator of Hazell's in Mountain Ash) developed the same theme. He argued that 'wherever groups are able to plan for themselves this should not be regarded as an obstacle to good planning but welcomed as an example of democratic enterprise.' He continued:

> Wherever we are able to preserve voluntaryism we should do so. Compulsion is always a confession of failure and I see no virtue in the abandonment of voluntaryism where it can be made to succeed.[41]

Here, succinctly, was a coherent philosophical, organisational and political alternative by two co-operators to the state nationalisation programmes of Labour.

In 1951 Hazell asked the Labour Government about its attitude towards co-operatives.

> Are you still neutral towards us? Are we still to be classed with the multiples and joint-stock companies? Or will you, like us, be non-neutral? On this our future and yours depends…[42]

He did allow himself a cry of anguish: 'Neutrality, what crimes are committed in thy name!'

The journey Hazell travelled in relation to the Labour Government was a long one. While he would still work for its return to power, he had reached the point of challenging it outright in its further extensions of the role of the state and its attitude towards co-operation.

There was early one ironic exception. Labour's Agricultural Act of 1947 was seen by Hazell as 'a producers' bargain', with '[g]uaranteed prices, assured markets, all reasonable security for the farmer with the consumer left to fight his own battle…' Hazell's co-operative-based analysis, with the interests of the consumer to the fore, led him to criticise the absence of a programme to nationalise the land. Hazell lambasted '[t]he lush farmer on his feather bed' and hill farmers who had 'all benefited by the continued attention paid to them by all or any colour governments' and complained that:

Kings and queens have had their entrances and exits. The kings of the soil remain. The British kulak is more firmly entrenched. No Government has yet had the audacity to talk of collective farms for these islands.[43]

How uncharacteristic that Hazell, normally a man so reasonable, could argue for the collectivisation of agriculture and use the Russian Revolution term 'kulak'. While out of keeping with his general viewpoint, his outburst displayed the extent to which he thought agriculture favoured the farmer and was organised against the interests of the consumer.

Council Life

Hazell was unhappy at the way that district councils' powers were markedly reduced in the post-war period. Compared with the pace of wartime and the challenges of planning for reconstruction, the role of the district council became emasculated after 1945. Whereas Hazell considered that 'practically every act of social reform' since 1900 had added to councils' 'duties and prestige', the Labour Government had removed many of their functions.[44] Through his involvement in the restructuring of the delivery of local services he saw education, hospital provision, public health (including midwifery, mental health, vaccinations and immunisations), fire services and planning transferred away from the Urban District Council to the County Council and other bodies. The Council's gas and electricity utilities (including its only profitable one) were nationalised. Little more remained, Hazell joked, than the Civic Sunday and the Chairman's Chain of Office. Overall the responsibilities of the urban district council were much reduced and limited to highways, sanitary inspection, the Shops Act and 'that headache of which no one has yet proposed to relieve us – housing!' He reflected: 'Some of [those on the housing waiting list] have waited a lifetime, living meanwhile in apartment-rooms or by the sufferance of relatives' and said that housing was a councillor's nightmare and to rehouse the population would take years.[45]

Hazell now represented the Council on bodies such as the East Glamorgan Joint Planning Committee; the National Electricity Consumers Council; the County Fire Services Committee, and the General Meeting of the British Gas Council. However, these were advisory bodies, and he had no authority, responsibility or control over decisions and resources. Hazell appreciated the importance of the broader bases now involved in planning work and wrote articles in the Aberdare Leader explaining how planning would touch 'your life at every point' in the Aberdare Valley.[46]

New powers assumed by district councils, such as road safety, entertainments and national savings were marginal compared with powers that were lost. The removal of powers, thought Hazell, could be 'a process which may have to be reversed with experience of the benefits of de-centralisation.'[47]

From the tenor of his comments, it would appear that Hazell had already decided to stand down from the Council at the next election. Although only re-elected as a Councillor the previous year, his article read like a valedictory. Having been returned uncontested for 25 years, he placed on record his appreciation of the electorate's support, adding:

> There are seven dreary miles between this doorstep and the Town Hall. The writer has travelled them, unpaid and unsung, thousands of times. The joy has been in service and the feeling of making life more liveable, more full, for his fellows.[48]

Perhaps Hazell's last significant act as a local Councillor was in early 1949 when he and Abel Morgan were the only two members who opposed the resolution that Mountain Ash was a convenient and effective unit of local government. Hazell and Morgan reflected the long held local view that the 4,000 people of Ynysybwl considered themselves closer to Pontypridd than the Cynon Valley. Although Hazell and others met the Assistant Commissioner and discussed the situation of Ynysybwl, the Local Government (Boundary Commission) Committee of the local authority decided not to take a census of opinion of the Ynysybwl population on whether to remain part of Mountain Ash or become part of Pontypridd.[49]

On 2 May 1950, Councillor William Hazell attended his last full meeting of Mountain Ash UDC after 27 years as a member. The Chairman said everyone regretted his decision to stand down because they would lose the benefit of his vast experience of local government. Several members 'expressed their indebtedness to Councillor Hazell for the kindly counsel he had always given them.' It was reported that, aged 60, he stood down 'in order to live a little life on my own account' while Hazell said that he had chaired 'everything worth chairing' in that Authority.[50] However, it is difficult to avoid concluding that his leaving was due to the much reduced powers of the local authority and its incapacity to deliver change. Without his beloved education and health, yet still with the burden of housing, he would be unable to make sufficient positive difference to the lives of others, and his time would be better invested elsewhere.

Life's Challenges
The late 1940s brought a series of personal misfortunes. In 1947, Hazell suffered a serious injury in the pit when his hand was crushed by a fall of stone. He was sufficiently prominent in the co-operative movement for the accident to be reported on the front page of the *Co-operative News*. The following year, his house was burgled and his drawers and bureaux ransacked. As ever, counting his blessings, he said that while the thieves had stolen the glitter, they had left the gold untouched. Although the spending money had vanished, he listed the other things that the robbers could not take, which would have been real losses, such

as his faith in the decent people around him, his dreams, or his memories, saying he felt thankful for what the thieves had left him.[51]

At the start of 1949, Hazell wrote of making his New Year's resolution. Light heartedly, he reported that his would be to act with less discretion. He said that 'even if it means shredding some habits of a lifetime', he was defecting from the ranks of the 'careful, cautious, tactful...' However, in spite of becoming indiscreet, 'I hope to preserve the kindnesses, the amenities, of co-operative living; no evil-motivated, cruel revelations shall ever pass my lips...' More seriously he added: 'Many pitfalls doubtless await my humble feet in this New Year.' Quoting G B Shaw who said that 'A lifetime of happiness would be hell on earth', Hazell riposted 'This danger does not exist for me' adding: 'I am reconciled to the inevitable: New Year, new trials; new trials, new courage needed.'[52] Certainly, he was accustomed to life's difficulties being unavoidable. The death in May of Bill Collins, the journalist who had been a lifelong champion of the movement, would have been a considerable personal loss to Hazell. Collins had been a close friend and his unofficial tutor, mentoring him in his writing, and Hazell was one of many at his funeral in Glyntaff, Pontypridd.[53]

At the turn of the decade Hazell had to give up working in Lady Windsor Colliery due to suffering from 'dust' on his lungs after working underground for 43 years. He later wrote of the experience of having pneumoconiosis or silicosis. Although not in the first person, the article is deeply autobiographical, referring to a man of 60 with 20 per cent disability, who 'on top of the wear and tear and accidents of 45 years' work in the mines is very heavily handicapped.' He described the victims who suffered for 50 per cent, 60 per cent or 100 per cent disability by 'their pitiful breathing and obvious lack of the joy of living'. He recounted how men:

Detail of Taffs Wells Branch Opening, 1920
(Pontypridd Museum)

William and Deborah Elizabeth, 1910
(Margaret West)

The Hazell children in Clive Terrace around 1920
(Margaret West)

William Hazell sometime in his 'cocksure twenties, hardening thirties and dogmatic forties'
(Margaret West)

Ynysybwl Co-operative Society Management Board, 1920s
(*The Gleaming Vision*, p 51)

Opening Taffs Wells Branch, 1920
(Pontypridd Museum)

Taffs Well Branch, 1920
(Pontypridd Museum)

Remodelled Taffs Wells Branch, 1927
(The Co-operative Cymru/Wales, South Wales Coalfield Collection)

Rhydfelin Branch Opening, 1929
(The Gleaming Vision, p 110)

Market Square Premises with The Arcade next door
(Pontypridd Museum)

Opening the Church Street premises, Pontypridd, 1932
(The Co-operative Cymru/Wales, South Wales Coalfield Collection)

Church Street, Pontypridd, 1934

(The Co-operative Cymru/Wales, South Wales Coalfield Collection)

Hazell 'losing three weeks of life' in Roden Convalescent Home, 1934

(Margaret West)

The Ynysybwl Co-operative Society Board visiting the Lowestoft CWS Factory, 1936
(*The Gleaming Vision* p 95)

WHEATSHEAF
SOUTH WALES SUPPLEMENT
No. 167.—AUGUST, 1937

Co-operation Fights Capitalist Exploitation

TRANSFORMING WAGE SLAVES INTO FINANCIERS AND EMPLOYERS

By COUNCILLOR W. HAZELL

(President of Ynysybwl Society and Chairman of Brecon, Mon., and East Glamorgan Association)

AT a recent conference in South Wales the story was told how a traveller found life "down below" much improved compared with the conditions on a previous visit! Looking around, he questioned an old inhabitant about the reasons for the change. He was told: "Oh, things are much improved here since the Co-op. took us over."

ment of our times; its 7,000,000 members are monuments to its precepts and its 250 factories, mills, and workshops are monuments to its practice.

Our movement has led the way in transforming the hell of iniquity known as "employment in the distributive trades." It pioneered the weekly half-holidays and the abolition of the fining of apprentices and premiums for learning the trade. Its influence has been a most potent factor in reforming and diminishing that particularly hellish system, a veritable Hades of its own, known as "the living-in system."

Trades unionism has been encour-

cost than either so-called "big business" or big banking. *Reynolds* tells us that the comparison is as follows:—

Per £100 of paid-up capital—

			s.	d.
Co-operative directors cost...			0	0½
Lewis's Stores	,,	... ...	1	2
Barclay's Bank	,,	... ...	7	0

The movement is daily producing its own directors, managers, and staffs. It supplies city and town councils with many of their most useful members, and Parliament with capable debaters, legislators, and statesmen. Its members, instead of singing the old distich, "God bless the squire and his relations and keep us in our proper stations," stand on their hind legs and consider themselves as good as the Churchills and Cecils. Which, of course, they are.

Our traveller saw, in the comparative freedom from tied—debts and truck—shops of the modern artisan, a new

'Co-operation Fights Capitalist Exploitation', 1937: One of hundreds of articles written by Hazell over forty years

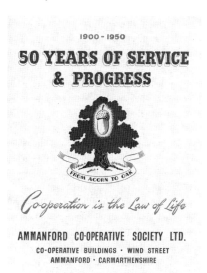

'Hazell's history of the Ammanford Co-operative Society, 1950

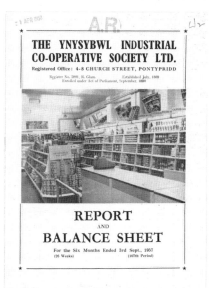

Ynysybwl Co-operative Society Report and Balance Sheet, September 1957, showing the Pontypridd Self-Service Store
(National Library of Wales)

Ready to
Speak
(Margaret West)

The Centre of
Attention
(Margaret West)

Opening
Hazell House,
1963
(Margaret West)

after sleepless nights of struggles for breath, rise to cough away a little more of the remainder of their lungs. They pant at the least exertion, they walk slowly, with constant pauses for wind, up the hilly streets of the Welsh valley towns. They can now no longer take their previous mountain-top walks – to climb so far would kill them. Most were officially scheduled for 'light work', but no work was light for them.

At one point, he referred to having 'an intimate knowledge of the economic and human factors involved', and said:

The early delightful freshness of our capacity to appreciate – that goes. Our ability to enter upon new things with zest and enthusiasm – that goes. Our sensitiveness thickens. We become cynical, harder to stir deeply. All the forces which make for human misery frighten and frustrate and baffle us.[54]

Hazell retired with no occupational pension from his four decades in the pit and did not receive one until he qualified for his state pension, six years later, in 1955,[55] although Gwlad may have been entitled to a state and/or an occupational pension. Hazell may have claimed unemployment assistance, supplemented by whatever he may have earned from his writings or expenses received from co-operative or council work, although the latter also ceased when he stood down from the Council in 1950.

Leaving the colliery and the Council within a very short space of time were significant milestones. While not comparable to the traumas he had faced in the mid-1930s they presented, nonetheless, considerable challenges. The financial difficulties of having to give up working in the pit became quickly apparent. In January 1950, he wrote that 'The lady of the house has of late... been advocating strict economy' as 'the only way to avert a domestic financial crisis'. Using humour to explain the household's apparent economic difficulties, he said that he had 'agreed to consider the matter carefully', which he said was home slang for obedience. He continued: 'I ventured to suggest one day (having seen that the door was open for a quick escape) that economy was the art of buying a complexion to match a hat, instead of buying a hat to match a complexion', to which Gwlad responded that 'I might consider reducing my cigarette bill to the relative length of the family purse', which would have been a considerable sacrifice for Hazell and his favourite 'Jaycee' CWS filtered brand.[56]

When his father died aged 92, in October 1949, Hazell said that his ancestors had not been thrifty for 'not a bean did they leave for me and mine', although he added the remark 'but, why worry when you are on the sunny side of ninety?' While a friend had suggested that 'thrift consisted mainly of worrying about what became of last month's money' Hazell countered that:

> it is quite the reverse in my home. The worry here is how to save [i.e. reduce expenditure] out of our if-and-when problematical next month's income.[57]

Even so there was still sufficient income in the household to purchase a television when few others had them and also in 1952 a new CWS washing machine, which made the Hazells early adopters of dry goods upon which the development of the new consumer society would, in part, be based.[58]

Although Hazell may have stopped working in Lady Windsor Colliery he appears to have continued being a member of the canteen committee. John E Morgan noted that 'in the second week in May (1950) it began to be whispered that all was not well with the Pit Canteen finances.' More than £700 was owing to the Co-op Society alone. The YCS Secretary took steps and representatives of Miners Welfare, Food Ministry officials and others attended a meeting at the colliery. An Inquiry was held. Morgan doubted that 'the business will be allowed any publicity' for a number of reasons including:

> the fact that such a prominent person as Mr Hazell is a Canteen Committeeman and is also the chairman of the Coop Society to

whom so much is owed. It is to his credit that some time this year, he strongly urged that a cash register should be got for the canteen. He should, however, have insisted and followed it up. He and the committee should also have demanded annual balance sheets, etc at the appropriate time.[59]

At this stage Morgan was deeply embittered towards the lodge and made forthright attacks on others in Ynysybwl. By the standards Morgan used against them, this was mild criticism of Hazell indeed.[60]

The Tories Back in Power

In early 1951, conscious of the changing composition of the electorate, Hazell looked at the previous half century of social and labour development 'when sickness was almost a crime – and old age even a worse one!' He was conscious that:

> An ever-increasing factor in the nation's political life is that at every succeeding general election more and more people are voting who never suffered under purely capitalistic and Tory rule. Jarrow and the depression are to them just history.
>
> They have never been members of a hungry family, or witnessed economic oppression in its most cruel aspects. They have never known victimisation as a consequence of joining a trade union or suffered social ostracism for membership of a Labour Party. Here is the fertile ground for reactionary propaganda.[61]

In October 1951, he spoke to 'a half-Tory audience' at election meetings in Cardiff, and his worst fears were realised with the election of a Conservative Government.[62]

When, in 1952, the new Conservative Government changed the regulations for unemployment assistance he bitterly complained that men, disabled and partially disabled in the coal industry by pneumoconiosis or silicosis were going to be subject to the Means Test to get assistance. He explained that such people faced the end of their extended benefit under the Insurance Acts and now faced a Household Means Test to retain inadequate compensation payments, assessed by the medical board. As wife's earnings and children living at home would be taken into account by the means test investigators, he asked whether children would, once again, have to leave home so that 'the old man' might have a chance of getting assistance? He questioned 'how will they and their families live?' In what was surely a painfully intimate personal description he wrote:

> the man must spend his savings – a hard blow to a thrifty man – any little property must be submitted for inspection and assessment. This dear little home and family built up over the years is now a *case* under Clause 62.

He continued:

> Only those who have undergone it can know what mental torture the test involves. The first investigation, however kindly conducted, spells humiliation and cruelty to all involved. This first process is, however, not the worst. Mental cruelty is followed by actual physical cruelty – the struggle to live upon the assistance grudgingly given.

He identified the difference between the 'right' of unemployment benefit, compared with discretionary 'assistance', which from time to time would be checked up on. 'Every town has its list, every street has its victims' and described visiting a co-operative society in West Wales, where all the anthracite miners on the committee were victims of 'dust'. He asked whether miners and their families were once again to be subject to the means test and referred to the 50,000 South Wales miners who had marched in Cardiff against the means test asking 'Do you wonder the miners marched?' For the first time since the Popular Front he used an article to make a direct call to action, saying that, while the miners had marched, it was for others, too, to make their influence felt and 'move those who can remedy things'.[63]

Retirement from the Pit – More Time for YCS, the Movement and for Writing!

Finishing work down the pit and on the Council changed the balance of Hazell's life, allowing him greater time for further public service. He reported: 'Someone had always been able to persuade me to fill in every evening with efforts on behalf of our neighbours in Wales or Timbuctoo.'[64] Now with more hours available in the day Hazell spent even more time on co-operative activity, assumed new areas of public life, and took on more extensive writing projects.

Hazell went daily to the offices of YCS in Church Street, Pontypridd, to work with Sam Davies, the Society's Secretary, until his premature death in 1951, and then with Owen Jones, the General Manager. The location of Pontypridd gave YCS a strategic trading advantage as the point where the train lines converged, giving easy access to the 200,000 people living in the Rhondda, Aberdare and Merthyr valleys. As a natural shopping centre with multiples of nearly every trade, plus old established firms, transport authorities estimated that that between 30,000 – 40,000 people visited the town on the market days of Wednesdays and Saturdays. The Society's shops and arcade benefited; sales and membership increased and in 1952 YCS trade reached nearly £1.5 million per annum. By 1953 YCS had capital of a half-million pounds.[65] Showing that it was still in the vanguard of retail development, the Society opened its first self-service store in Pontypridd.

While it was said that financially the Society had no equal, such self-congratulation contrasted with reports of apathy in the co-operative movement in the late 1940s and 1950s, when few attended meetings or voted in elections. Nor had the personnel of the Board of YCS changed much for some years, and members' mentalities were set in an earlier era. In spite of the steady post-war growth, the co-operative movement in Ynysybwl nurtured on titanic inter-war industrial struggles, the Depression and wartime, was ill-prepared for prosperity and the rise of consumerism. As late as the mid-1950s it was observed that 'Sometimes the Society's officials and committee... wonder how long such prosperity can last.'[66]

On The Committee

By the 1940s, as well as his immersion in YCS Hazell was deeply entrenched in the 'weird and wonderful' world of the national co-operative movement's topsy-like committee system. He was one of thousands of co-operators from local to national level who were involved in the running of the movement. Such was Hazell's degree of involvement that he was little short of a full-time lay official. Already a member of the national Congress Standing Orders Committee, and various other bodies, in 1947 he became Chair of the Western Section of the Co-operative Coal Trade Association. He spent time on the National Executive of the Coal Trade Association and on the Milk, Bakery, and Meat Trade Associations in a long association with Co-operative National Committees.[67]

He accrued more roles as he climbed through the tiers of the movement, gaining increased responsibility and influence. When Sam Davies died in 1951, Hazell was elected to represent the Western Section on the Central Board. The 93-member Central Board was nominally the management committee of the Co-operative Union, responsible for the policy direction of the movement nationally as well as for its machinery and governance. It considered large issues such as purchase tax and the introduction of self-service, and oversaw the running of the Co-operative College. However, this large and unwieldy group, which had been operating for 82 years, experienced constant tension between democratic accountability based in local voluntary effort and achieving competitive business efficiency. Hazell did not serve his full three-year term as the Central Board was abolished at the 1952 Margate Conference, even though the Board opposed its own abolition due to concerns that the Wholesale Societies would become dominant.[68]

The Co-operative Union nominated Hazell for public appointments and he took these positions seriously. He made a distinction between service and membership explaining 'Real service on public bodies (not "membership", which may mean little) compels one to learn.'[69] In 1950 he was appointed to the Transport Users' Advisory Committee (Wales), retaining his membership throughout the decade. He became a member of the Welsh Regional Hospital Board and the Wales Gas Consultative Council, as well as the Pontypridd and Llantrisant Divisional Health Executive.[70] In 1955 he joined the Rhondda Valley Local Advisory Committee of the Ministry of Pensions and National Insurance. However, he saw room for reducing the numbers of such quangos. In the economic field he questioned whether the Welsh Board of Industry, the Industrial Association of Wales and Monmouthshire, the National Industry Development Council and the Welsh Economic Development Council were all needed, suggesting that:

> this recurring madness is only likely to cease when all suitable titles and name[s] for futile bodies become exhausted. One name would fit the whole bag-full but it could not be printed here.[71]

Life's Pleasures

Attending co-operative and labour events allowed Hazell to explore much of England and Wales. Many pleasant interludes resulted in articles on places visited, drawing on local literary or historic references, the lives of authors, plot scenes of novels, as well as the co-operative movement locally. Whether Bath Spa or Brighton or following the course of the Wye from its source in Plynlimon to Chepstow, his writings in the late 1940s and early

1950s come over as a veritable travelogue, helped by having access to a friend's car. Hazell loved the natural environment and was still walking in the high Brecon Beacons in his 60s. While attending the Co-operative Party Annual Conference in Llandudno, in 1947, he and Gwlad went up Snowdon 'determined to stand on Snowdon's summit with my wife for once in a lifetime', although the heavy mist prevented them having any view. From 1949 he attended the annual All-Wales Labour rally in Newtown to commemorate Robert Owen,[72] hearing Herbert Morrison give the address in 1952, and Aneurin Bevan in 1953, as well as Attlee.

Hazell's relationship with Gwlad and their sharing of social activities was exceptional at a time when couples in the valleys were more inclined to occupy separate social spheres. Such social sharing was also in contrast to his first marriage, although when he was married to Deborah Elizabeth he was at a different stage of life with greater familial responsibilities. In 1954, Hazell and Gwlad were said to be very happy and comfortable together at a time when his 'main occupation' was "studying for a diploma in the art of living – a 20 year course."[73]

Hazell made the most of cultural opportunities. The first post-war National Eisteddfod was held in Mountain Ash in 1946, where the great pavilion had previously been one of the Ministry of Food's depots for six years. The programme was worked for, said Hazell, by the Council, colliery officials, business fraternity and miners young and old. Both Aberdare and Ynysybwl Co-operative societies made generous donations and many co-operators worked on the various committees. Hazell reported: "All Welsh life and culture is represented here – from millionaire to miner and peasant, and geographically, from Caernarvon to Cardiff.'[74] When the National Eisteddfod went to Caerphilly in 1950, YCS was one of the first subscribers to guarantee funding for the event, donating £100 and confirming the Society as part of the national cultural fabric.[75]

Hazell attended the opening day of the Festival of Wales and went to see the Gwendoline Davies bequest at the National Museum. When Jacob Epstein's 'Majestas' was dedicated at Llandaff Cathedral at the 'Hallowing of the Nave' ceremony in April 1957, this cultured man was so impressed that he returned a further three times in subsequent weeks.[76] Invitations to Hazell as a representative of the co-operative movement conferred on it a social status he appreciated.

He was not, though, much interested in sport, considering himself 'a mere outsider and a sporting upstart'. Nor did he much favour going to the cinema as a leisure pursuit, describing it as 'Hollywood tripe'. He admitted, though, 'without shame to having sat entranced' through Walt Disney's *Snow White and the Seven Dwarves*, saying he had met them all in meetings, on the street, or at the Co-operative Congress. His review of the film *Blue Scar*, about South Wales coal mining in 1949, praised its sincerity while observing it 'may not set the Taff or the Thames on fire...'[77]

While to his grandchildren Hazell would appear an austere man who was not interested in material wealth, he had a humourous side. At Christmas he was happy to join in as Santa Claus. During the winter of 1945-6 he 'had the somewhat doubtful honour' of being impersonated at a local guild gathering, and concluded a 'dose of personal deflation' was good for pointing out his petty weaknesses. While he wrote more of his family than his friendships, Hazell was an active part of the community.[78]

Post-War Writing: Hazell and History

Some of the extra time available to Hazell in retirement from the pit was used to write. He produced two short centenary histories of Ammanford and Tredegar Co-operative Societies in 1950 and 1951, each of which followed a formula that was broadly familiar in that genre, before embarking on the much more ambitious history of the Ynysybwl Co-operative Society, *A Gleaming Vision*, which was the most detailed account of a co-operative society in Wales produced in the 20th Century.

Hazell had not undertaken a venture of that scale previously and at times his inexperience showed. The book's weaknesses were apparent. He was quick to play down any right to be considered a historian, saying 'the writing of a few "Jubilee Brochures" and one full-length history of a local society barely entitles him to claim, say, a few months' apprenticeship to the noble art.'[79] However, Hazell was unduly self-critical, for overall he made a significant contribution to co-operative history with considerable skill. In essays that showed an understanding of the historical method, of assessing and discounting evidence, the way that interpretations change over time, and of the value and limitations of oral history, Hazell wrote of the need for 'a fully documented *History of Co-operation in South Wales and Monmouthshire*'. He wondered whether the University of Wales or the National Library could be induced into funding 'Co-operative historical research in Wales'. Writing when the economic strength of the movement was at its zenith, and taking for granted the future position of the movement in history, Hazell could optimistically refer to 'all future students and historians of co-operation in the principality', and confidently write that '[w]hatever may be the future of Co-operative effort, no social historian can deny the notable part played by the Co-operative societies of Wales in the nineteenth and twentieth centuries.'[80] In his writings, Hazell captured a legion of co-operative pioneers who would otherwise be lost to history. He also undertook primary research which challenged the orthodoxy that Cwmbach was the first co-operative society in Wales and mapped the origins of many societies saying that his limited investigations convinced him that systematic research would uncover many other 'brave pioneering enterprises in the days before co-operation had a legal existence.'[81] While writing a book length history taxed him, Hazell was an outstanding lay historian of the movement.

In 1950, Hazell called for the publication of a monthly or quarterly co-operative historical journal – a regular and specialised journal – even if it meant stopping the publication of one of the movement's other journals. His vision included establishing a Chair of Co-operation at one of the universities and recognising the importance of preserving co-operative records, Hazell lamented their disappearance saying he 'tears his hair and weeps' at records discarded 40 years earlier.[82]

Areas of research that were needed were identified by Hazell. In 1953 he called for the writing of a history of the South Wales valleys over the previous half-century and felt that much of the material could be found in the pages of co-operative publications, 'for the progress of co-operation is always like a barometer to gauge genuine social and industrial conditions in South Wales and everywhere else.'[83] Such a historical perspective was lost for a half century, and is only now, once again, being reclaimed.

Local historians were held in high regard by Hazell. He described them as 'the salt of the earth' to whom the debt was immense for 'out of these local histories and sketches national historians build up their weightier volumes'. Fittingly, his last article traced so far, in August 1959, was entitled 'Headaches of the Historian: "If You can Write History You'll Be a Man"'.[84]

Hazell used history to educate, to illuminate contemporary discussions, and to highlight injustice. He also wrote much more widely than just on co-operative history, roaming over issues of time and subject. In July 1924, Hazell wrote of working conditions in the Scottish mines in the 18th Century as a means of calling men to join the union. In 1933, he described how the common land around Pontypridd, including mineral rights, had been handed over free to the landed classes by an Act of

Parliament in 1860.[85] In 1948, he said that 'The [Chartist] men of Llanidloes were transported *for you!*'[86] Hazell loved history, and for his contribution in articles over decades, he deserves to be considered alongside Ness Edwards, Bert Coombes and Mark Starr as one of the writer-proselytisers of the South Wales coalfield.

Hazell and Wales

Hazell thought a lot on the nature of Wales and Welsh issues and wrote regularly of Welsh culture, highlighting its qualities. He considered himself an adopted son of Wales and felt that Wales had been generous to him.[87] Hazell had a strong sense of Wales as one – rural and industrial, north and south 'now, for good or ill, make one pattern, one life; and this pattern continually changes before our eyes'.[88] As early as 1926 he had written on the importance of 'educating and training Young Wales and the nation of the future.' In 1955 he complained that the recent White Paper on the railways had not addressed the need for better north–south communications in Wales. 'We call ourselves a nation, a principality, yet there is no real main line between our capital city of Cardiff in the south and Carnarvon in the north.' It was easier, he wrote, to get to Edinburgh than Llandudno or Bangor.[89]

He viewed the broad sweep of the history of Wales from the Ice Age, through Romans and Normans to the industrial revolution, Chartism and beyond. He wrote of the Silures, opposition to the Anglo-Saxons, the guerrilla resistance of the Welsh people against the Normans, as well as more obscure areas such as gavelkind – the law of inheritance in Wales.[90] Wales, he said, had always been more democratic than England and quoted Michael Llewellyn who said that feudalism never really touched *real* Wales. Hazell explained that the feudal system only existed in the 'Norman-conquered lowland'. In the areas of '*true* Wales'...

'The democratic system, Jack's as good as his master, survived and persisted'.[91]

Hazell's sense of Wales was one where the best and most noble impulses – such as in the Laws of Hywel Dda – were akin to co-operative principles. Hazell likened co-operative pioneers to Saint David, as practical saints with a social gospel, who succoured the poor and cheered the workers. He described co-operators as St David's successors in his own country and identified the country's strong democratic impulse as explaining why South Wales was the most loyal with purchases per member, second only to Scotland, and where loyalty to the CWS was second to none. Indeed, when he considered the wonders of Wales and Glamorgan, he pondered whether the greatest wonder was not

> the co-operation of a million of its people in the co-operative
> societies of its towns and cities. Confident in the principle
> of mutual help and communal effort, they go forward, amid
> conflicting currents of individualism and state-dependence, to be
> a commonwealth of sturdy, thrifty, neighbourly, kindly men and
> women who believe, not only in themselves, but in their fellows
> also. They seek peace and pursue it.[92]

This eloquent description captured his essence of the co-operative movement as well as the way he saw Wales. It synthesised his values and principles and reinforced his earlier description of co-operators as 'the salt of the Welsh earth', saying co-operators attacked the worst enemies of the nation 'selfishness, exclusiveness, commercial acquisitiveness, vested interests and exploitation.'[93]

Hazell appreciated both Anglo-Welsh and Welsh language cultures. He was told that 'by becoming equipped in the two languages, English and Welsh, I should be able to live in two worlds at the same time!'[94] And it is evident from his writings that to some extent he did. Although the family of his first wife, the Pasks, were not Welsh speakers, Hazell would have been

173

exposed to it in the pit and the village for decades. Moreover, Gwlad was a Welsh speaker and would have introduced him to Welsh language culture. By December 1941 he had an obvious facility in the Welsh language and a decade later was sufficiently competent to judge that an 18th Century Welsh language pamphlet displayed subtlety and used ridicule. He used Welsh quotes in his writings and commended the reading of *Rhys Lewis* in the Welsh 'if you can', but failing that there was a good English version. He was still waiting, though, for a great Welsh novelist.[95]

Hazell had warmth towards the Welsh language and Welsh language culture recognising one of the main objects was to keep the language alive and that the first line of defence was in the hearth and home. He was conscious of the way that Welsh-speaking Wales sustained its cultural history. He used an article on 'The Fortifications of Wales' to explore different forms of Welsh defences such as castles. However, he proposed that the 'real defences and protections of *Welsh life and living*' consisted of fortifying the spirit of Wales through its values and qualities of 'Welshness' which abide in the heart and soul rather than through *things*.[96] While the Welsh in the 1850s were 'then, still a race apart, with its language, traditions and culture intact,'[97] now some of its more important defences were 'the language, the Eisteddfod, the educational system, and the love of music', which were the '"outward and visible" expressions of deeper emotions within'. In that regard he also felt that:

> True spiritual progress, as apart from denominationalism, must be fortified and confirmed – that is my conviction. Without it, even the Welfare State is endangered.[98]

However, Hazell became unhappy with some aspects of how that defence came to be manifested. In 1946 he had seen in the national eisteddfod shared characteristics and values, and 'a growing vein of inspired idealism, co-operation and true internationalism'.[99] However, during the following decade, the National Eisteddfod Council:

> decreed, in their unwisdom, that the Welsh national event must be for ever a one-language festival. Songs must be sung, choirs must sing, poets must pen, Welsh only... Everything is to be done in language-exclusiveness. The next step to this is racial exclusiveness – surely Wales will never take this second step? Not the Wales I know and cherish... Not this Wales![100]

Hazell's words suggest that he was mindful of the policies of Nazi Germany, the menace of fascism and six years of war. While Hazell affirmed that 'Everyone is now agreed – this Welsh language must live. It must be nourished and sustained...' he contrasted the exclusiveness and lack of vision of the national eisteddfod with the spirit of tolerance and internationalism of the Llangollen International Eisteddfod. Hazell criticised the national eisteddfod saying: 'There is nothing of the Llangollen spirit here' adding that although he was an adopted Welshman, he was also a citizen of the world 'which co-operation has taught me is one despite all its divisions'.[101]

On issues of Wales, Hazell's disdain was reserved for Plaid Cymru. At various times he dismissed its ideas and actions and considered that the insularity of the Welsh nationalists had no place in co-operation 'Each for all and all for each means the same in Penzance as in Swansea.'[102] He derided their proposals for the nationalised industries and utilities of a Welsh Coal Board and Welsh Electricity Authority, and argued that any Welsh Water Board would charge customers in England higher prices for Welsh water.[103] He described Plaid Cymru as a 'curious tribal remnant' that 'are now able to gather under their tattered colours the most nondescript army the political battlefield has ever seen or ever will see between now and 1984.' He saw 'in the shadow cast by the Red Dragon of Wales, the same old anti-Labour and anti-Co-operative crowd camouflaged with leeks and daffodils, and each carrying a bowl of Liberal-Communist broth.' Hazell ridiculed Plaid's policy of advocating that Welsh miners break the All-British wage agreement, for which miners had worked for many years, 'to cheerfully go back to a sectional, Wales agreement...' He dismissively concluded: 'Talk about fairy-tales.'[104]

Hazell and Writing

The post-war years were a very productive writing period for Hazell. While he had articles published regularly from the early 1920s, the five years after the war showed a dramatic rise in output. Of the articles traced, Hazell had 150 articles printed in the five years from 1946 to 1950, with a typical output of around 30 each year. For 1949, 37 articles have so far been traced. Articles printed in the *Co-operative News* appeared, at times, seemingly weekly from early 1946 until the end of the decade.

Not only was Hazell's output prodigious, his eye was wide-ranging. It is impossible to encapsulate his breadth, covering everything from William Caxton and early printing to the change in the colour of the livery of YCS vehicles from green and cream to red. For example, in April and May 1953, he published a hard-hitting piece on state control, a criticism of the Wales Tourist and Holiday Board's plans for a beauty competition on the grounds of ageism and sexism, an appreciation of the Quaker contribution in the Rhondda and a light piece on street teas during the coronation. Decades later he would have loved blogging.

Hazell wrote regularly on international affairs, expounding his world view, whether on European boundaries, the lessons that the USA could learn from Britain or on the moral leadership that Britain could offer a new world. He looked to the British Empire to give South Africa its freedom, establish an Irish Free State which would later become a United Ireland, and allow Egyptians to govern their land and the Nile, amongst others.

When the Soviet Foreign Minister, Gromyko, was reported as objecting to compromise, Hazell railed against him as he did against the United States Congress for its uncompromising use of the veto in the United Nations. His erudition was clear when locating the challenges facing De Gaulle in France in the context of Voltaire and Rousseau and the French Revolution.[105]

Hazell captured something of everyday life in his writings, whether bowls in the park, band practice, coach trips to the seaside or sheep grazing in valleys' villages. He wrote about his street, with its street teas for VE and VJ days; suppers when the local baritone won the National Eisteddfod, and celebrations when Hazell won a local council election. As he said:

> We in the valleys are community-bound. Cords of friendship
> and understanding, and knowledge of each other's problems,
> attainments, and limitations, bind us together in bonds more firm
> than any Act of Parliament could ever prescribe.[106]

And using the valleys idiom 'ours is a nice street ours is' he encapsulated both its inclusiveness and yet its sense of being apart from the rest in an article on the street's annual Guy Fawkes bonfire. Organised and built by the boys in the street, the bonfire was held on the nearby open space, and Hazell, and other neighbours, used the opportunity to throw out unwanted furnishings. Once the first layer of the bonfire was set, watch was kept on it. Indeed, 'fire guards' had existed in his street long before 1939, after 'jealous Avenue boys, no doubt' once lit the bonfire some days prematurely. 'Anyhow, we take no chances now'. He conveyed the way in which his whole street took part, and contrasted it with more aspiring areas:

> You never hear of a bonfire in the avenue, or the close, or the
> crescent. They are much too Third Programme for that. They may
> run a study circle or art class, but bonfires! Why they come and
> look at ours, pretending to be just casually strolling round.

By implying that the Guy was 'that horrible man [with official-looking personage] who came with notebook a few days ago, demanding to know the promoters' names'[107] and if they had appropriate permissions, Hazell made a 'Passport to Pimlico'-style poke at authority and the 1940s regulatory regime. At the end of the 1940s and beginning of the 1950s, some of Hazell's articles became more personal in tone. Hazell had said little of Auntie Gwlad previously in his writings. However, from 1949, he started to refer to her playfully.

There were often gender aspects of Hazell's analysis, such as in the relationship between the domestic environment and women's changing roles. In noting the revolution in the Welsh kitchen in his lifetime, he lamented that as a member of a housing committee he had helped abolish 'the most typical of all the rooms of a Welsh cottage for at least three centuries past'. He concluded that 'the dearest, homeliest, room in the house' had been 'banished from our municipal housing estates' in conformity with the Ministry of Health's 'Housing Manual'. He welcomed hot and cold water from chrome taps, and tiled walls recognising that 'in this TV age, and with many women working in factories, what time could there be to-day for polishing brasses and fenders and dusting a hundred pieces of china on an open dresser?'[108] Gender awareness was also displayed in Hazell's use of language. In using the form of words 'In honouring him or her…'[109] Hazell recognised that both men and women could hold the position of president of a co-operative society, subtly challenging prevailing assumptions. Although no woman had held the role in Ynysybwl Society, it showed Hazell's awareness of the possibility expressed in a way that did not become common until decades later.

Hazell's light-hearted 1947 gender analysis of Cinderella and her ugly sisters was just a precursor to his sharper-edged dissection of the Welsh Tourist and Holiday Board's 'Miss Wales' beauty queen competition in 1953. Displaying much greater awareness and sensitivity than the Tourist Board, although couched in humour, Hazell criticised the competition on grounds of age and gender as well as marital and parental status. Analysing the qualification criteria for the role, he asked why should the person be a preferably Welsh-speaking "Miss" with charm, intelligence, personality, able to wear the Welsh national costume with grace and distinction, and be around 25 years of age? He seriously suggested, 'Why not a *Mrs.* Wales?' Taking it further, if this was about the future of Wales, 'then why not even a Welsh mother and child?' He made clear that he was not enamoured with beauty competitions 'national, seaside or local', suggesting tongue-in-cheek that this might be 'sour grapes', as he had never been accused of being attractive and would soon reach that "isn't he wonderful" age. However, he proposed different criteria to value worth and suggested alternative women who should be considered for the respect they warranted. One woman he met every morning

> trudging through all weathers, winter and summer, bucket, flannel and brush in hand, in order to clean out the colliery offices, filthy with coal dust... She is over 60 years of age and a widow.[110]

Hazell then nominated a Captain in the Salvation Army who ministered to the sick in their homes. Neither would be eligible under the Board's criteria. Two other women activists from the Women's Co-operative Guild would not possibly wish to enter such a competition, anyway. After making a number of points that would have sat comfortably with feminists 20 years later, he extended the argument further by asking 'But after all, if we are against all colour and racial bars, why should the sex-bar still operate?' and he proposed co-operative men who deserved recognition for their work. He concluded by 'respectfully suggesting' to the Tourist Board that they should enlarge the scope of the activity as well as its age limit.

Such writing, from the pen of a man in his 60s, who had

lived all of his adult life in the valleys, was advanced. It would have been so had it come from a valleys male in his 20s writing two decades later. The principles that underpinned Hazell's 1922 article calling for equality for women in the co-operative movement still held firm. Even if not always well expressed, his progressive outlook, evident in that first article on women's equality, came through in his writings.

Hazell was a voracious reader of 'almost every kind of literature'[111] and a real book-lover. He was a religious man who knew his Bible well. His writings were rich with references from the scriptures. He also drew freely on literature, quoting prose and poetry. While he called on Kipling, Gray's Elegy and Yeats, and wrote of literary figures such as Wordsworth or the artist Frank Brangwyn[112] his greatest admiration was reserved for Johnson and Boswell for 'here we stand on holy ground'.[113] Many writers and texts, including John Bunyan's 'Pilgrim's Progress' were marshalled to underscore some point about democracy, support his principles, or illuminate some aspect relevant to co-operation.

He was a learned man who taught himself some Latin as well as Welsh. Realising that language was always in a 'state of flux', he delighted in tracing the origins of a word, such as 'premises', back 'to the Middle Ages – to propositions, syllogisms, and Aristotle', when an Arabic word was taken in the 13th and 14th Century, translated into Latin, and used as a form of logic.[114]

The inspiration for Hazell's writing came from a huge range of sources both formal and informal. He undertook research, reading original documents, such as the Report of the Registrar General for 1839. He devoured official publications, including Forestry Commission Annual Reports and identified themes for writing. He lauded the work of the Forestry Commission and considered that the 'man-made hell' of the Rhondda and the 'industrial desert' of Merthyr were being tempered by the operations of foresters.[115]

Hazell appraised the Annual Report of the Medical Officer of Health for Glamorgan, which most people would not encounter, giving an accessible summary of its main points, with appropriate personal wrapping and interpretation. Sanitary conditions, maternal health, child welfare, the impact of radio control for the ambulance service, as well as the new home help service were considered. He highlighted the inadequacy of the Lunacy Acts to deal with senility and looked at the testing of food and drink as well as sewage treatment and water analysis. Performing a role of popularising education, he said that readers would share his appreciation of the new National Health Service and its staff, which were 'All in the interests of Glamorgan's health – which means you and me'.[116]

As a natural teacher Hazell became competent in plying his craft. In 'Fireside Motoring' he took imaginary car journeys without leaving his armchair. He held imagined conversations with Robert Owen[117] as well as with industrial chimneys to appreciate their changing role. Such imaginative approaches addressed subjects in creative ways. He still delighted in learning as well as teaching. His inquisitiveness came through still in his mid-60s, and his mind remained fresh, even as his body weakened.

Hazell, the Rhondda and the Valleys

Decades before the historian Gwyn Alf Williams posed the question 'When was Wales?' Hazell asked his own existential question about the human spirit in his long, searching piece 'Does the Rhondda Make Sense?' It started with a bus journey to Tonypandy, when 'I found myself asking, does this long string of shapeless townlets, this dreariness, this collection of colliery tips make sense?' Observing that its sense was in its *faith in man and his future*, he also considered the Rhondda from other perspectives. While the physical environment held buildings which 'wrecks of a soulless industrialism', he saw the Rhondda's social development as the '*power to build up personality*' and recognised 'three generations of toil and sacrifice' in building the communities. He opposed planners who would remove the population from the valley in a mass evacuation as it would 'rip the heart and soul out of the Borough' as well as 'the loss which the arbitrary breaking-up of these town communities would entail'. Architects should not look for easy sites on which to build, but should 'tackle the harder propositions on the lower slopes of... the hills'.[118] He lamented the lack of investment in the infrastructure of the valleys by coal companies which had taken their surpluses for the benefit of Cardiff or the Vale of Glamorgan. He said that even if half the wealth the valleys had produced had been spent there, there would be museums, art galleries and other public facilities. He concluded that only in education did the Rhondda outclass the coastal plain and only the eye of history could give the necessary perspective to make sense of the Rhondda.

Hazell was in awe of the Rhondda valleys as is evident in the nature and number of articles he wrote on them. For him, the nature of Rhondda people was different from those of Merthyr 'in outlook and purpose' and he questioned whether the different industries had not shaped their populations differently?[119] Hazell sought to pin down the 'real soul-mystery' of the Rhondda, which he felt had not been adequately captured by Jack Jones' *Rhondda Roundabout* or Richard Llewellyn's *How Green Was My Valley* and returned to the theme on a number of occasions. He identified 'the wonderful assimilation and mixing of such varying component parts which have produced such a coherent community spirit', in ways not evident elsewhere and saw in 'this assimilation, this mixing, this welding of men and tongues, the hope of mankind'. Expanding his panorama further, he saw that such fusions should be taken forward nationally and by the United Nations as the basis for tackling international evils such as disease or environmental enemies.[120]

The environment was one of Hazell's recurring themes. He complained early and often about the despoiling of the landscape and weaved the issue into a range of articles including his critique of nationalised industries. Just as he had criticised private coal companies in the 1920s and 1930s for their conduct so he decried the behaviour of the NCB. In a couple of telling phrases he condemned the new masters:

> just a few years ago a flag was unfurled high on the pit-head gear and a notice prominently exhibited – "This colliery belongs to the people." Cannot this three-lettered giant, the N.C.B., be made to understand that this valley and its hillsides belong to the people also?

The NCB was spoiling the landscape by tipping above Ynysybwl:

> to the right and left, down to the river's edge and high, high up to within sight on the "Roman Road"... The bracken and whinberrys; the hedges and walls; the sweet rough herbage and grass, all now covered and killed by vast dirt mounds! For why? [Originally] to enhance a colliery company's balance sheet and later to add output-prestige to the N.C.B. But man shall not live by prestige alone.[121]

The introduction of the five-day week was seen by Hazell as an opportunity to bring pressure on government ministries 'to hasten the long overdue work of levelling and beautifying those hateful, horrible rubbish-tips' so that they could be used as sites for recreation.[122]

Yet even before the first pit closures occurred in South Wales Hazell could look forward to a valleys life beyond coal, saying: 'perhaps we over-estimate the power and permanence of a selfish industrialism – it will pass', adding: 'If beauty is truth, and truth, beauty, then this ugliness is all a huge lie, it must defeat itself.' He consciously gave an environmental interpretation to a Marxian concept, stating that there was some truth in Marx's saying that the capitalist system carried within it the seeds of its own destruction.[123]

Just as Hazell was able to see a future for mankind in the fusions of the Rhondda, so too could he envisage the most famous coal-producing area in the world in a period after the industry had disappeared.

> The day will come, must come, when its coal seams are but a memory, and its pit-shafts, filled in, its workers diverted to other industries… [But] **the things of the spirit, and men's aspirations… will live on when change and decay will have overtaken material things**.[124]

His comments, seen from the more environmentally-conscious and post-industrial perspective of the early 21st Century, are apposite.

When the Rhondda received its Borough charter Hazell wrote 'Revolution in the Rhondda'. He smiled at the ironic prospect of Will John, ex MP, and Mark Harcombe, MBE, as he described them, who 'had faced authority's power, the bludgeon of the State, and even imprisonment and poverty, in what they deemed the workers' cause' greeting the Duke of Edinburgh. He looked forward to the prospect of 'Will and Mark, and many other Rhondda leaders cheer[ing] and clap[ping] the Duke!' Acknowledging the changes that had taken place since the war in the coal industry, improvements in the miners' status and jobs for women, he said the Rhondda had been revolutionised, though nor quite in the way that had been expected by the miners' leaders at the time of the Tonypandy riots. 'Better this way, I think, and most good citizens with me.'[125]

In his writings, Hazell addressed a range of issues that emerged from post-war society. The coming of the five-day week for miners was an opportunity which reminded him of the war-time 'holidays at home' scheme run by the local councils and he quoted the Chairman of the Rhondda UDC, who said it would require revolutionary change towards public amenities. Hazell advocated that local authorities should negotiate access to landowners' hills, as Mountain Ash UDC had done in the past. Ever aware of potential new markets, Hazell saw co-operative societies in coastal destinations 'having a field day' with catering and co-operative cafes, and a co-operative coach service being established to take them there.

The five-day week was also considered a great opportunity for co-operative education, and not just schools and classes, but with rallies and rambles combining pleasure with education. However Hazell recognised that window shopping in St Mary's Street and Queen Street in Cardiff was a more likely destination for many on Saturdays, when half the 'valleys' population was there. When the two-week paid holiday was introduced in 1947, Hazell made the surprising recommendation of 'doing nothing and doing it well. For two blessed weeks, laziness instead of being... a sin, must be the virtue of virtues...' There were, he said, 50 other weeks in which to think and do things.[126]

Limits to Utopia

Hazell's view of the potential of the movement at times appeared to have no limit. Throughout his life, his writings displayed an absence of cynicism and a freedom from disillusion or despair. He was a proselytiser who called for those who had become cynical and disillusioned to 'Start again now'.[127] His capacity to deliver messages of hope, constructiveness in approach and a commitment to building, in spite of the circumstances in which he, the movement, and the world, at times, found themselves, required unswerving belief rooted equally in co-operation and in faith in people through Christianity.

While sincerely rooted, his ambition for the movement went far beyond that which was realistically attainable. So panoramic was his vision that he considered that co-operation could make a solid contribution to achieving world peace. He wrote that 'we have found in the co-operative movement more goodwill among men, more of the genuine desire to work together, more of human tolerance, than anywhere else on earth.'[128] Even before the 'iron curtain' had settled across Europe he wrote that against the 'shattering, explosive crushing power' of the atomic bomb, international co-operation could be an antidote as a 'binding, cohesive, restoring and healing power'. He pointed to the International Co-operative Alliance as uncorrupted by war and united in outlook and 'There have been no first, second, and third internationals in co-operative history'.[129] While his utopian project of building an economic and social commonwealth through co-operation was understandable, his aspirations in building world peace through co-operation were less well-grounded.

One matter which, exceptionally, qualified his optimism for positive change was that four million people regularly did the football pools.[130] He revisited the theme in 1950, describing it as 'a social problem of staggering magnitude', and contrasting the constructive products of the workers pennies over the last 80 years with their money spent on the football pools, which were 'contributions poured down a purely capitalist sink of corruption'. Frustrated, he said that world peace could be attained if working people used as much energy opposing war as they did on the pools. Socialism would be attainable 'in our time' if people spent as much time and money building it as they did 'speculating on the three-thirty and the four aways!' He asked readers who were democrats, trades unionists or socialists how 'the pools' related to their democratic instincts or principles? He said that the

> 'whole system strikes at the root of moral responsibilities and perverts the moral insight. That the many have to lose in order that few may be enriched is certainly morally wrong.

That phrase captured the essence of Hazell and his philosophy of life. Attacking the motivations of those doing the pools he said:

In the new socialist world there will be nothing for nothing: failing to understand this[,] you do not comprehend socialism. The joy of life and living will render escapism superfluous. Craving for adventure will be abundantly satisfied in the highest adventure of all – building the brave new world and bringing the Kingdom of Heaven right down to earth, where it ought to be.[131]

This utopian view showed a side that was out of touch with, or at least out of sympathy with, the many millions of people who had 'a flutter' on the pools each week and gained some enjoyment from it. It was beyond Hazell to comprehend the need that some people had for a permanently unrealised hope of escaping from daily drudgery. His inspiration was rooted elsewhere. As a deacon, elder and Secretary of Glyn St English Presbyterian Church, Hazell attended adult Sunday School at least until 67 years of age. Still taking annual examinations on his study of the gospels and passing with the highest possible grades, Hazell placed his faith elsewhere.[132]

CHAPTER 5

Consumers Arise!

WITH THE REMOVAL OF rationing in the mid-1950s, and the disappearance of black and grey markets, Hazell realised that the movement faced new challenges. When margarine, butter and meat became freely available in mid-1954 it brought to an end over 14 years of controls during which time YCS had not been exposed to the rigours of the market place. Hazell, like hundreds of able business men and women on co-operative committees across South Wales, had decades of studying markets and consumer behaviour. While serious chain store competition had not yet permeated the valleys and co-operatives still had hegemony, Hazell, with his wide reading and involvement in national discussions, was aware of developments elsewhere. He recognised the threat that chain stores posed as they reduced costs to consumers, and welcomed their competition saying it would keep co-operation on its toes.[1]

In a number of articles and reviews in 1955 Hazell explored consumers and business from different perspectives.[2] In a ground breaking article 'The Miner – No Longer a Minor: His Shopping Habits To-day and Yesterday', Hazell looked at the coalminer as consumer rather than producer. In presenting the coalminer-consumer as a primary agent of social change, Hazell went against long traditions of the South Wales coalfield, which considered the point of production to be key. He saw that the co-operative movement's 'long battle for the recognition of the consumer as the ultimate person of importance is within sight of being won.'[3]

Locating the miner in changes that were happening in South Wales and beyond, he reviewed consumption in the South Wales Coalfield back to the 1890s. He contrasted Victorian buying patterns in the family budget of big weekly orders of 'plain food' potatoes, flour and bread with contemporary purchases of:

> tinned foods, out-of-season items, imported luxuries and "frills", or clothes and footwear changes. With wives and daughters buying in the higher price footwear ranges and in 'children's lines, for many, the best is not too good'.[4]

At a time when he considered the movement to be taking self-service and pre-packaging too cautiously, Hazell knew that understanding shoppers' preferences and recognising changes in consumption patterns required new thinking by co-operative managers. Robert Southern, General Secretary of the Co-operative Union, said that the movement had been primarily set up for food, which still constituted its chief trade. However, he identified sales of white goods and distribution mechanisms as increasingly important but markedly under-developed in the movement and trade battles were to be expected.[5]

Many of these pressures were not yet evident within YCS. The ending of rationing saw Hazell reporting to the annual meeting that trade figures had exceeded all expectations and that the target of £2m per annum was in sight. This compared with trade in 1938 of £836,164.[6] Ynysybwl was a seen as a 'large, sound and effectively managed co-operative business concern'.[7] An exhibition of CWS products in Pontypridd town centre saw more than 4,000 visitors attend in the first two hours. Hazell opened the event which he described as the greatest held in the town by any trader, or group of traders. He highlighted the contribution that YCS made to Pontypridd saying: 'They have educated men and women in mutual help and communal living;

they have pointed the way to a commerce freed from personal greed and fortune-building; they have always been in the van of social progress.'[8]

For Hazell the co-operator these were positive times. He reached the peak of the movement in South Wales on becoming Chair of the Western Sectional Board. In August 1956, he attended the opening of Co-operative House, Swansea, which replaced its predecessor destroyed 15 years earlier by the Luftwaffe.[9] Hazell wrote: 'the momentum and rhythm of a people's movement have been re-established,' adding: 'Looking from the High Street one may see where the new joins the old, like a seam, irregular in parts, but showing clearly the break between not only buildings but also in traditions, social habits and shoppin[g] [sic] customs.'[10]

The summer months of 1956 were heady. As Chairman of the East Glamorgan Federal Bakery Board, Hazell opened 'a gigantic modern bakery plant' in Taffs Well. The joint venture between Ynysybwl, Cardiff, Taff Bargoed, Ton, Treorchy and Dowlais and Barry societies with the CWS, which provided 50 per cent of the capital, was steered by Hazell from the start.[11] Also, the Society's 21st branch was opened in Nantgarw Road, Caerphilly, by Ness Edwards MP, who described it as having 'aesthetic values… combined with utilitarian purpose in order to make the new shops really attractive in every way' in contrast to the 'co-operative back-street shop of dingy memories'.[12] Local authorities, including Pontypridd and Caerphilly, union branches and miners' institutes did their banking through the Society. With a membership of over 17,000 and a strong capital base, the Society's balance sheets were consistently commended by co-operative accountants.[13] Fittingly, it was described as 'a living, practical demonstration of what can be accomplished by an enthusiastic, self-governing local democracy of working men and women.'[14] The position of YCS was seemingly unassailable. However, the introduction of National Savings provided competition which slightly reduced the Society's capital. Aimed at attracting small savings, which was the backbone of the co-operative economy, it was considered to be an act of deliberate political bias by the Government against the movement.

However, one segment of the market emerged with which YCS was not in touch – youth. Hazell had been conscious of the place of young people in society and wrote about them during the late 1940s and 1950s. He admired the strength of co-operative children's choirs and supported the work of co-operative youth club, classes, guilds, meetings, conferences and concerts.[15] However, with society beginning to change, he reflected on 'Welsh youth, the youth of the valleys, and more especially co-operative youth'. He reported that a meeting of the Western Educational Association considered that 'too much was being done for youth, and not enough by them', a view with which he concurred. Hazell contrasted it with the Urdd Gobaith Cymru, where the emphasis was on 'giving, not getting – on service, not sops – on purpose, not puddings'. He returned to the theme in 1953, this time in a more curmudgeonly way, saying he was 'sick and tired of this perpetual "Appeal to Youth", fed up to the neck with it'.[16] When in 1956 the film *Blackboard Jungle* and Bill Hayley's 'Rock Around the Clock' helped create the first youth culture based around music and clothes, Hazell was part of a broader attitude that would struggle to come to terms with the changing role of young people in society. Teenagers, for the first time with discretionary disposable income, created a dynamic new market in the late 1950s and early 1960s and successive cohorts of young people reshaped consumer practices. As they grew into family responsibilities and middle age, unlike their parents and for the first time in three generations, it was not to the co-op that they went for their shopping.

At this key time of retail development, Morgan William Rees was made General Manager of YCS. It was an appointment in which Hazell would have played a central part. It was reported that: 'In accordance with their traditional policy, Ynysybwl Society have filled the vacant post… by means of promotion within the society's staff.'[17] Having lost Sam Davies prematurely and now without Owen Jones, the professional backbone of the Society for the previous three decades had gone. Morgan Rees had begun work 36 years earlier, in 1919, as a warehouse boy. He had much practical experience, having managed the Rhydfelin and Caerphilly branches as well holding roles in the local community, illustrating that co-operative managers, and not just committee members, were actively engaged, and was a pillar of the community.[18] While Rees' track record in managing branches and social involvement was beyond doubt, these could not have equipped him for the challenges confronting YCS. Of the benefits to making internal appointments in the traditional way, 'new thinking' and 'fresh blood' were not among them. The rise of chain stores was reshaping shopping in ways that tested the co-operative movement, and fresh thinking would be needed at this time of dramatic changes in retail. The absence of the Society's papers does not allow analysis of Board discussions about retail and societal changes at that time. My suspicion is that there would have been little, and the filling of the General Manager's post with Mr Rees would have been seen as a safe appointment.

At the time of Rees' appointment, the YCS Management Board comprised a cinema manager, a retired railway goods clerk, two housewives, a retired police sergeant, three ex-miners, a factory worker, one grocery manager and a retired grocery manager, a BR locomotive driver, a pithead baths superintendent and a retired railway official. There was not one working miner on the Board, which says much about how the Society's leadership had become more occupationally diverse. However, what they did share was that they were older. Their photo in *The*

Gleaming Vision records an ageing, and sometimes aged, group, with approximately a third retired.[19] In the coming years that would prove telling.

In 1957, a fascinating series of articles called 'Gateways to the Boardroom' cast light on the inner workings of co-operative societies and Hazell's thinking on the co-operative movement's relationships with trades unions and local authority membership. Hazell described the difficulties of transition that some unionists encountered moving 'from the cause of the producer...to a cause which is nine-tenths a consumers' organisation' and from being an employee to employer. While he considered that the coming of the Welfare State and full employment had required unionists to rise above a 'cruder trade union outlook' and narrow sectional interest, and the advent of nationalised industries had brought progress in union thinking, some trades unionists found it not easy to adapt. Trades unionism, he thought, had become a centralised movement subservient to a centralised head office and had lost its character of voluntary association. No doubt coloured by the experience of the South Wales miners with their strong tradition of autonomous union lodges, Hazell supported the decentralising process that the shop stewards movement had carried out efficiently. However, he believed that only the co-operative movement now possessed what he considered to be a pure voluntary association of co-operation where 'boards... have full and undoubted local autonomy'. With a swipe towards political parties he said 'strait-jacket regimentation would be anathema in a co-operative boardroom' as there was no group or caucus system, which could only exist as cliques or underground groupings 'which are detestable whichever way one looks at them.'[20]

On links with local authority membership, Hazell recognised that there could be two-way traffic between co-operation and municipal service. He considered that co-operators could obtain a useful 'financial apprenticeship' in the council chamber, although the 'critical financial faculties of the local councillor have become somewhat dimmed since the coming of... block grants, and other Exchequer aids'. He saw civic duties in noble terms with a councillor, alderman or mayor as one of the highest forms of service to others. In an interesting ranking of perceived worth, though, he saw the co-operative movement as being 'the true elevation' and that local government was of 'incalculable value' for those aspiring to that 'greatest honour'. While reversing what others might consider relative standings, Hazell also recognised the negative impact that municipal service could have in the co-operative boardroom as, in some, 'the local government aroma pervades the air almost to the exclusion of the co-operative attar.'[21]

The essence of co-operation was further questioned in the relations that could exist between building a 'co-operative commonwealth' and working to retain market share in an increasingly consumer-oriented capitalist economy. As austerity receded into the past, the contradictions and limitations of achieving radical social transformation through the pockets and purses of consumers came more to the fore.

Hazell and the State

During the late 1940s and throughout the 1950s, Hazell was preoccupied by the increasing role of the state. He warned against the expansion of state activity undermining voluntary delivery and individuals' personal responsibility. Hazell realised that as the state took over roles previously been undertaken by the people, the voluntary action that was key to people delivering services on their own behalf would be undermined. Hazell also foresaw competition emerging between municipalities and co-operatives and was sure that 'voluntary co-operation would hold its own in any future collectivised state'. Intriguingly he advanced the idea that service and enterprise could replace the profit motive in business.[22]

Hazell's concerns extended across a range of services and industries. While he supported and praised the National Health Service, the loss of voluntary effort and local democratic accountability since the services transferred to the state pained him. His position was clear in relation to an adjunct service, convalescent care, where he extolled the virtues of the "Porthcawl Rest". He described it as 'one of the glories of voluntary effort' which still remained under a democratically-elected committee and depended upon collected donations and subscriptions.

> No one has yet had the audacity to even hint that the 'Rest' should be nationalised, regionalised, or governmentalised in any way. Like a co-operative society, it runs itself and is proud of it.[23]

Supported by unions, co-operative societies and public appeals, the Chair, Harry Williams of Cilfynydd, was a member of the YCS Board. The 'Rest' had over 30 staff, had been used by more than 125,000 people and had recently extended its work to include paraplegics, particularly those injured in the mining industry.

Hazell's reservations about other aspects of the Welfare State come through clearly. He believed that there needed to be more individual discipline in the Welfare State, which he referred to as 'over-paternal'.[24] Hazell highlighted the risks inherent in that responsibility being displaced by the state and elsewhere listed the services offered by YCS at each stage in taking an individual member through life, from birth to death.

Some of Hazell's writings were very hard-hitting. His most powerful railing against the state appeared in an article entitled 'A Congress Creed: Democracy for Man – Not Man for Democracy' where he called for the next Co-operative Congress in Llandudno to come out with an equivalent of the Magna Carta which would 'bring us nearer in ideals and action to the free and just society which will some day have to be organised.' Aldous Huxley, he said, had once thought that under perfect State socialism, 'charity would be not merely superfluous... but actually criminal', and questioned whether a century of co-operative experience was 'now to be discarded in the name of a new democracy.' Hazell's half-century of co-operative experience and idealism counterposed the state's capacity to 'card-index, note, record, number and administer' with

> discovery, believing, journeying, questing and searching by the chart of a slender hope, an awful longing, and the keeping alight of the dying smoking flax of a pure idealism: this is not for bureaucracy, but for joyous, co-operative, hopeful, travelling.

He continued:

> the people are in danger of perishing upon a cross of ideologies and spurious-State worship, an erection which is democracy degraded into anti-democracy and a Socialism which is no longer social but retains only the 'ism'.

He discounted 'the determination to have a ready-made, labelled, cellophane-wrapped, creased-and-folded new world', which he saw was an implicit danger in 'the reformer's eternal temptation to produce the finished article'. While he did not describe it as such, he indicated that the moral value of things were in the way they grew *organically*. He called on the Llandudno Conference to 'say all this and much more', and make itself into the 'gathering which marked the turning of the corner in Britain's post-war social and economic progress.[25]

Whereas Hazell lauded planning in 1947 and could still acknowledge its advantages in the mid-1950s, he considered it a tragedy that a village or hamlet could never again 'grow naturally from the soil and surroundings, the occupations and even the whims and fancies of the Welsh people.' He thought there was a loss in everything being 'planned and geometrical, orderly and tidy.'[26] Hazell said that co-operators were not against planners and organisers, for they did it all the time, 'But how much planning? How much state organising? That is where we disagree…' He said has the time not arrived to say that 'democracy was made for man and not man for democracy?' Saying that principle had been sacrificed on the altar of expediency for far too long, he asked 'Do our [Labour Party] "friends" really expect us to commit hari-kiri [*sic*]…?' Rising to the argument he asked

> Do 'Democracy' and 'Socialism', in their 1953 interpretations, really entail the extinction of Co-operation as we have known it, or are its boundaries to be so circumscribed that we must scrap our dairies, bakeries, mills and factories and suffer relegation to keeping a few kiosks and sideshows which the State is unwilling, at present, to run?[27]

He pointed out that as the state became more omnipotent, so distrust grew of its efficiency and referred to calls for management of the nationalised coal and railway industries to be decentralised. Could decentralised groups, such as co-operative societies, take over their functions, he wondered? He believed that such steps could revitalise the co-operative movement and 'The defeatism, frustrations and disappointments of the past decade will disappear and vanish…' He added 'The fear of totalitarianism in catering for consumer-needs will recede once more, and bureaucracy lose its terrors' to be replaced by 'the joy and deep satisfaction of true voluntary effort, which is the real essence of a democracy made for man, as against a pseudo-democracy for which men are being mis-made'.

While his critiques continued, Hazell later noted that changes were taking place. Speaking on 'Public Ownership Today and Tomorrow' at a Western Sectional Board educational school, organised by the Abersychan and Pontypool Co-operative Society, in February 1954, Hazell considered that the 'tide of excessive top-control in the nationalised industries has definitely receded'. He noted a trend towards decentralisation, with much more regional and area control being introduced.[28] Some weeks later, in the *Co-operative News*, he undertook an analysis of publicly-owned bodies, including the Coal Board and the gas, electricity and airline industries. He said that while nationalisation had swept away old vices, it had introduced new ones, with some industries being strangled by bureaucratic controls. He pointed to growing demands for decentralisation and delegation of functions in the administration and management in all publicly-owned undertakings, and that public pressure had helped address the top heavy structure of the Coal Board. Arguing that it was necessary for a service to be near the users and consumers, he welcomed the greater autonomy of the Divisional Boards.[29]

Hazell's critical assessments continued for the rest of the decade. In 1954, in the third year of Tory Government, he pointed out the limitations on relying on state-delivered forms of collectivism.

> Some co-operators have thought they saw the end of the gleaming vision [of the Co-operative Commonwealth] in some political New Jerusalem whose foundations were State-laid. Over the years, however, the consumer co-operative ideal has held its ground, while political fortunes have followed the usual up-and-down pattern.[30]

In November 1957 he revisited the issue of state-running of the coal industry, against which he had first written in 1946. He had already exquisitely described the NCB as 'the three lettered giant'.[31] This time he wrote:

> In the year 1946 [*sic*] King Coal's kingdom was, on New Year's Day, officially changed into a republic. The mines had been transferred to the State; the monster's claws had been clipped and his power strictly limited. A notice board said, 'This mine now belongs to the people'; the flag was hoisted with its three initials, N.C.B.

It seemed to the writer, who was present at the simple ceremony, that the feeling of most present was not the easy rejoicing some had expected but a sober thoughtfulness of what the future would unfold…

Eleven years have passed, and such is the whirligig of time and its strange revenges that thoughtful ones now inquire whether the board is just a new type of monster…? What kind of men is it breeding and evolving? They are better off, but are they better men? Will nationalisation take the place of the older, voluntary, betterment methods such as co-operation and friendly societies with their self-government and character-building, thrift-inducing ideals?

In the ultimate, one knows that neither empire, kingdom, republic, soviet, nor even the N.C.B. can regenerate the spirit of man… 'What shall it profit a man if he gain the whole world – and lose his soul?'[32]

And that, for Hazell, was the essence – the nationalised coal industry was seen to lack a soul, was dehumanising for those who worked in it, and was an affront to Hazell's faith in the human spirit, as well as being a less good form of collective organisation and service delivery than co-operation. State delivered services and industries were producing lesser men as a result. The clarity and strength of such sustained arguments over an extended period confirm Hazell as a thinker in British co-operation.

Hazell and Communism

Hazell displayed an easy familiarity with the writings of Marx, Engels, Lenin and Stalin. In 1946, he wrote in not too complimentary terms on G D H Cole's most recent book – the latest on Marx. Hazell cautioned against reading what Cole and others thought of Marx as they often 'cancel each other out. Read them if you can, understand them if you may, quote them if you dare – buy them only if you must.' Instead, he recommended:

The only sensible thing to do for the average working man is first to take three winter courses in economics and industrial history, and then and **only then**, read *Das Kapital* as three volumes. With your accumulated knowledge, a stiff dose of common sense and a few lucky guesses, you may come as near the truth as Cole or anyone else.[33]

This was an intellectually confident Hazell whose learning and experience gave him the wherewithal to analyse and criticise academics.

While Hazell could admire Marx, he underwent a profound change in his attitude to the Communist Party in the 1940s. While he had been prepared to embrace the Communist Party as a brother in support of the Popular Front up to 1939, its treachery 'when Stalin kissed Hitler over the Russo-German pact' earned Hazell's enduring contempt and exposed the Soviet Union's perfidious nature along with its progeny in the CPGB.[34]

After the war, with the establishment of communist dictatorships in central and eastern Europe, Hazell's respect for Marx became qualified. He saw how Marx's thought was ideologically (ab)used and referred to the Communist Manifesto as having been written 'when Communism was an ideal not an Imperialist ideology.'[35] Hazell regularly counterposed the lives and thought of Robert Owen and Karl Marx, and by 1953 concluded: 'How much wiser, better and happier the world might have been to-day if it had turned towards Owenism rather than Marxism.'[36]

Hazell's preparedness to work closely with the Communist Party against fascism in the Popular Front and in the Second World War changed after 1945, when he became a staunch critic. There are various examples of him lampooning the actions of that Party. When the South Wales Area NUM Executive, which was heavily influenced by the Communist Party, decided no longer to use the NCLC educational facilities, but rather to set up its own education scheme, Hazell was suspicious. He referred to the change as a surprising development before asking rhetorically '(or was it?)', suggesting the change was in the interests of the Communist Party. Using humour to make a serious point, Hazell parodied the situation by recounting the tale of a local Communist telling him that that all the education that Hazell or anyone else needed was to be found in the [Daily] Worker, to which Hazell now asked 'Can it be that the standard [of the paper] is deteriorating, and that other means to a desired end have become necessary?'[37]

Hazell recounted a story from a local council election, when a comment was directed to him on the Dictatorship of the Proletariat. He did not attempt to answer on a public platform and kept to municipal topics as questions normally were about sewers and salvage and he did not wish to risk taking his audience out of its depth. He did though point out that someone in the 1940s would not say the same things, nor write them down in the same way as, say, in 1848.[38]

While he was happy to describe individual communists as friends, Hazell was deeply antagonistic to state communism and authoritarianism and unsympathetic to its British apologists. This was apparent in an impassioned essay, worthy of Orwell, written in October 1951 in favour of the reasonable and against logic.

> The logical Marxians – and who so logical as they – have given us horrors we never dreamed of, even after reading all Jack London's and Upton Sinclair's social epics. Bourgeois, capitalist imperialists, deviationists, social escapists – all these tryannise over our thoughts and produce that monstrosity only possible to economic logicians, the classless society, and the State monster which, quite logically, swallows up the individual in its caricature of society and its cartoon of humanity.

He said:

> To the disgust and non-comprehension of my logical friends, I consistently refuse to look for the classless society or a State which

is all-in-all, achieved by naked force and overwhelming power. I have suffered too much for the sins in logic of my fathers to confuse my values.[39]

Hazell described 'The ultra-logical terror in France in 1792-3', and the guillotining of thousands, linking it to contemporary Eastern Europe, which 'adopts the terror to-day under other logical titles – liquidation and the purge.' His critique was relentless, saying that even China, the traditional home of philosophy and culture, where arguments in pre-Communist days had been settled on the basis of the reasonable as well as what was logically correct, now adopted police and military terror as a state instrument. He said that what terrified him about the authoritarian right and left 'is not the theories they annunciate so logically, but the fanatical spirit which enthuses them, and the methods by which their theories are pushed doggedly to logical absurdities.' His rejection of the requirements of Party or other orthodoxy where individuals were required to subsume their own sense of reason was clear.

> Instead of any Utopia of any brand, I look to the Reasonable Age, of which co-operation[,] as I understand it[,] is the forerunner, and in which co-operative effort, voluntary and free, will play many parts, together with trade unions and churches untrammelled by any State fetters.

He continued:

> The reasonable spirit... humanises all our thinking. It does, admittedly, make us less sure of our own super-correctness and near-infallibility. All the better. What is obstinate dogmatism of all sorts in human behaviour but logical fanaticism of the worst type?[40]

This was the voice of an older, wiser man. Having outlived his 'cocksure twenties, the hardening thirties and the dogmatic forties, [when] one is so sure of all the answers' he was now in his 'mellowing and tolerant sixties', when 'one hesitates to prescribe…'[41] However, Hazell was clear on an alternative which was as much about a sense of spirit as organisational:

> Co-operation cannot be systematised. It is one of our glories that we never called it a system. It is a movement… It can move and adapt itself. Being in essence plastic and adjustable… ever-changing and ever remaining the same…[42]

In 1954 Hazell wrote a review of George Orwell's *1984*, which had just been televised. He considered the book to be a classic, which he had studied when first published. Hazell said Orwell described a 'devilish state of society, perilously near to us' which was 'a genius-created likeness, by an artist in his realm of literary realism unsurpassed', describing a world where a de-humanised existence had reached its culmination. Against a back-drop of the state takeovers of the co-operative movement in Central and Eastern European, the threat of the atomic bomb, and the Cold War, Hazell asked his readers to consider the 'monstrous dehumanisation of human values already in evidence in the world around you' and invited them to 'Sit up and take notice of a modern seer who scrutinised modern tendencies and trends and traits with an ultra-microscope'. For Hazell developments in the nationalised industries, the extending tentacles of the state and the undermining of personal and collective responsibility which were visible in Ynysybwl made it not difficult to imagine 1984. In what was a personal manifesto he wrote:

> Is it not the lesson that we must resist unceasingly any encroachment upon the fundamentals of human liberty and the spirit of man?

He added:

> On us in the churches, in the Labour Party, in the co-operative movement rests a great and grave responsibility. The fate of the race in 1984 can only be averted by our faithfulness to the ideals we have proclaimed. Every tendency to hero-worship, whether

it be of Big Brother, or Winston, or Nye, or Ike, should be seen
as unworthy of our manhood. The insidious creeping cancer of
totalitarianism must be clearly perceived and rejected.

The isms that spilt, the ideologies that divide, the schisms that
confound and confuse, must be religiously avoided. The spirit of
man must remain intact, inviolate and undivided.[43]

The article evoked strong responses. While Frank Jones of
Manchester liked the article, he said that Hazell had 'missed [the]
point' that the 'horrors of peace' required armed strength. Sidney
Aitken of Birmingham added Hazell 'does not understand', that
the 'problems of humanity will not be the same in the future
as they have been... [for] a new man is being developed under
socialism...'[44] Correspondence in the letters page of the *Co-
operative News* ran for over two months, the biggest response to
any piece of Hazell's writing.

However, Hazell's criticisms of communism did not mean
that he was any more reconciled to capitalism. He would
remind readers of inter-war conditions and the consequences of
unfettered markets:

I think of a long lifetime spent in profit-dominated private
industry, where the only incitement [*sic*] in a material sense
was the fear of the sack! What incentive did I then have, what
encouragement?[45]

For Hazell there was still a need for 'transforming capitalistic
jungles' and it was to co-operation that he still looked for
delivery.[46]

In his introduction to Orwell's *The Lion and the Unicorn'*,
Bernard Crick's dissection of Orwell's component parts of his
socialist politics fitted Hazell to a tee. Orwell never lost 'his belief
in the innate decency of ordinary people nor his belief in the
growth of socialist values' which Crick described as 'moralistic
socialism'. It is difficult to give a better description of Hazell's
own beliefs.[47]

The 1950s National Co-operative Debates

The changes in post-war society, including the rise of the consumer and changes in shopping patterns led in the 1950s to the most important national debates in the history of the co-operative movement. Although co-operatives had been established and grew in competitive environments their primary purpose had been to supply necessities. There was in many senses a paradox between the conditions under which co-operation thrived, with social solidarity and basic goods, and that of a consumer-based society focussed on the luxuries and wants, rather than the needs, of the individual. Tensions within the movement became increasingly evident between the autonomy of local societies with democratic participation and moves towards a more streamlined movement with a stronger role for the CWS, which some argued would bring increased efficiency.

Hazell actively engaged in the debates through co-operative structures, his articles and public speaking. He understood that the movement faced challenges, although he may not have appreciated how the developing consumer society was creating market forces which co-operative societies could not match. Nor could Hazell have been aware that the consumer coming to the fore would undermine co-operation itself. The movement which for over a century had been the consumer's greatest advocate now faced the irony that new patterns of consumption and consumer choice would prove the greatest threat yet to its vitality.

When a Committee of Inquiry was established into the CWS in 1953 Hazell stood unsuccessfully to be the representative from the combined South Western and Western Section. In February 1954, Hazell criticised the centralising forces within the movement and contrasted the trend towards decentralisation in the nationalised industries with a strong trend in the opposite direction within co-operation. While much more regional and area control was being introduced in the nationalised industries, within the co-operative movement local and sectional committees were 'marked out for destruction'. He referred to the 'paradoxical spectacle of the same speakers on different platforms advocating centralisation for co-operative institutions, and on the other hand, devolution and more local control for nationalised concerns!' [48]

The following week, in an article provocatively entitled 'Is the Movement Going Totalitarian?' Hazell identified a growing number of indicators towards 'totalitarian thought and philosophy in the Union's higher circles'. He pointed to a 'successive introduction of seeming[ly] innocent and minor proposals [which] had disarmed opposition and lessened [their] eternal vigilance…'. Two all-powerful bodies, the Central Executive and the General Purposes Committee, had been created while the Central Board (of which he had been a member) which 'acted as a spur to efficiency and a brake upon reaction… was destroyed, mainly by the block votes of certain wholesale bodies'. The process, he judged, was 'insidious in its gradual unfolding'. Consequently, he argued, only Congress, which met only once a year, and which was a 'totally unsuitable instrument for this purpose' could check on national committees. Now, following 'the decapitation of democratic checks at the top', attention was turning to the 'inoffensive but energetic district councils at the bottom', which were 'modest bodies… close to the retail societies [which] were still doing good work.' He evoked the language and example of the Soviet Revolution in saying 'the whispers, the hints, the tendencies, all point in one direction. All power to Manchester.' All that was missing from this broadside was a series of exclamation marks. They came shortly afterwards. The co-operative movement, he declared, was moving towards 'the totalitarian structure already standing condemned in the nationalised industries! What irony!' He continued that the movement's committee structure, which had put men and women from all sections and districts 'personally in touch with national business, meeting frequently with national leaders, receiving national minutes and able to interpret and explain and expound to rank and filers' across the country was considered older than ancient. Although he did not identify it as such, what he considered to be the lifeblood of the movement was being threatened. He said that:

> arguments for totalitarianism are as specious as they were in the days of the great dictators. Economy, efficiency, co-ordination, functionalism, quick-acting bodies, centralised leadership, and hey presto!

Hazell asked co-operators if they felt that totalitarianism was too high a price to pay for efficiency and economy, before concluded with a stark warning:

> But remember, before you acquiesce. It will be a co-operative system no longer. It will be on a level with the centralised trusts and combines. Its democratic glory will have departed.[49]

As the perennial debate between centralised efficiency and democratic participation continued Hazell placed himself with the local societies.[50] Two months later in an article on the CWS Special Committee of Inquiry he observed:

> One might have hoped that... the larger the wholesale colossus grows, the plainer and more urgent the need for a measure of decentralisation. Clearly, a great opportunity lost.'[51]

Hazell likened the movement to a mosaic – an assembly of bits and pieces, within which there was a unity of purpose.[52] Within that mosaic local societies were an essential element. He later wrote:

> While the present democratic structure of the Co-operative Movement remains intact, those necessary evils, the boards of management, will remain with us. When they are defunct or suppressed we shall have a Movement, but it will not be "co-operative".[53]

It is not known how Hazell's views were received in the Central Executive of the Co-operative Union. From 1955 and 1959, he attended some Executive meetings, which comprised around 20 representatives from across the Co-operative Union. There he took part in discussions on establishing the key Independent Commission on co-operation. Led by Gaitskell and Anthony Crosland, it was charged with looking at the future direction of the movement.

At the May 1958 Scarborough Congress, Hazell's continued resistance was evident when he intervened in the debate on the Commission: 'We are told that the matter is urgent, and it may be so, but I am more concerned about arriving at right decisions than about arriving at quick decisions.' He continued: 'In the main, it is going to be in the board rooms of the societies of this country that these issues will be decided. Let us hope that we may arrive at the right decisions.'[54]

When Anthony Crosland, the Commission's Secretary, came to Cardiff to speak about its Report at a Western Section conference Hazell questioned Crosland's analysis that the last ten years of prosperity had been good for co-operation. Hazell said that the movement had been born, grown, and could thrive in poverty, but that full employment and higher wages did not mean that the extra money would be spent in co-operative stores. Showing a clear understanding of changes in social and economic behaviours, Hazell said that it was now necessary to 'take account of profound psychological changes', such as miners taking continental holidays. The 145 delegates were amused at the way Hazell tellingly criticised Crosland's financial recommendations and such was the nature of Hazell's critique that Crosland felt the need to respond strongly.[55]

The November 1958 Special Congress, convened in Blackpool specifically to consider the Report of the Commission, had 'an almost terrifying intensity'. It was said that there had never previously been a Congress like it where 'forthright talking was the order of the day and short shrift was accorded those few delegates who wandered from the point.'[56] When Hazell went to the rostrum as the fourth speaker in the debate, he found delegates restive and was met with cries of "vote". Unperturbed, Hazell reminded Congress that there was no definition of which was the movement's most successful competitor, whether 'cash and carry' or other, nor was there an agreed form as to what should be the co-operative response.[57]

In his subsequent analysis of the Special Congress Hazell said he was saddened at the way co-operators wished to ape the methods of capitalism – 'the eloquent advocacy of purely copy methods' – which he likened to being caught in the same chains as capitalism. 'One waited in vain for the new ideas, the pioneering method, the novel... way...' Giving examples of innovation as means of inspiration both in the co-operative sector and the private sector, he wondered where the new ideas at Congress were or whether co-operation really had 'said the last word?'[58] While accepting Congress's decision to support the Commission, he subsequently described the Commission's conclusion on amalgamation into 200-300 societies as naïve.[59]

Another important issue for South Wales societies, the role of the CRS, was raised in the Scarborough Congress. Since its first act in taking over the Cardiff Society in 1936 the CRS had been contentious; now it was playing an increasingly controversial role in becoming a major retailer in competition with independent societies. Opposition to the CRS had long existed in, and been led by, societies in South Wales, not least because CRS had developed one of its strongest footholds in the region. Hazell took part in the Congress debate, making a measured and apparently conciliatory intervention: 'This is a modestly-worded resolution... and it does not attack the CRS but simply seeks information as to the position.'[60] He went on to say that while some looked upon the

CRS as a sort of saviour, others saw it as a Frankenstein while the truth lay in-between. After Congress passed a resolution setting up a Special Survey Committee to inquire into the CRS, the Ynysybwl Society nominated Hazell for membership. Placing an advert in the *Co-operative News* seeking support for his nomination from other societies, YCS described Hazell's name as 'a bye-word in Co-operative affairs' who had virtually dedicated his life to the movement. However, Hazell was unsuccessful.[61]

Hazell did not quite reach the top levels of the co-operative movement. Perhaps his highest accolade was being nominated by the Western Sectional Board to be President of the Brighton Co-operative Congress in 1957. The Congress Presidency was the pinnacle for any lay member in the movement and, although he was not selected, being nominated was an honour, recognising his lifetime of co-operative work. Hazell made what would appear to be his only trip outside Britain when he attended the Annual Meeting of the Danish Co-operative Movement on a Co-operative Union delegation in May 1956. Although not intended as such, it was just reward for his decades of dedication to the movement and would have affirmed his still strong beliefs in the international reach of the movement. Less glamorous but more typical was the visit to a Lowestoft canning factory the following year.[62]

CHAPTER 6

Last Words...

Semi-Retirement and Nominal Winding Down

In the 1950s, probably at the behest of Jack Bailey, Hazell wrote a number of articles entitled 'In Wales Now' for the *Co-operative Party Monthly Letter*, which Hazell used as an opportunity to write irreverently. In 1957, Hazell was invited, but declined, to contribute a regular co-operative column for *The Cymric Democrat*, a paper which primarily served the Labour Party across Wales, produced in the Rhondda. Perhaps feeling that he was winding down, rather than looking for new responsibilities, Hazell said that he would supply articles but could not become the paper's regular correspondent.[1] In his last years of writing, Hazell's articles mainly appeared in the *Co-operative Review* and the *South Wales Supplement*. When the *South Wales Supplement* apparently ceased publication in 1958 he lost his major outlet, for Hazell had contributed regularly over four decades and had written 43 articles or other pieces between July 1955 and December 1958, compared with seven which were published elsewhere. With the demise of the *Supplement*, Hazell may have judged that, as well as retiring under the age rule, it was timely to cease writing.

Hazell attended his last meeting of the Western Sectional Board on 2 May 1959, at which point he was required to retire from committee memberships because of the co-operative movement's age-limit rule. A retirement function was organised by the Ynysybwl Society on 29 June, where tributes were paid by the Sectional Board and by the Western Section of the Co-operative Party. A presentation was made on behalf of the Ynysybwl Society and the programme for the event aptly bore the phrase "Those having torches will pass them on to others".

The personal impact of his retirement, which he presented almost as a bereavement, can be sensed from Hazell's article: 'On the Shelf: Can One Retire Gracefully?' He wrote: 'However well man or woman may have schooled themselves to meet it, compulsory retirement comes as an *emergency* – a *crisis*.' It meant:

> a severance from active service in a Movement to which they have given voluntary, unpaid toil, for often a lifetime. All the accumulated knowledge and experience, all the lessons learned, all the problems solved, all the constructive efforts, now count for nought.[2]

A month later he parodied his situation:

> As the years fly by, and the moss grows on us and our ideas tend to become fixed; the guillotine knife descends and we are released from our burdens of office. The impartial age-limit! It cuts away the fossilised, the hide-bound; those whose minds have ceased functioning.[3]

However, even though Hazell was required to stand down from offices in the Co-operative Union, he could continue as President of the Ynysybwl Society and represent it at Co-operative Congress and at meetings of the CWS. He could also remain active in the Co-operative Party.

Hazell had lost none of his powers. When cautioned before speaking at a Co-operative Day gathering by an unnamed inviter about the audience who 'although we call them co-operators, they are merely purchasers in our shops', an 'unthinking mass' sprayed each night by advertising 'propaganda and imporperganda' and were 'merely machine-made victims of a dope age', who 'cannot even *dream* for themselves', Hazell dismissed the advice and made clear that he still dreamed. Giving a wide-ranging talk aimed at challenging his audience, he drew on Tennyson, Keats, Orwell and Howard Spring and contrasted Ghandi and Lansbury with the Kaiser and Hitler; Robert Owen, Wesley and Wilberforce with Napoleon Bonaparte, and Christ and Paul with Tiberius and Nero before evoking 'the Man of Nazareth' as a source of appropriate inspiration rather than nuclear power or atomic destruction. He then linked the argument to the findings of the Independent Commission, which he said erred in confusing real value with power and size.[4] This was classic Hazell.

While Hazell recognised it was much harder to educate the membership of the co-operative movement than to produce dividends, he still considered the role of education to be essential.[5] If new-style consumers were replacing co-operators, Hazell felt that co-operative education could give members 'the solidity, the rightness, the unfailing strength of co-operative principles, as against today's economic trading and commercial trends', and which would set them 'like granite against the doubters, the defeatists, the multiple-admirers and those who succumb to the glittering facades of state-subsidised totalitarianism.'[6] This though was whistling in the wind for although some societies were quite active, Hazell considered leadership in educational work in the Western Section to be almost defunct.[7] The educational and cultural association that had underpinned the economic aspects of co-operation and had been central to the vision of creating an alternative economic and social system was withering.

Co-operative Party

Hazell had long been a supporter of the Co-operative Party, writing in 1937 that as a movement they should never regret entering politics for the protection of consumer interests. In 1955 he was elected to the Co-operative Party National Committee, representing the Western Sectional Board, holding the position until 1959 when he stood down owing to the age rule. Intriguingly, at the Co-operative Party's Annual Conference in Skegness over the Easter weekend 1957, Hazell and Will Coldrick MP spoke on behalf of the National Committee against the emergency resolution which demanded a postponement of 'H' bomb tests, and getting rid of the nuclear bomb, which was narrowly defeated. The debate occurred at a time when the issue was at the top of the British political agenda. The debate – fittingly on Easter Sunday – was very heated and emotional.[8] Although appalled by the prospect of nuclear war, Hazell did a clinical dissection of the resolution which he described as supporting unilateralism, anticipating the position taken by Bevan at the Labour Party conference later that year.

In South Wales Hazell was active in the Brecon, Monmouth and East Glamorgan Federation of the Party in the mid-1950s, though it was organisationally poor and the Executive Committee meetings were spasmodic. The Party in South Wales undertook some political work, including protesting against the invasion of Suez,[9] but such was its weakness that Hazell wrote that it was not possible to be optimistic and 'we cannot, simply cannot, afford to allow the present position to continue.'[10]

In August 1956, Jack Bailey addressed the inaugural meeting of the Western Sectional Council of the Party, which was established to stimulate Party activity, with Hazell in attendance. Bailey identified that there were too few society [based] parties and it was agreed that more society parties could be formed. By the late 1950s, the situation was apparently transformed. In a burst of activity, conferences were organised in 1958 and 1959 to generate new enthusiasm. Some 40 to 50 people attended the first, organised by the Blaina Society in Abertillery in September 1958. The Ynysybwl Society provided much support to the Party and a follow-up conference in Pontypridd on 26 September 1959 was opened by Hazell and considered 'a splendid success'.[11]

Although age was taking its toll and Hazell felt frustrated

and annoyed at his physical frailties,[12] that he had not lost his sense of challenge was clear in a CWS South Wales Divisional meeting. There he pointed to revolutionary changes with the decline of the Lancashire cotton industry and with coal in South Wales 'virtually on its way out', and proposed that the CWS should enter new industries such as plastics. Fred Pickup of the Dry Goods Committee responded that he did not believe that the Lancashire cotton industry was on the way out, and said that there were no better equipped cotton mills in Britain than those of the CWS. He also said that 'the CWS had no intention at all of going in for plastics manufacture', which showed that in some areas Hazell had clearer foresight than Manchester officials.[13]

However, in other areas Hazell was less insightful. At the Annual Co-operative Party Conference in Llandudno in Easter 1960, Hazell expressed concern that the Macmillan position of 'Never Had It So Good' was, in fact, artificial prosperity based on credit (he said 'hire purchase') which was susceptible to collapse and argued that Party campaigning be undertaken on this basis. While his analysis may have been prudent, it was a perspective which dated back to the 1921 lockout and out of sympathy, or perhaps out of touch, with the spirit of the times.[14]

Hazell's retirement from national and sectional roles coincided with the spreading of 'multiple' stores, the relaxation of hire purchase arrangements, the increasing purchase of consumer durables, price-cutting, and the emergence of the teenage market. Such market changes were debated at the 1961 Co-operative Congress. The movement's Grocery and Provisions Trade Association Executive stated that while this area was the 'backbone' of the movement's trading activities, co-operative grocery departments were losing ground to competitors. A 'dynamic evolutionary change' was described where national trade in footstuffs had increased by 9%, of which multiples had increased their sales by 22% and co-operative societies by 4%.

The Association argued that societies were not adapting quickly enough and said that: 'Those who do not adapt themselves to changing conditions will not survive.' Hazell intervened in the debate criticising the Association's view that 'the small shop is out' and that the largest possible stores and supermarkets must be aimed for, commenting that the debate had been presented 'from the city point of view' and conditions varied. He argued that from the perspective of his Society 'the small shop is not going to go' as some people still wanted service, as opposed to the 'cash-and-carry, non-dividend, cut-price stores – cut-throat, I call them…', which the Society had also opened.[15] Hazell's cosseted position was possible because competitors had not yet penetrated the valleys. However, while the Ynysybwl Society remained in a comparatively stronger situation than many societies elsewhere in Britain, the ground was shifting quickly.

Later that day, Hazell took part in a discussion on the opticians service and in an amusing intervention said that while short vision was well catered for in the movement, long vision of the 'Co-operative Commonwealth' was needed.[16] However, overall, the 1961 Congress showed that in the most vital area, that of market change, Hazell was no longer able to see even a short distance into the future. Tides of business change were about to sweep over Hazell which would henceforth put YCS permanently on the back foot.

Three years later, Hazell presented his last quarterly report to the Ynysybwl Society, saying supermarkets were establishing stores at the centre of communities with high trade volumes. He acknowledged that co-operative branches with less trade had become uneconomic, that 'the previously accepted manner of trading must be altered' and rationalisation of branches had to be expedited.[17]

In 1963, Hazell opened a new Department store in Caerphilly, which was named Hazell House in his honour and assumed pride of place within the Society. However, it had been planned before the Second World War, when assumptions about future trading were different.[18] While it might have been the aspiration for a forward-looking Society at that time, shifting shopping patterns and the move away from large department stores meant that such stores at the start of the supermarket age would quickly become white elephants. The pace of change in retailing would catch the Ynysybwl Society and its President unprepared.

Final Days

As he grew towards the end of his life, Hazell drew a line under previous differences. In a letter to Lilian and David he reflected on his life, writing:

> Thank you for all gifts, not only now, but over the years. I cherish all kind thoughts. In fact, I have no resentments, at all, of any kind. We must understand each other.[19]

This acknowledgement of earlier rifts was also a move towards final reconciliation.

Christmas 1963 was 'very, very, quiet'. Gwlad went to Glyn St Chapel on Christmas morning, with the 'usual faithful present'. He was now affected by the 'hostile' weather and was sitting on top of the fire; by April the east wind was blowing 'and on this hill, particularly troublesome'. As Hazell's health declined, he concluded that he was probably going to cut out the morning service in Glyn Street in future as there was no bus in the mornings and the weather was against him. 'I have kept it up as long as I could & probably longer than I should.' He warned Lilian and David that when he and Auntie visited them in Chippenham

> I may disturb your nights by coughing. I generally get one severe spasm of it in the small hours. I have now 2 pillows please note.'[20]

By mid-1964 he was doing little letter writing. Ivy visited but when she left 'everything went very flat.' Gwlad was able to get out to the local shops, got plenty of rest and ate fairly well while 'I go on my painful, sleepless way', usually getting up at 3.30am making a cup of tea and read.[21] Hazell was pleased to see his great grandchild, Richard, born on 2 April 1964.[22]

Despite his physical limitations, Hazell remained active, including attending meetings of the Institute Committee. In July 1964, YCS, in which he had been actively involved for nearly 50 years, celebrated its 75th Anniversary. In October, the [Pontypridd] Observer, Leader & Free Press carried a biographical tribute headed 'Tower of Strength in the "Co-op" Movement', describing him as 'a worthy leader of a worthy organisation.'[23] That month he attended a delegate conference of Co-operative, Trades Union and Labour Party representatives at the Aberdare Society, where Bob Edwards MP spoke on national and international problems and Hazell moved the vote of thanks. Hazell also went for a three-day visit to London to attend a conference, which he enjoyed. In November, Gwlad wrote that he was 'going to a Consultative meeting to-night at 7pm (in P'pridd) & tomorrow, we shall be both attending the Opening of a new Co-op Women's Guild in Glyn Coch Housing Estate.' Such demands were onerous. Yet he retained his strong character and his sense of service and regularly visited the Society's offices in Pontypridd. He remained tall and dignified in older age – the sort of man who would still raise his hat on meeting the woman who ran the B&B in which he was staying.[24]

While Hazell may have been described in the local press as a tower of strength within the co-op, he was no longer strong physically. In October 1964, Gwlad wrote to Lilian and David thanking them for their kindness and welcome, saying that it had done them both good. Dad was reported as being a little better, and had been coughing less. She was getting out into the 'country' for a short walk each day, and described herself as having good health. However she was concerned about William as 'Next week will be most trying for him – the half-yearly meetings of the YCS with two elections thrown in', one of which was for the Society's Presidency.[25]

In November 1964, at 74 years of age, Hazell once again embarked on the cycle of five Half Yearly Meetings of YCS taking place over four consecutive nights. The first, on Monday 9 November 1964, was in Ynysybwl, followed by Abercynon, two meetings in Caerphilly and Abertridwr on Wednesday, finishing in Pontypridd on Thursday 12 November. On the agenda, for the item 'Election of the President', Hazell was the only nomination.

Hazell successfully conducted the first three meetings. However, on Wednesday 11 November, as he was leaving the Caerphilly department store to travel to Abertridwr for his second meeting of the evening, he collapsed and died a few feet from the plaque which he had unveiled a year previously to mark the opening of Hazell House. Having given his life over to the movement, it was fitting that he died undertaking co-operative business, after chairing a meeting of his beloved Society while leaving a building named in his honour. He had been President of the Society for 29 years and a member of Management Board almost continuously for 49 years. The cause of death was bronchopneumonia and emphysema.[26]

There was also symmetry in the timing of Hazell's death for it coincided with the demise of a major co-operative publishing activity in which Hazell had played a prominent local part for nearly 35 years. In September 1964, it was learned that, owing to increased costs, the CWS Board was discontinuing its publication of *Home Magazine* (formerly *Wheatsheaf*), which had lasted for over a century; the wrap-around local pages prepared by individual societies, including YCS, were also to cease. Hazell probably continued editing the local pages, 'which have been so popular with our members for such a long period of time', until they ceased, weeks before his own passing.[27] When it was announced that a successor magazine called *Good Shopping*, would be produced from December, YCS decided to produce and insert its own local news sheet in the magazine. The first issue of the news sheet dated 1 December 1964 was a cheaply produced cyclostyled sheet and poor quality compared with the professionally produced, glossy pages which the Society had provided monthly for over a half a century. It led with a moving dedication to William Hazell.

> Mr William Hazell, Society President for the last 29 years, historian, visionary, social worker and scholar, a quiet dedicated man. How can a lesser writer begin the task of recording in cold type the debt which we, the members of the Ynysybwl Co-operative Society, owe this gentle giant[?] His length of service is worth recording for itself alone. Yet it was not in the length, or period, that his stewardship was so notable. It was in the quality and dedication that his service excelled and shone, and indeed, will continue to shine so long as we who knew him and truly appreciated him survive to cherish his memory. For his worth was the pure gold of a consecrated personality.
>
> Co-operation was his ideal, and to this he was completely and utterly convicted [*sic*]. It was not mere lip-service, not just a job of work to do, not a means of achieving personal social aspirations, it was a cause to which he devoted his life.
>
> 'Why, man, he doth bestride the narrow world
> Like a Colossus, and we petty men
> Walk under his huge legs, and peep about.' (Shakespeare)[28]

This moving eulogy captured the essence of William Hazell. The irony is that the words were not *about* Hazell, but were *by* him. The tribute was one Hazell had written for Sam Davies 13 years earlier and recorded in *The Gleaming Vision*.[29] Now copied almost verbatim for Hazell, they demonstrated that, with Hazell's passing, those who followed were not of equal stature. It was the end of an era.

Hazell was cremated at Glyntaff, Pontypridd, on 15 November 1964. Four Ministers from Ynysybwl, Aberdare and Pontypridd officiated at his funeral. The cortège included representatives of the length and breadth of the co-operative movement as well as Glyn St Chapel and Lady Windsor Lodge. A tribute to his life's work was paid by *The Co-operative Review*.[30]

Gwlad continued to live in Clive Street and stayed in close contact with the family. In January 1972, during the miners' strike, she wrote 'It is bitterly cold here…' adding:

> If anyone is coming down in February… warn them to put on
> plenty of warm clothing, as this house is very cold. My stock of
> coal is low & I cannot use more than two electric fires at a time,
> as the original wiring is not ample enough for more. I manage to
> keep warm with cardigans & coats, and only have coal fire twice a
> week. Let us hope the miners will soon have a square deal.[31]

Gwlad had not been to Pontypridd since the winter started and only now went out on the occasional mild day. She too, looked back and thanked Lilian for her kindness 'throughout the years'. The last surviving letter to come out of 24 Clive Street was written by Auntie Gwlad dated 5 May 1972. She was looking forward to afternoons in the Park in Pontypridd, and recalled that in the previous year it was well into June before she felt sufficiently strong to go there. She had felt well enough to attend the Gospel Hall Sisterhood nearby in Augustus Street, and in the absence of the usual organist had to 'volunteer'. She said 'Believe me a quiet 'cloistered' life is the best for me, until the last call comes'. Six months later, on 12 November 1972, Gwlad died of bronchopneumonia in Dewi Sant Hospital, Pontypridd, aged 83.

Hazell's estate in 1964 was £2,601. After Gwlad's death, the sale of 24 Clive Terrace raised just over £3,000, which was split between the five remaining children. The Probate Registry said the total estate was worth £8,426. When the house was broken up, the book shelves were sold for £40 and the books – Hazell's lifeblood – made £2.5.0d.[32]

Casting a Long Shadow

Even in death Hazell cast a long shadow. On the day his father died Willie wrote to Lilian from Canada:

Do you think he was ashamed of me, or disappointed, or do you think he understood I was trying to live a bigger braver life in going away[?] If it is the former, you'd better tell me when I reach you in June.

Wishing to live up to his father's expectations and seeking his approval even in death, Willie was a stern self-critic. Canada was hard for him. 'It's a tough sort of life here – hostile for me… but – I pray this decision is right – to run away again might do me no good…'[33] He continued:

I am glad you have two good and tried Hazell men, Les and Austin, with you. Please forgive me, the black sheep, for being away at such a time.

Of his father, Willie wrote:

Life must have been very difficult for him and how brave he must have been to carry on with Church, and all, feeling so tired. I was not even surprised because he had such a hard life in the mine, and worked for us – and others – as well.

Years later, Willie would alter his perspective of their father and say that Hazell had paid more attention to the co-operative movement than he had to his children. Lilian meanwhile continued to have pride in their father's work.[34]

YCS after 1964

Although Hazell had many roles as a miners' leader, councillor and JP it was his contribution to Ynysybwl Co-operative Society and its members which defined his life's work. At the time of

Hazell's death, the Society was apparently at the peak of its strength. When he became President in 1935 the Society had 3,345 members, and its sales were less than £160,000. When he died in 1964 it was a Society of over 20,000 members and sales were over £2 million. With members' share capital worth more than £600,000, shares in other co-operative businesses including clothing, chemists, printing, youth centres and caravanning valued at over £50,000, and with over £274,000 on deposit with the CWS or in bonds with six South Wales local authorities, the Society was in valleys terms an economic colossus.[35] Its property alone was valued at £334,000.

It is difficult now to imagine a single enterprise that could incorporate a butchery, hardware, travel bureau, cafeteria, building, painting and decorating service, a carriage and coach building workshop, ladies hairdressing, toys, TV radio and repairs, footwear, optical and funeral services, sports, and with separate showrooms for baths and fire grates. It also had transport, milk and bread depots, was a leader in the East Glamorgan Federal Bakery and offered footwear repair through Mid-Glamorgan Boot Repair Co-op. In 1966 the Co-operative Directory reported the Society had a supermarket, 18 self-service and seven counter service shops. It was, in effect, a mini business empire. The brand new Department store in Caerphilly, the Central Stores in Ynysybwl, with its multiple departments and as well as the Pontypridd establishments complemented a network of branches that extended from Trehafod at the mouth of the Rhondda Valleys to Machen at the south-east tip of the coalfield.[36]

The Society still had an educational and cultural function, with an active Education Committee. Cilfynydd Co-operative Girls Choir was 'ready to render service to any cause' and 40 young people had just completed their studies classes for junior co-operators in Abercynon, Cilfynydd, Hopkinstown and Treforest. The Society ran educational day schools, and had four branches of the Women's Guild, although a fifth in Abercynon had temporarily closed down.

Yet while the Society might appear strong, and would continue to grow in size, the social and economic circumstances which underpinned the movement and the relationship between the Society and its members were changing. The YCS supplement of 1 December 1964, which carried news of Hazell's death, gave a clear warning about a new economic reality with an acknowledgement that the Society would have to address uneconomic branches. By the end of the 1960s, the Ynysybwl and Aberdare Societies looked but failed to amalgamate; had it occurred benefits of scale might have been achieved. However, both institutions were wedded to an approach more rooted in the past than the future. Without amalgamation both societies faced long-term comparative decline. The YCS Report and Balance Sheet for the year ending 3 September 1979 recorded that 'some of the Society's smaller units no longer make any contribution to the Society's revenue and early consideration will be given to their future'. The Society was also giving 'urgent priority' to establishing a large unit in the area.[37] However, the dynamism of earlier days had gone and the Society was responding to events rather than shaping them.

As the Society's economic results deteriorated John Butler, the Secretary of Co-ops UK, visited to 'read the riot act' about poor performance. Later he would attend to oversee the discussions on YCS becoming part of the national CRS. Butler was bemused by the experience. A combination of geography and democracy resulted in his attending a remarkable series of eight meetings – two meetings in each of four areas with all votes counted in the last of the meetings. Butler recalled the disorganisation around the last meeting.[38] Democratic accountability of members meetings, introduced to provide organisational strength across different valleys, was now considered a hindrance to efficient management and good governance. In 1981, the Ynysybwl Society gave up its status as an independent co-operative society and transferred its undertakings to become part of the CRS.

After the miners' strike of 1984/5, Lady Windsor Colliery closed in 1988. The Miners Institute in Ynysybwl, no longer in receipt of deductions from miners' pay, closed its doors and the last surviving institution set up to meet the needs of miners and their community was demolished. It was 100 years from when the first of them – the Ynysybwl Co-operative Society – had opened its doors.

APPENDIX

The Legacy –
Hazell's Writings

Hazell is known to have written for more than a dozen publications from the local
newspaper to the Ocean Colliery Company Magazine as well as 10 co-operative
outlets. Those traced to date are:

The Aberdare Leader

Agenda

Colliery Workers' Magazine

The Co-operative News

Co-operative Official

Co-operative Review

Co-operative Party Monthly Letter

Millgate

Ocean and National Magazine

The Producer

Scottish Co-operator

Wheatsheaf South Wales Supplement

Wheatsheaf Ynysybwl Local Pages

Pamphlets and Book

1900-1950 50 Years of Service and Progress, Ammanford Co-operative Society,
1950.

1901-1951 Jubilee Time at Tredegar, Tredegar Industrial and Provident Society,
1951.

The Gleaming Vision, Ynysybwl Co-operative Society, 1954.

Articles

Nearly 400 of Hazell's articles have been traced. It is certain that a complete list of his writings has not been tracked down, and it is unlikely that a complete list can ever be compiled. There are gaps in holdings of key publications such as the South Wales Supplement. Also, what would possibly have been a major outlet – the local Ynysybwl pages of the *Wheatsheaf/Home Magazine*, which were published for decades – are not extant. Furthermore, in the 1920s, as well as from 1942 to 1946, the *South Wales Supplement* did not carry by-lines or name its authors; at that time he was writing regularly so was probably published, unacknowledged, in the Supplement. However, those writings that do exist indicate the scale and range of his writings.

'Plea for the Personal Touch: One of the Movement's Greatest Needs in the Present Troublous Times', *Co-operative News,* 13 May 1922, p 2

'Cash or Credit Trading', *The Producer*, June 1922, p 241

'Had the Pioneers Lived in 1922', *The Producer*, August 1922, p 293

'No Afterthought: No Side Show. Women's Representation Must be Increased. How Ynysybwl Practices Equality, *Co-operative News*, 23 September 1922, p 13

'Lessons Learnt on Welsh Hills', *The Colliery Workers' Magazine*, Vol. I No. 4, April 1923, p 90

'A Full Life', *The Colliery Workers' Magazine*, Vol. I No. 10, October 1923, p 254

'A Page of Mining History', *The Colliery Workers' Magazine*, Vol. II No. 7, July 1924, pp. 180-1

'The Raging Red Beast. Let Destroy What Statesmen Only Cage. Thoughts for Anti-War Sunday', *The Co-operative News*, 20 September 1924, p 2

'A Leaf from a Councillor's Diary', *The Colliery Workers' Magazine*, Vol. II No. 10, October 1924, pp. 260-1

'The Return of Empire Day. Co-operative Reflections for May 24th', *The Co-operative News*, 23 May 1925, p 9

'A Labour Councillor's Dairy: Public Health (Meat) Regulations, 1924', *The Colliery Workers' Magazine*, Vol. III No. 11, November 1925, pp. 255-256

'Notes from A Labour Councillor's Diary', *The Colliery Workers' Magazine*, Vol. IV No. 1, January 1926, pp. 15-16

'Weeding the Co-operative Garden: Some Virulent Growths and their Antidotes', *The Co-operative News*, 4 December 1926, p 2

'Is the Co-operative Congress Unwieldy?' *The Co-operative Official*, Vol. VIII No. 85, April 1927, pp. 145-6

'One Way Traffic for Co-operation: The Efficiency of a New Rule-of-the-Road', *The Co-operative News*, 28 May 1927, p 2

'Strictly Non-Political', *The Colliery Workers' Magazine*, Vol. V No. 7, July 1927, pp. 114-5

'The "Father of Co-operation" and Holkham: Robert Owen as a Prospective M.P.', *The Co-operative News*, 13 October 1928, p 3

'Is There a Co-operative Solution to the problems of the Coal Industry?', *The Co-operative News*, 5 October 1929, p 2

'"The Producer" as a Propagandist's Vade-Mecum', *The Producer*, October 1929, p 261

'What of "Amalgamation": Co-operative Officials and Modern Tendencies in Co-operative Organisation', *The Co-operative Official*, Vol. X No. 117, December 1929, pp. 459-461

'Our Christmas – Yesterday and Today', *Ocean and National Magazine*, December 1929, Vol. 2 No. 12, pp. 363-4

'Slum Problem: Co-operators Welcome Government Action', *The Co-operative News*, 5 April 1930, p 2

'Amalgamation – An Alternative', *South Wales Supplement*, June 1930, pp. ii-iii

'A Democratic Romance', *South Wales Supplement*, July 1930, p i

'Present-Day Retail Trade Tendencies: Is the "One-Man Shop" Doomed?', *The Co-operative News*, 20 September 1930, p 2

'Unanimity Achieved at Lady Windsor', *Ocean and National Magazine*, February 1931, pp. 43-4

'Effect of Falling Prices in Trade', *South Wales Supplement*, April 1931, p iii

'Co-operation Ousts Competition: Commercial Travellers Superseded by Telephones', *South Wales Supplement*, August 1931, pp. iii-iv

'Pontypridd to Bournemouth: A Co-operative Pilgrimage in 1931', *South Wales Supplement*, September 1931, pp. ii-iii

'Why Not Have a Co-operative Census?', *The Co-operative Official*, June 1932, Vol. XIII No. 147, pp. 237-8

'How a Management Committee Spends Its Fees', *South Wales Supplement*, September 1932, pp. i-ii

'"The Gateway of the Rhondda" Co-operative and Other History of Pontypridd and District', *South Wales Supplement*, March 1933, pp. i-ii

'Before the Truck Acts: The "Company" Shops of South Wales', *Co-operative Review*, Vol. VII No. 41, September 1933, pp. 224-6

'"Taken As Read": Notes on Minute Taking and Minute Keeping', *The Co-operative Official*, October 1933, Vol. XIV No. 163, p 425

'Employment and Economic Conditions', *The Co-operative News*, 23 June 1934, p 2

'Early "Education" in Wales', *South Wales Supplement*, August 1934, pp. i-ii

'Food Taxes and the Pioneers', *The Co-operative Official*, Vol. XV No. 117, December 1934, p 580

'Co-operators on Local Authorities: Communal Service v. Private Interest', *South Wales Supplement*, April 1935, pp. iii–iv

'Miracle of the Valleys', *Co-operative Review*, May 1935, pp. 109-112

'In This Year's Congress City: A Co-operator Visits the National Museum of Wales', *The Millgate*, Vol. XXX No. 357, June 1935, pp. 487-9

'Practical Propaganda for Propaganda Week', *The Co-operative Official,* June 1935, Vol. XVI No. 183, pp. 311-12

'John Morgan', *The Wheatsheaf Local Pages*, September 1935, pp. i–ii

'A Co-operator on the People's Outlook', *The Co-operative News*, 14 November 1936, p 2

'Co-operators Too Modest: Let the World Know', *South Wales Supplement*, December 1936, p ii

'Nuffieldism in Practice', *South Wales Supplement*, March 1937, p ii

'Co-operation Fights Capitalist Exploitation: Transforming Wage Slaves into Financiers and Employers', *South Wales Supplement*, August 1937, pp. i–ii

'Trading Estates: Co-operative and Otherwise', *Co-operative Review*, October 1937, pp. 298-9

'State Trading Estate Criticised: Helping "Private" Enterprise to Make Very Private Profits', *South Wales Supplement*, October 1937, p i

'The Voice that is Silent', *South Wales Supplement*, November 1938, pp. i & iv

'Committees', *South Wales Supplement*, March 1939, p ii

'Some Aspects of Stamp Club Trading', *The Producer*, April 1939, pp. 101-2 [Hazell provided the content, rather than authored]

'"Omitting Personalities" Some Reflections on Peace Alliance or "Popular Front"', *Aberdare Leader*, May 20 1939

'Iron Smelters at Ynysybwl', *Aberdare Leader*, 24 June 1939

'Who Pays the Bill?', *South Wales Supplement*, July 1939, pp. i & iv

'1889-1939 Ynysybwl Society's Half-Century of Co-operation', *South Wales Supplement*, November 1939, p i

'Pages from the Diary of an Educational Administrator: Report of H.M.I. on the school at "X"', *Aberdare Leader*, 24 February 1940

'Marx and Robert Owen: A Gibe at "Reactionary Humbug"', *South Wales Supplement*, April 1940, pp. i & iv

'Extras for Troops Plan', *The Co-operative News*, 10 August 1940, p 2

'Ration Anomalies', *Co-operative Review*, September 1940, pp. 302-3

'Twenty-Five Years in College', *Co-operative Review*, November 1940, pp. 387-8

'Co-operators and the Peace', *The Co-operative News*, 1 March 1941, p 2

'The Origin, History, And Practice of Functionalism', *The Co-operative Official*, July 1941, pp. 261-2

'CWS Directors' Salaries', *The Co-operative News*, 2 August 1941, p 2

'Owen's Kindergarten', *Co-operative Review*, October 1941, pp. 306-7

'Howell Harris: Field Preacher – Co-operator – Soldier', *South Wales Supplement*, November 1941, No. 218, pp. i & iv

'Are They British Restaurants?', *The Co-operative News*, 22 November 1941, p 2

'Pan-Celtic National Anthem', *South Wales Supplement*, December 1941, No. 219, pp. i-ii

'The Walls Speak', *South Wales Supplement*, March 1942, No. 222, p ii

'Co-operators and the Sub-Normal', *The Co-operative Official*, March 1942, pp. 77-8

'Mignonette and Onions', *The Co-operative Official*, April 1942, pp. 109-10

'Sixteen to One: What Unity Would Achieve', *South Wales Supplement*, May 1942, No. 224, p iii

'A Jewel of the South Wales Coast', *South Wales Supplement*, June 1942, p iii

'Some Method Will Replace Business for Financial profit – Will It Be Ours?', *The Co-operative News*, 21 November 1942, p 10

'We Are Come to Worship': The Unending Quest', *The Co-operative News*, 26 December 1942, p 7

'Beveridge Report is Ambulance Work. "Unholy Trinity" of Interest, Rent and Profit Untouched', *The Co-operative News*, 13 February 1943, p 10

'Why Not an Inclusive Union Subscription for Press, Party, and I.C.A.', *The Co-operative News*, 6 November 1943, p 2

'Our Christmas Legend "The Vision Splendid" of the Pioneers', *The Co-operative News*, 18 December 1943, p 9

'The Sign is a Babe. Thoughts for Christmas', *The Co-operative News*, 25 December 1943, p 9

'Headaches for Headmasters!', *The Co-operative News*, 26 February 1944, p 9

'The Whole Nation is in Debt to Strikes', *The Co-operative News*, 10 June 1944, p 2

'What Milton Said About Press Freedom', *The Co-operative News*, 26 August 1944, p 9

'Health Ancient and Modern: Does Cold Water Kill?', *The Co-operative Official*, Vol. XXV No. 294, September 1944, pp. 260 & 286

'Outcast of the Air. Why is Co-operation Debarred from the National Forum of the Radio', *The Co-operative News*, 23 September 1944, p 10

'Retail Society "Brains" Might Usefully Have Collaborated in Drafting the AMALGAMATION PLAN', *The Co-operative News*, 12 December 1944, p 10

'A Co-operator at the Westminster Conference of Urban Authorities', *The Co-operative Official*, March 1945, pp. 77 & 79

'Ignoble Act of Telling Lies', *The Co-operative News*, 16 June 1945, p 2

'In Praise of the Starry-Eyed Idealist', *The Co-operative News*, 25 August 1945, p 9

'Phantom of Piccadilly', *The Co-operative News*, 15 September 1945, p 9

'Midianites – Merchantmen', *The Producer*, October 1945, pp. 27-8

'Atomic Bomb May Give Savages a Chance', *The Co-operative News*, 27 October 1945, pp. 11 & 13

'Is It a Mirage?', *The Co-operative News*, 22 December 1945, pp. 9–10

'Effect of Town Planning on the Local Store', *The Co-operative News*, 5 January 1946, p 9

'An Eighteenth Century "New Deal"', *The Co-operative News*, 19 January 1946, p 7

'Rebecca of Wales: Turnpike Tolls Caused Riots', *South Wales Supplement*, March 1946, pp. i–ii

'Honouring a Practical Saint', *The Co-operative News*, 2 March 1946, pp. 9 & 14

'"…and our education will proceed"', *The Co-operative News*, 23 March 1946, pp. 11 & 13

'Gas: Review of an Industry which is Down for Nationalisation', *The Co-operative News*, 30 March 1946, p 9

'Vitamins in Politics', *The Co-operative News*, 6 April 1946, pp. 9 & 10

'New Emblem But Not New Name: Confound Your "Isms"', *The Co-operative Official*, Vol. XXVII No. 314, May 1946, pp. 137-8

'"Dictatorship of the Proletariat"', *The Co-operative News*, 11 May 1946, p 9

'Forest of the White Saint', *South Wales Supplement*, June 1946, pp. i–ii

'Nutritive Value of Canned Foods', *Co-operative Review*, June 1946, pp. 116–17

'The Referendum', *Co-operative Review*, July 1946, p 128

'The South Welcomes the National Eisteddfod – pageant of song', *South Wales Supplement*, July 1946, pp. i–ii

'The Bells Rang Out at Rochdale', *The Co-operative News*, 6 July 1946, p 9

'Learning May Again Flourish in the Shrines Where Sanity Rules', *The Co-operative News*, 13 July 1946, p 9

'Secrets of the Rhondda', *South Wales Supplement*, August 1946, pp. i–ii

'John Gilpin and Charles Lamb', *The Co-operative News*, 3 August 1946, p 9

'But Lincoln Was Wrong', *The Co-operative News*, 10 August 1946, pp. 9 & 10

'Round the Marble Arch or Up the Garden Path', *The Co-operative News*, 17 August 1946, pp. 9 & 10

'In the Path of Kings', *The Co-operative News*, 7 September 1946, pp. 9 & 13

'Mr R. Browning to Miss E. B. M. Barrett. A Great Romance Recalled', *The Co-operative News*, 14 September 1946, p 9

'September was a Magic Month for Cromwell', *The Co-operative News*, 28 September 1946, pp. 9 & 10

'Social Suicide – A New "Guide to the Pools"', *The Co-operative News*, 26 October 1946, p 2

'Folk Museum Gift for South Wales: Castle Presented to the Nation', *South Wales Supplement*, November 1946, pp. i–ii

'Co–operation Must Remedy New Coal Problem', *Co-operative Review*, November 1946, pp. 215-6

'When Uncle Sam Bought a 'Frig'!', *The Co-operative News*, 9 November 1946, pp. 9 &14

'Churchyard Magic', *The Co-operative News*, 16 November 1946, p 9

'Thomas Hughes', *Co-operative Review*, December 1946, p 239

'Around Fleet Street', *The Co-operative News*, 7 December 1946, p 9

'Discussing the Pros and Cons of the Perpetual Pension', *The Co-operative News*, 14 December 1946, pp. 9 & 14

'They Bought Gold', *The Co-operative News*, 21 December 1946, p 2

'The Art of Putting Things, *The Co-operative Official*, January 1947, Vol. XXVIII No. 322, pp. 2 & 12

'After Two Wars' – A Comparison', *The Co-operative News*, 11 January 1947, p 9

'History Made by Friends Parting', *The Co-operative News*, 18 January 1947, pp. 9 & 14

'When Libel Didn't Mean a Thing', *The Co-operative News*, 15 February 1947, pp. 9 & 14

'Richard Jeffries, Writer Who Loved the Country', *The Co-operative News*, 8 March 1947, p 9

'This Renewed Interest in Dickens', *The Co-operative News*, 15 March 1947, pp. 9 & 14

'Lost Libraries of Yesterday, *The Co-operative News*, 22 March 1947, p 9

'St. Tudno Speaks', *The Co-operative News*, 29 March 1947, p 9

'A "Good Word" for Aberystwyth', *South Wales Supplement*, March/April 1947, pp. i–ii

'At the Sign of the Red Pale', *Co-operative Review*, April 1947, p 88

'Britain's Power in Moral Leadership', *The Co-operative News*, 26 April 1947, p 9

'In the Days of the Magnets: Cyfartha Castle's History', *South Wales Supplement*, May 1947, pp. i–ii

'May Day is a Challenge', *The Co-operative News*, 3 May 1947, pp. 9 & 10

'Truants' Report on Old Brighton', *The Co-operative News*, 10 May 1947, pp. 9 & 14

'The Philosophy of Henry Ford', *The Co-operative News*, 24 May 1947, p 9

'Pyjama Holiday (or Vacation in Vacuum)', *The Co-operative News*, 14 June 1947, pp. 9 &14

'Some Problems of the Five-Day Week: A Plea for South Wales', *South Wales Supplement*, July 1947, pp. i–ii

'Nil Desperandum', *The Co-operative News*, 5 July 1947, pp. 9 & 14 [Named as Walter Hazell]

'The Pioneers' Fifth Objective', *The Co-operative News*, 19 July 1947, pp. 9 & 14

'Just Sitting: Being a Spot of Wilful Reiteration', *The Co-operative Official*, August 1947, Vol. XXVII No. 328, pp. 222-3

'That Vice – The Questionnaire', *The Co-operative News*, 23 August 1947, p 2

'If You Are Forestalled Do Not Despair', *The Co-operative News*, 30 August 1947, p 9

'Bid Ben, Bid Bont?', *South Wales Supplement*, September 1947, pp. i–ii

'Co-operative Youth: Was W.L. Stedman Right?', *South Wales Supplement*, September 1947, pp. iii–iv

'Why Did Robert Owen Leave Manchester for Lanark?', *The Co-operative News*, 13 September 1947, p 9

'A Curate Bought a Book 200 Years Ago', *The Co-operative News*, 20 September 1947, p 9

'To Llanthony by Magic Carpet', *South Wales Supplement*, October 1947, pp. i–ii

'In Praise of People Who Light Fires', *The Co-operative News*, 4 October 1947, pp. 9 & 14

'Book Titles: What's In a Name?', *The Co-operative News*, 8 November 1947, pp. 9 & 10

'Hooray for Cinderella', *The Co-operative News*, 15 November 1947, pp. 9 & 10

'Be Yourself', *The Co-operative News*, 29 November 1947, p 7

'When Spencer Tossed a Coin And Killed a Romance', *The Co-operative News*, 13 December 1947, p 9

'The Potters' Art at Nantgarw: Ceramics Debt to Wales', *South Wales Supplement*, January 1948, pp. i–ii

'These Imports Are Justified', *The Co-operative News,* 17 January 1948, pp. 9 & 10

'Glorious History of Caerphilly Castle', *South Wales Supplement*, February 1948, pp. i–ii

'In Defence of Compromise', *The Co-operative News,* 14 February 1948, p 9

'The Most Important Co-operator in Wales', *South Wales Supplement*, March 1948, pp. i–ii

'Chartism in Owen's Country', *South Wales Supplement*, April 1948, pp. i–ii

'Planning of East Glamorgan – Significant Trends discussed', *Aberdare Leader*, 10 April 1948

'Future Development of Aberdare Valley: Mountain Ash Lacks Building Sites', *Aberdare Leader*, 17 April 1948

'Lesson of the Forth Bridge', *The Co-operative News,* 24 April 1948, pp. 8-9

'Obituary', *South Wales Supplement*, May 1948, p ii

'Hewlett of Briton Ferry', *South Wales Supplement*, May 1948, pp. iii–iv

'Son of a Marlborough Mother Freed the Slaves of England', *The Co-operative News*, 29 May 1948, pp. 8–9

'"Progress Report" from Ynysybwl, *The Producer*, June 1948, p 10

'Kingsley's Year', *The Co-operative News*, 26 June 1948, p 9

'Cardiff Civic Centre', *South Wales Supplement*, July 1948, pp. i–ii

'Built Miners' Institute of Sugar – It Was Too Good to Eat', *The Co-operative News*, 10 July 1948, p 7

'On Being Burgled', *The Co-operative News*, 17 July 1948, pp. 8–9

'Joining the Classics Club', *The Co-operative News*, 24 July 1948, pp. 6–7

'Greatest Love Story of South Wales: Eisteddfod Town's Romance', *South Wales Supplement*, August 1948, pp. i–ii

'The Real Torch of Greece', *The Co-operative News*, 7 August 1948, pp. 6–7

'Links Across the Channel: Cardiff Greets Bristol', *South Wales Supplement*, September 1948, pp. i–ii

'Exaltation of Literature', *The Co-operative News*, 25 September 1946, pp. 8–9

'The National Museum of Wales: Treasures of the People', *South Wales Supplement*, October 1948, pp. i–ii

'Passing of the Gleaners', *The Co-operative News*, 23 October 1948, pp. 6–7

'Remember, Remember', *The Co-operative News*, 30 October 1948, pp. 6–7

'Day Dreams in Llantwit Major Churchyard', *South Wales Supplement*, November 1948, pp. i–ii

'Don't Remember', *The Co-operative News*, 13 November 1948, p 6

'The Revolution That Began With Steam', *The Co-operative News*, 27 November 1948, p 8

'Sentence – Twenty-Five Years' Hard', *South Wales Supplement*, December 1948, pp. i–ii

'Toys Line The Gateway to Paradise', *The Co-operative News*, 11 December 1948, pp. 6–7

'The Treasure of Swansea: Cause for Civic Pride', *South Wales Supplement*, January 1949, pp. i–ii

'Why Britain Needs Books', *Co-operative Review*, January 1949, pp. 17–8

'Intelligent Boy's Guide to Parasites', *The Co-operative Official*, Vol. XXX No. 345, January 1949, pp. 21–2

'Away With Discretion', *The Co-operative News*, 8 January 1949, p 6

'W Hazell Rises to "National Level"', *The Co-operative News*, 22 January 1949, p 10

'Food Rations of Bygone Days in Wales: Hunger Amid Plenty', *South Wales Supplement*, February 1949, pp. i–iii

'The "News" Would Have Cost You Sixpence", *The Co-operative News*, 12 February 1949, pp. 8–9

'The New Capital and the New "Capital"', *South Wales Supplement*, March 1949, pp. i–ii

'The Beautiful Vale of Neath', *South Wales Supplement*, April 1949, pp. i–ii

'Weston-Super-Mare: The Blackpool of Somerset', *The Co-operative News,* 9 April 1949, p 10

'Ynysybwl Society's Diamond Jubilee', *South Wales Supplement*, May 1949, pp. i–iii

'A Welsh Town Library's Fine Record', *South Wales Supplement*, June 1949, pp. i–ii

'W. J. Gruar Restores Faith', *South Wales Supplement*, June 1949, p iii

'I Knew Bill Collins', *South Wales Supplement*, June 1949, p iii

'The Co-operative Pilgrim's Progress', *The Co-operative News,* 4 June 1949, p 10

'Wales Produces Her Flashbacks', *South Wales Supplement*, July 1949, pp. i–iii

'South Wales and I.C.A. Appeal for Contributions', *South Wales Supplement*, July 1949, p iv

'The Magic Carpet of National Membership', *The Co-operative News*, 2 July 1949, p 6

'Old Man Datum – Movement Hamstrung', *The Co-operative News*, 9 July 1949, p 10 [By W.H.]

'These Are True Stars', *The Co-operative News*, 16 July 1949, p 10

'Was Taffy Such a Thief?', *South Wales Supplement*, August 1949, pp. i–ii

'A Real Film of Welsh Mining: *Blue Scar*'s Sincerity', *South Wales Supplement*, August 1949, pp. iii–iv

'Gloucester and the Man Who Wrote "Invictus"', *The Co-operative News*, 6 August 1949, pp. 6–7

'Chippenham A King's Gift to His Daughter', *The Co-operative News*, 13 August 1949, pp. 8–9

'Trowbridge and Sleepy Bradford on Avon', *The Co-operative News*, 20 August 1949, pp. 8–9

'The Journey Ends at Salisbury', *The Co-operative News*, 27 August 1949, pp. 8–9

'Dai Morgan has his Shackles Removed', *South Wales Supplement*, October 1949, pp. i–iii

'Mr. E.J. Meredith', *South Wales Supplement*, October 1949, p iv

'He Wrote A People's Anthem and Rhymed Against the Corn Laws', *The Co-operative News*, 1 October 1949, pp. 8–9

'In Defence of Committees', *South Wales Supplement*, November 1949, pp. i–ii

'We Salute a Welsh Lady of Literature: Historian, Novelist and Poet', *South Wales Supplement*, November 1949, pp. iii–iv

'Glorious Fifth!', *The Co-operative News*, 5 November 1949, p 9

'Skyhooks', *The Co-operative News*, 12 November 1949, p 10

'Silence is Not Always Golden', *The Co-operative News*, 26 November 1949, pp. 2 & 14

'A Happy Christmas', *South Wales Supplement*, December 1949, pp. i–ii

'School for Santa Claus', *The Co-operative News*, 24 December 1949, p 2 [By "W.H."]

'You Can't Nationalise Me, Says Santa Claus', *The Co-operative News*, 24 December 1949, pp. 10 & 14

'Newport, the Town of Busy People', *South Wales Supplement*, January 1950, pp. i–ii

'Calendar Time Comes Around Again', *The Co-operative News*, 7 January 1950, p 10

'The Virtue of Economy is Mainly Ancestral', *The Co-operative News*, 7 January 1950, p 10

'Honouring a Practical Saint: St. David's Perfect Life', *South Wales Supplement*, February 1950, pp. i–ii

'He Talks Like a Book', *The Co-operative News*, 18 February 1950, p 10

'He Gave His Name to Downing Street', *The Co-operative News*, 4 March 1950, p 10

'Wales and the Lake Poet', *South Wales Supplement*, April 1950, p iii

'Incentive', *The Co-operative News*, 6 May 1950, p 8

'Ruskin The Prophet of Brantwood', *The Co-operative News*, 27 May 1950, p 10

'Wales in Robert Owen's Time: Why He Did Not Return to Newtown', *Co-operative Review*, June 1950, pp. 135–7

'Ammanford's Jubilee', *South Wales Supplement*, June 1950, No. 320, pp. i–ii

'History and All That', *The Co-operative News*, 24 June 1950, p 8

'So Caerphilly is Shining its Shoes', *South Wales Supplement*, July 1950, pp. i–ii

'Pryce Pryce-Jones Also From Newtown', *The Co-operative News*, 1 July 1950, p 10

'Pools Without Healing', *The Co-operative News*, 8 July 1950, p 10

'New Light on F.D. Maurice', *Co-operative Review*, August 1950, pp. 187–8

'Just Plain "eighteen"', *The Co-operative News*, 12 August 1950, pp. 8–9

'Adding Lustre to Porthcawl: A Notable Inhabitant', *South Wales Supplement*, September 1950, p iii

'Rhondda Still has its Songsters', *South Wales Supplement*, October 1950, pp. i–ii

'There's Fun Everywhere If You'll Look For It', *The Co-operative News*, 7 October 1950, p 10

'A Maker of Dreams', *The Co-operative News*, 11 November 1950, p 1

'The Thunder of a Falling Feather', *Scottish Co-operator*, 23 December 1950, p 11.

'"Dusty Fiddles" – Out with the Waits', *South Wales Supplement*, December 1950, No. 326, pp. i–ii

'LOST A Co-operative Commonwealth', *The Co-operative News*, 9 December 1950, p 10

'Our Quiet Christmas', *The Co-operative News*, 30 December 1950, p 6

'Looking Back – 50 Momentous Years', *South Wales Supplement*, January 1951, pp. i–ii

'1900 and all that', *The Co-operative News*, 6 January 1951, p 8

'Price Tribunal for International Disputes', *The Co-operative News*, 20 January 1951, p 10

'Exit MAGAZINE – enter DIGEST', *The Co-operative News*, 27 January 1951, pp. 8-9

'There's a Welcome of the Hillside', *South Wales Supplement*, February 1951, pp. i-ii

'If I Were a Dictator', *The Co-operative News*, 24 March 1951, p 8

'Welsh Literary Weapons of Yesterday and Today', *South Wales Supplement*, April 1951, pp. ii-iii

'I'm all in Favour of the South Shore', *The Co-operative News*, 28 April 1951, p 10

'Can you find your way to Pontypool?', *South Wales Supplement*, May 1951, pp. i-ii

'What to Show a Festival Visitor to South Wales', *South Wales Supplement*, June 1951, pp. i-ii

'In Praise of Sand', *The Co-operative News*, 30 June 1951, p 10

'Robert Owen Speaks Again', *South Wales Supplement*, July 1951, pp. i-ii

'Is the Labour Party 'NEUTRAL'?', *The Co-operative News*, 7 July 1951, p 10

'Everyone Builds Castles at Barry', *South Wales Supplement*, August 1951, pp. iii-iv

'A Place to Stand and Stare', *South Wales Supplement*, September 1951, pp. iii-iv

'Labels', *The Co-operative News*, 8 September 1951, p 10

'Changing the Moon Every Noon', *South Wales Supplement*, October 1951, pp. i-ii

'Joining the Reds', *The Co-operative Official*, Vol. XXXII No. 378, October 1951, pp. 377-8

'Logic Which Can Be Terribly Inhuman', *The Co-operative News*, 20 October 1951, p 10

'Tiger, A Feline Story with a Moral', *The Co-operative News*, 27 October 1951, p 8

'Co-operative Triumph in Tredegar', *South Wales Supplement*, November 1951, pp. i-ii

'The Armless Hand', *The Co-operative News*, 15 December 1951, pp. 8-9

'Welshman's £1,000 put Yale on Its Feet', *South Wales Supplement*, January 1952, p i

'O.K. Capt'n carry on. A Tribute to An "Obstinate Man"', *The Co-operative News*, 19 January 1952, p 8

'First Welsh College was International', *South Wales Supplement*, February 1952, p iii

'Little England Beyond', *South Wales Supplement*, March 1952, pp. i-ii

'Cavalcade', *The Co-operative News*, 1 March 1952, pp. 8-9

'Something for Nothing at Pontypridd', *South Wales Supplement*, April 1952, pp. i-ii

'The Railway Pioneer of Wales', *South Wales Supplement*, May 1952, pp. i-ii

'Congress Owes a Big Debt to JACK CADE 'Captain of Kent'', *The Co-operative News*, 17 May 1952, p 8

'Such a Friendly Town', *South Wales Supplement*, July 1952, pp. i–ii

'Let's Do a Spot of Grumbling', *The Co-operative News*, 19 July 1952, p 8

'Clubbing Together', *South Wales Supplement*, August 1952, pp. i–ii

'Sheep Graze in Rhondda Streets', *South Wales Supplement*, November 1952, pp. i–ii

'W Hazell finds a welcome in the Smiling Land of Gwent', *South Wales Supplement*, December 1952, No. 350, p ii

'First Lodgings', *South Wales Supplement*, January 1953, pp. i–ii

'Vaynor could be Excused for Vanity', *South Wales Supplement*, February 1953, pp. i–ii

'First Welsh Jones in Robert Owen's County, *South Wales Supplement*, March 1953, pp. i–iii

'A Congress Creed: Democracy for Man – Not Man for Democracy', *Co-operative Review*, April 1953, pp. 82-3

'"Summer Meadow": A "Noble" Quarter Century', *South Wales Supplement*, April 1953, p iv

'In Search of Miss Wales', *South Wales Supplement*, April 1953, pp. i–ii

'Street Teas a Speciality for the Coronation', *South Wales Supplement*, May 1953, p iv

'W. Hazell Looks at the Congress Town', *The Co-operative News*, 16 May 1953, p 10

'W. Hazell's Appeal to Maturity', *The Co-operative News*, 20 June 1953, p 10

'I Remember: W Hazell Recalls his Adopted Valley Home', *South Wales Supplement*, July 1953, pp. i–ii

'Robert Owen Memorial: Statue Should Focus Opinion on His Teachings', *Co-operative Review*, September 1953, pp. 206-7

'Two Men of the Marches', *South Wales Supplement*, September 1953, pp. i–iii

'The Black Knight at "Fairy" Castle', *South Wales Supplement*, October 1953, pp. i–ii

'Was Daniel Owen the Welsh Dickens?', *South Wales Supplement*, October 1953, pp. iii–iv.

'This Nation of Shopkeepers', *South Wales Supplement*, November 1953, pp. i–ii

'What is this Means Test?', *South Wales Supplement*, December 1953, pp. i–ii

'Are Chances Missed in New Towns', *The Co-operative News*, 20 February 1954, p 12

'Is the Movement Going Totalitarian?', *The Co-operative News*, 27 February 1954, pp. 2 & 13

'This "Rest" is No "Rest"', *South Wales Supplement*, March 1954, pp. i–ii

'A New Charter for the Rhondda: Mayor and Co-operation', *South Wales Supplement*, April 1954, pp. ii–iii

'Movement Would Gain By Decentralisation', *The Co-operative News*, 17 April 1954, p 10

'Howell's Ducats Built a School by the Taff', *South Wales Supplement*, May 1954, pp. iii–iv

'Pryce Pryce-Jones also from Newtown', *Ynysybwl Industrial Co-operative Society (Local Pages)*, inside front & back covers of *Co-operative Home Magazine*, June 1954 (apparently reprinted from *Co-operative News*)

'One Hundred Years of "Wild Wales"', *South Wales Supplement*, June 1954, pp. i–ii

'By Coach to Paradise', *South Wales Supplement*, July 1954, pp. i–ii

'The Chimneys Speak', *South Wales Supplement*, August 1954, pp. i–ii

'And so to Tenby', *South Wales Supplement*, October 1954, pp. i–ii

'Llangollen versus Exclusiveness', *South Wales Supplement*, October 1954, pp. iii–iv

'The Next South Wales Borough?: Pontypridd Petitions the Queen', *South Wales Supplement*, November 1954, pp. i–ii

'A Stalwart Retires', *South Wales Supplement*, December 1954, p iii

'A Little Bit of France in Wales', *South Wales Supplement*, December 1954, p iv

'The Challenge of '1984'', *The Co-operative News*, 25 December 1954, p 2

'Glamorgan's Greatest Wonder', *South Wales Supplement*, January 1955, pp. i–ii

'A Thing of Beauty: A Prose Ode to the Welsh Dresser', *South Wales Supplement*, January 1955, pp. iii–iv

'City Under the Sand', *South Wales Supplement*, February 1955, pp. i–ii

'The Jewel of Towy Side', *South Wales Supplement*, February 1955, p iii

'The Western Mail look at Distribution', *South Wales Supplement*, March 1955, pp. i–ii

'Distribution in Europe: New Book on Wholesale and Retail Efficiency', *Co-operative Review*, March 1955, pp. 64–6

'The President', *Agenda*, March 1955, pp. 35–8

'See Wales First: Tourist Board's Appeal to the Welsh Nation', *South Wales Supplement*, April 1955, pp. i–ii

'In Wales Now', *Co-operative Party Monthly Letter*, April 1955, pp. 6–9

'In Wales Now', *Co-operative Party Monthly Letter*, May 1955, pp. 9 & 12–14

'The Shop Windows of Wales', *South Wales Supplement*, May 1955, pp. i–ii

'In Wales Now', *Co-operative Party Monthly Letter*, June 1955, pp. 12–14

'Revolution in the Rhondda', *South Wales Supplement*, June 1955, pp. i–ii

'Under the Sea to London', *South Wales Supplement*, June 1955, pp. iii–iv

'Flintshire Pilgrimage', *South Wales Supplement*, July 1955, pp. iii–iv

'Did Prince Madoc Anticipate Columbus? Persistent Legend of the White Indians', *South Wales Supplement*, August 1955, pp. i–ii

'Bannister's Record Broken – in 1880: Rhondda Boy's Four-Minute Mile', *South Wales Supplement*, September 1955, pp. i–ii

'N.H.S. – What It Means to Glamorgan', *South Wales Supplement*, September 1955, pp. iii–iv

'Does the Rhondda Make Sense?', *South Wales Supplement*, October 1955, pp. i, ii & iv

'The Bar Crossed', *South Wales Supplement*, October 1955, p iv

'Happy Birthday to You', *South Wales Supplement*, November 1955, p i

'The Miner – No Longer a Minor: His Shopping Habits To-day and Yesterday', *Co-operative Review*, November 1955, pp. 258-60

'Calenig – the Children's New Year Greeting', *South Wales Supplement*, January 1956, pp. i–ii

'It was the Singing that Did It! The Rugby Legend in Wales', *South Wales Supplement*, January 1956, pp. iii–iv

'Welshwoman Startles Wales', *South Wales Supplement*, February/March 1956, p iv

'The Fortifications of Wales', *South Wales Supplement*, April 1956, pp. i–ii

'The Unity of the Co-operative Mosaic', *The Co-operative News*, 14 April 1956, p 14

'Gold Coins Stretched for a Mile', *South Wales Supplement*, May 1956, pp. iii–iv

'Wooden Walls of Wales', *South Wales Supplement*, June 1956, pp. ii–iii

'Land of Beautiful Bridges', *South Wales Supplement*, June 1956, p iv

'The Sun Shone on Swansea's Opening Day', *South Wales Supplement*, August 1956, pp. i–ii

'There's Magic to be Found on the Highway: Fireside Motoring with W. Hazell', *South Wales Supplement*, October 1956, pp. i–ii

'Story of a Vanishing Society', *South Wales Supplement*, November 1956, p iii

'The Railways of Wales', *South Wales Supplement*, December 1956, pp. iii–iv

'Men and Events of 1956', *South Wales Supplement*, February 1957, pp. i–ii

'Forty Years at the Table: W Hazell Tells of Some Reactions to "Agenda"', *Co-operative Review*, February 1957, pp. 41-2.

'Co-operation Owes Much to Wales', *South Wales Supplement*, March 1957, pp. i–ii

'Secret of the Twyn', *South Wales Supplement*, April 1957, pp. iii–iv

'Magic of the Hills', *South Wales Supplement*, May 1957, pp. i–ii

'Gateways to the Boardroom: 1 – The Educational Approach', *Co-operative Review*, May 1957, pp. 106-7

'Gateways to the Boardroom: 2 – Municipal Service and Trade Unionism', *Co-operative Review*, June 1957, pp. 134-5

'Those Who Give the Community Service', *South Wales Supplement*, July 1957, pp. iii–iv

'Alan Skuse: Wages Expert Living an Abundant Life', *Co-operative Review*, July 1957, pp. 160-1

'Gateways to the Boardroom: 3 – Employee Representation and the Popular Gate', *Co-operative Review*, August 1957, pp. 174-6

'A Lakeland Day', *South Wales Supplement*, August 1957, pp. i–ii

'The White Saint and the Fountain of Light: Clydach Valley (II)', *South Wales Supplement*, September 1957, pp. i-ii

'The Artist in Wales', *South Wales Supplement*, October 1957, pp. ii & iv

'Clydach Valley (III) Where the Monks Tended their Flocks', *South Wales Supplement*, October 1957, pp. iii-iv

'Vale of Clydach (IV): Invasion of the Monster – Coal', *South Wales Supplement*, November 1957, pp. i-ii

'The Peter Pan town which didn't want to grow up', *South Wales Supplement*, December 1957, pp. iii-iv

'When Dante Visited Wales', *South Wales Supplement*, January 1958, p ii

'Cardiff Prepares for the Empire Games', *South Wales Supplement*, January 1958, pp. iii-iv

'The Green Corn Ripens', *South Wales Supplement*, February 1958, pp. ii-iii

'Epstein and Llandaff', *South Wales Supplement*, March 1958, pp. i-ii

'The Heroic Clergyman of Anglesey', *South Wales Supplement*, April 1958, pp. i-ii

'The Pioneer Co-operators of South Wales', *South Wales Supplement*, May 1958, p ii.

'New Books About Wales', *South Wales Supplement*, June 1958, p iii

'Music, Teachers, Coal – the Rhondda Exports all three', *South Wales Supplement*, July 1958, pp. ii-iii

'Roar of Dragons, or was it only a Purr?', *South Wales Supplement*, August 1958, pp. i-ii

'Legend of the White Rock', *South Wales Supplement*, September 1958, p iii

'Aberystwyth –Town with Three Faces' *South Wales Supplement*, October 1958, p iii

'Why Not a Statue Here?' *South Wales Supplement*, November 1958, pp. i-ii

'Thunder of a Falling Feather', *South Wales Supplement*, December 1958, pp. i-ii

'Golden Service', *South Wales Supplement*, December 1958, p iv

'Beyond the Chains: History Warns – There Must be New Approach', *Co-operative Review*, February 1959, pp. 34-5

'Amalgamation Road: *"Travel in Hope and Prepare for Eventualities"'*, *Co-operative Review*, March 1959, pp. 69-70

'On the Shelf: Can One Retire Gracefully?', *Co-operative Review*, May 1959, pp. 103-5

'A Good Word for the Flick-Knife', *Co-operative Party Monthly Letter*, Vol. 16, Number 6, June 1959, pp. 5-6

'Spoken on Co-operative Day: *"Be Willing and Eager to Go Hand in Hand!"'*, *Co-operative Review*, July 1959, pp. 152-3

'Headaches of the Historian: *"If You can Write History You'll Be a Man"'*, *Co-operative Review*, August 1959, pp. 178-9

Select Bibliography

MANUSCRIPT COLLECTIONS

Brecon, Monmouth & East Glamorgan Federation of the Co-operative Party, Minutes of Executive Committee, 1948-1964

Co-operative Coal Trades Association, National Executive, minutes and reports

Co-operative Congress Reports

Co-operative Party annual reports and conference proceedings

Co-operative Party National Committee minutes, 1956-9

Co-operative Party Western Section, Affiliation Fees Book, 1936-1973

Co-operative Society Mergers 1915-2004, National Co-operative Archive, 2004

Co-operative Union Central Board, minutes

Co-operative Union Western Sectional Board, minutes and reports

Co-operative Union Western Section Co-operative Coal Trades Association, minutes and reports

Hazell/West/Brooks family papers

John E Morgan papers

Lady Windsor Lodge minutes

Mass-Observation Archive, Sussex University: Topic Collections 66/20/F Ynysybwl 1947

Mountain Ash UDC Minutes (UDC) (GRO)

Air Raid Precautions Committee Minutes (ARP)

Allotments Committee Minutes

Communal Feeding Committee Minutes (CFC)

Council Houses Management Committee Minutes (CHMC)

Education Committee Minutes (EDC)

Entertainments Committee

Finance Committee Minutes (FC)

Fire Prevention Committee Minutes (FPC)

Housing Committee Minutes (HC)

Maternity and Child Welfare Committee (MCWC)

Municipal Undertakings Committee Minutes (MUC)

New Industries and Development Committee minutes (NIDC)

Public Health Committee Minutes (PHC)

Road Safety Committee

Sanitary & Public Health Committee Minutes (SPHC)

NEWSPAPERS AND JOURNALS

Aberdare Leader (AL)

Agenda

The Cardiff Citizen

The Colliery Workers' Magazine (CWM)

Co-operative News (CN)

Co-operative Official (CO)

Co-operative Party Monthly Letter (CPML)

Co-operative Review (CR)

Merthyr Pioneer

Millgate

Ocean and National Magazine, (ONM)

Pontypridd Observer (PO)

The Plebs

The Producer

South Wales Democrat/Cymric Democrat

South Wales Supplement (SWS)

The Wheatsheaf (later Home Magazine)

COLLECTIONS OF CUTTINGS

W W Price Biographical index, Aberdare Reference Library

Hazell/Brooks/Price/West family papers

John E Morgan papers, Swansea University

GOVERNMENT PUBLICATIONS

Census, 1891 and 1901

PUBLISHED WORKS

Alan Allport, *Demobbed: Coming Home After the Second World War*, Yale, 2009

Chris Baggs, *"[T]he whole tragedy of leisure in penury": the South Wales Miners' Institute libraries during the Depression'*, 68th IFLA Council and General Conference, August 18-24 2002

Lord Beveridge, *Voluntary Action*, George Allen & Unwin, 1948

Lord Beveridge and A.F. Wells, *The Evidence for Voluntary Action*, George Allen & Unwin, 1949

Maurice Bruce, *The Coming of The Welfare State*, B T Batsford, 1961, (1974 reprint)

Alun Burge, 'Miners Learning in the South Wales Coalfield, 1900-1947', *Llafur*, Vol. 8 No. 1, 2000, pp. 69-97

Alun Burge, '"A Task Worthy of the Most Sincere Devotion and Application": The Co-operative Movement in South Wales and Its History', *WHR*, December 2007, pp. 59-71

Alun Burge, 'From Cwmbach to Tower: 140 Years of Collective Entrepreneurship in the Cynon Valley, 1860-2000', *Llafur,* 2012, pp. 129-48

Alun Burge, *Co-operation A Post-war Opportunity Missed? A Welsh Perspective*, Bevan Foundation, 2012

W S Collins, 'Hazell of Ynysybwl', *SWS*, November 1935, pp. i & iv

Noel and Alan Cox, *Two Hundred Years of Welsh Paranumismatic History: The Tokens, Checks, Metallic Tickets, Passes and Tallies of Wales 1800-1993*, Lake, Cardiff, 1994.

Richmal Crompton, 'William and the Bomb', *William Carries On*, Newnes, 1942

A R Davies, 'Hazell of Ynysybwl: Historian and Writer of South Wales', *CR*, October 1954, pp. 224-5

E W Edwards, 'The Pontypridd Area', Margaret Morris, *The General Strike*, Penguin, 1976

David Egan, 'Abel Morgan, 1878-1972', *Llafur*, Vol. 1 No. 2, 1973, pp. 29-33

David Egan, 'The Unofficial Reform Committee and the Miners' Next Step', *Llafur*, Vol. 2 No. 3, Summer 1978, pp. 64-80

Gwynfor Evans, *Land of My Fathers*, Y Lolfa, Talybont, 2005, pp. 427-8

Neil Evans and Dot Jones, '"A blessing for the miner's wife": the campaign for pithead baths in the south Wales coalfield, 1908-1950', *Llafur*, Vol. 6 No. 3, 1994, pp. 5-28

Fedw Hir, Groundwork Merthyr and Rhondda Cynon Taf, n.d.

Hywel Francis and David Smith, *The Fed: A History of the South Wales Miners' in the Twentieth Century*, Lawrence and Wishart, 1980

Juliet Gardiner, *Wartime Britain 1939-1945*, Headline, 2004

David Gilbert, *Class Community and Collective Action: Social Change in Two British Coalfields, 1850-1926*, Clarendon, 1992

Peter Gurney, *Co-operative Culture and the politics of consumption in England, 1870-1930*, Manchester, 1996

Peter Gurney, 'Labor's great arch: Co-operation and cultural revolution in Britain, 1795-1926', in *Consumers against Capitalism? Consumer Co-operation in Europe, North America and Japan, 1840-1990*, pp. 135-71, eds. E. Furlough and C. Strickwerda, Maryland, Rowman & Littlefield, 1999

Peter Gurney, 'The Battle of the Consumer in Postwar Britain', *The Journal of Modern History*, Vol. 77 No. 4, December 2005, pp. 956-87

Alan Vernon Jones, *Chapels in the Cynon Valley*, Cynon Valley History Society, 2004

Philip N Jones, 'A Valley Community in Transition: Ynysybwl in 1967', *Llafur*, Vol. 9 No. 1, 2004, pp. 85-94

Richard Lewis, *Leaders and Teachers: Adult Education and the Challenge of Labour in South Wales, 1906-1940*, UWP, 1993

Michael Lieven, The Universal Pit Village, 1890-1913, Gomer, 1994

Michael Lieven, 'A Fractured Working-Class Consciousness? The Case of the Lady Windsor Colliery Lodge', 1921, *WHR*, Vol. 21, Dec 2003, No. 4, pp. 729-56

John E Morgan, *A Village Workers' Council – And what it Accomplished, being a Short History of the Lady Windsor Lodge, S.W.M.F.*, n.d.

Beatrice Potter, *The Co-operative Movement in Great Britain*, Swan Sonnenschein, London, 1904 impression

D. Ben Rees, Chapels in the Valley, The Ffynnon Press, 1975

Helen Thomas '"A Democracy of Working Women" The Women's Co-operative Guild in South Wales, 1891-1939', *Llafur*, Vol. 11 No. 1, 2012, pp. 149-69

John F Wilson, Anthony Webster & Rachel Vorberg-Rugh, *Building Co-operation: A Business History of the Co-operative Group, 1863-2013,* Oxford, 2013

ORAL INTERVIEWS AND CONVERSATIONS

John Butler, ex-Secretary Co-ops UK, conversation, Cardiff, September 2006

Hywel Francis, conversation, 4 October 2013

Marjorie Hazell, telephone conversations, 11 & 13 November 2007

Ron Hazell, telephone conversation, 16 February 2008

Ivor John of Briton Ferry interviewed by Aled Eirug, November 1978

Lilian Price, conversation, 28 January 2007

Norman Stevens, ex-co-operative official, interview, Exmouth, Devon, 15 October 2006

Tom Watkins interview with David Egan, held in SWML, 23 October 1972

Margaret and Bob West, multiple conversations, 2007-14.

Notes

Introduction: William Hazell's Gleaming Vision

1   Ynysybwl Co-operative Society, *The Gleaming Vision (GV)*, 1954, p 11.

2   *1900-1950, 50 Years of Service and Progress*, Ammanford Co-operative Society, 1950; *1901-1951 Jubilee Time at Tredegar*, Tredegar Industrial and Provident Society, 1951.

3   Letter John Thomas to John E Morgan, 3 March 1952, JEM collection. Thomas, a WEA lecturer, had taught Hazell.

4   'Headaches of the Historian: "If You can Write History You'll Be a Man"', *Co-operative Review (CR)*, August 1959, pp. 178-9.

5   Roger Davies, a retired Co-operative Group membership official, told the author that societies' records were thrown into skips when they were taken over by the national Co-operative Retail Services (CRS). This may well have been the fate of the YCS records. Some co-operative records that survived were later deposited in West Glamorgan Archives and at Swansea University.

6   Norman Stevens, ex-co-operative official, conversation with author, Exmouth, Devon, 15 October 2006.

7   E-mail from the late David Lazell to author, 19 October 2006.

8   'Gateways to the Boardroom 1 – The Educational Approach', *CR*, May 1957, p 106.

9   Letter John Thomas to John E Morgan, 3 March 1952.

10 See for example, David Gilbert, *Class Community and Collective Action: Social Change in Two British Coalfields, 1850-1926*, Clarendon, 1992; Michael Lieven, 'A Fractured Working-Class Consciousness? The Case of the Lady Windsor Colliery Lodge, 1921', *Welsh History Review (WHR)*, Vol. 21, Dec 2003, No. 4, pp. 729-56; Philip N. Jones, 'A Valley Community in Transition: Ynysybwl in 1967', *Llafur*, Vol. 9 No. 1, 2004, pp. 85-94.

11 See my '"A Task Worthy of the Most Sincere Devotion and Application": The Co-operative Movement in South Wales and Its History', *WHR*, December 2007, pp. 59-71.

12 'Robert Owen Speaks Again', *South Wales Supplement (SWS)*, July 1951, p ii.

Chapter 1: Starting Out

[1]   1910 marriage certificate; A R Davies, 'Hazell of Ynysybwl: Historian and Writer of South Wales', *CR*, October 1954, pp. 224-5; 1891 census.

[2]   'I Remember...W Hazell Recalls his Adopted Valley Home', *SWS*, July 1953, pp. i-ii.

[3]   Observer, Leader & Free Press, 17 October 1964; 'Why Did Robert Owen Leave Manchester for Lanark?', *Co-operative News (CN)*, 13 September 1947, p 9; Davies, 'Hazell of Ynysybwl', pp. 224-5; 'Discussing the Pros and Cons of the Perpetual Pension', *CN*, 14 December 1946, pp. 9 & 14.

[4]   'When Spencer Tossed a Coin – And killed a Romance', *CN*, 13 December 1947, p 9.

[5]   'Hooray for Cinderella', *CN*, 15 November 1947, pp. 9 & 10; 'Remember, Remember', *CN*, 30 October 1948, pp. 6-7; 'First Lodgings', *SWS,* January 1953, pp. i-ii.

[6]   Marjorie Hazell, conversation, 11 November 2007; Ron Hazell, conversation, 16 February 2008. Ron said she died of enteric fever.

[7]   1901 Census; Marjorie Hazell, 11 November 2007; Ron Hazell, family tree, 16 February 2008.

[8]   'Skyhooks', *CN*, 12 November 1949, p 10.

[9]   Marjorie, 13 November 2007; Margaret West, family letters and recollections to author.

[10]   'I Remember...', pp. 1-2.

[11]   Marjorie, 11 November 2007.

[12]   'First Lodgings', p i; Marjorie, 11 November 2007; W W Price Card index, Aberdare Library; 1911 Census; letter William to Lilian, 13 May 1933.

[13]   'In This Year's Congress City', *The Millgate*, June 1935, pp. 487-9; 'Co-operation Owes Much to Wales', *SWS*, March 1957, p i.

[14]   See report of death of William Pask, *Aberdare Leader (AL)*, 25 January 1919, accessed from National Library of Wales site http://cymru1914.org/en/view/newspaper/3581390/4/ART37 on 28 November 2013.

[15]   'First Lodgings', pp. i-ii; *AL*, 29 June 1940, in W W Price card index.

[16]   'The Miner – No Longer a Minor: His Shopping Habits To-day and Yesterday', *CR*, November 1955, pp. 258-9.

[17]   'I Remember...', pp. i-ii.

[18]   Chris Baggs, *"[T]he whole tragedy of leisure in penury": the South Wales Miners' Institute libraries during the Depression'*, 68th IFLA Council and General Conference, August 18-24 2002.

[19]   Jones, 'A Valley Community...', p 87.

[20]   'I Remember...', pp. i-ii.

[21] *GV*, pp. 7, 20 & 23. The 1911 Census recorded approximately 40% of the population spoke Welsh.

[22] 'W Hazell Looks At the Congress Town', *CN*, 19 May 1953, p 10.

[23] 1911 Census; information from Margaret West; W W Price index cards, William Hazell, Card 1.

[24] 'The Chimneys Speak', *SWS*, August 1954, p ii; 'I Remember…', pp. 1-2.

[25] *GV,* p 30.

[26] John E Morgan (JEM), unpublished account of the setting up of the ILP in Ynysybwl; lodge minutes 27 September 1907, 8 January, 25 March, 24 & 29 April and 12 December 1908, 23 March 1910; JEM, *A Village Workers Council,* (*VWC*), pp. 11-12.

[27] *VWC*, pp. 45 & 46.

[28] *GV*, p 25; *VWC*, pp. 8 & 69.

[29] *VWC*, p 42; 'An Able Administrator: Abel Morgan, Ynysybwl, and Western Section', *SWS*, No. 30 March 1926, pp. i-ii; David Egan, 'Abel Morgan, 1878-1972', *Llafur*, Vol. 1 No. 2, 1973, pp. 29-33; David Egan, 'The Unofficial Reform Committee and the Miners' Next Step', *Llafur*, Vol. 2 No. 3, 1978, p 77.

[30] Quoted in Gwynfor Evans, *Land of My Fathers*, Y Lolfa, Talybont, 2005, pp. 427-8.

[31] 'Revolution in the Rhondda', *SWS*, June 1955, p i.

[32] JEM, 'The Retarders', typed manuscript.

[33] Emphasis in original. 'Churchyard Magic', *CN*, 16 November 1946, p 9; 'Joining the Classics Club', *CN*, 24 July 1948, pp. 6-7.

[34] National Council of Labour Colleges (NCLC). 'I Remember', pp. i-ii; 'Gateways…1', pp. 106-7; R Lewis, *Leaders and Teachers: Adult Education and the Challenge of Labour in South Wales, 1906-1940*, Cardiff, 1993, pp. 20 & 49; Letter John Thomas to John E Morgan, 3 March 1952; 'The Mind of The Miner', *The Welsh Outlook* , 1916, partly reprinted in *The Plebs*, October 1916, Vol. VIII No. 9, pp. 209-12. See also my 'Miners Learning in the South Wales Coalfield, 1900-1947', *Llafur*, Vol. 8 No. 1, 2000, pp. 69-97.

[35] Lewis, *Leaders…* pp. 46 & 49.

[36] 'The CWS in South Wales', *The Wheatsheaf*, February 1917, p 127.

[37] Beatrice Potter, *The Co-operative Movement in Great Britain*, Swan Sonnenschein, London, 1904 impression, p 187; Co-operative Society Mergers 1915-2004, National Co-operative Archive, 2004, unpublished; Noel and Alan Cox, *Two Hundred Years of Welsh Paranumismatic History*, 1994; information provided by Martin Purvis, Gillian Lonergan and extracted from co-operative sources, including Co-operative Directories and Co-operative Congress annual reports. Return of Trade for 1899, Western Section, *Co-operative Congress Report, 1900*, pp. 238-9.

[38] *GV*, p 19; *VWC*, pp. 2-3.

39 Emphasis in original, *GV*, pp. 23 & 20.

40 *Pontypridd Observer (PO)*, 30 September 1939.

41 *GV*, pp. 79, 31 & 42.

42 *GV*, p 20.

43 See my 'From Cwmbach to Tower: 140 Years of Collective Entrepreneurship in the Cynon Valley, 1860-2000', *Llafur*, 2012, pp. 144-5.

44 *GV*, p 33; 'Twenty Five Years in College', *CR*, November 1940, p 387; *Merthyr Pioneer*, 1 December 1913; Gateways to the Boardroom 1...', p 107; "...and our education...", *CN*, 23 March 1946, pp. 11 & 13.

45 See Peter Gurney, *Co-operative Culture and the politics of consumption in England, 1870-1930*, Manchester, 1996, on the construction of a co-operative 'way of life' and its transformative aspirations.

46 *GV*, p 38; 'An Able Administrator...', p i.

47 In 1935 Hazell had been editing the publication 'for years'. Two decades later he was still the editor of the *Local Pages* of the now renamed *Home Magazine*. 'An Able Administrator...'; W S Collins, 'Hazell of Ynysybwl', *SWS*, November 1935, pp. i & iv; *GV*, p 126.

48 *GV*, pp. 33, 26, 34, & 24.

49 Interview Tom Watkins with David Egan, 23 October 1972 held in South Wales Miners' Library. *GV*, p 134.

50 *GV*, p 35.

51 *GV*, pp. 39-40 & 37.

52 *GV*, pp. 39 & 105.

53 'The Co-operative Pilgrim's Progress', *CN*, 4 June 1949, p 10.

54 'Looking Back – 50 Momentous Years', *SWS*, January 1951, pp. i-ii.

55 *GV*, p 40.

56 *GV*, p 124.

57 *GV*, pp. 37-9.

58 *CN*, 1 September 1917.

59 David Egan, 'Abel Morgan...', pp. 29-33; Ivor John of Briton Ferry interviewed by Aled Eirug, November 1978; 'An Able Administrator...'.

60 *GV*, p 37. Egan, 'Abel Morgan...'; Press articles from mid-1916 amongst JEM's papers, untitled typed manuscript and associated photos.

61 *VWC*, p 37. Emrys Hughes was later son-in-law of Keir Hardie, biographer and politician.

62 *VWC*, pp. 55-6.

Chapter 2: Life Between the Wars – Years of Endurance

[1]   Lodge minutes, 28 June, 17 July, 21 August, 15, 18 & 22 November 1918; 11 & 15 September, & 5 & 22 October 1919. See *VWC*, p 49 and Lieven, 'A Fractured…', pp. 729-56.

[2]   *VWC*, p 46; Lieven, 'A Fractured…', p 736; *AL*, 18 November 1944 (copy held in JEM papers).

[3]   'Alan Skuse: Wages Expert Living an Abundant Life', *CR*, July 1957, pp. 160-1.

[4]   Lodge minutes, 15 & 22 September 1920.

[5]   Lodge minutes, 20 October 1920.

[6]   Lodge minutes, 22 August 1919; 2 June, 18 August, 26 February & 16 March 1920; 1 October 1919 & 2 October 1918.

[7]   *GV*, pp. 36, 37, 40, 42 & 43.

[8]   *GV*, pp. 43, 47, 46, 52, 81, 109, 111 & 156.

[9]   *GV*, pp. 40, 52.

[10] *GV*, p 52.

[11] *GV*, pp. 36 & 31.

[12] Lodge minutes, 25 March 1921.

[13] Gen Meeting 7 April 1921 I am grateful to Anthea Fielding for transcribing this section of JEM's diaries.

[14] Lodge minutes, 9 April 1921; *VWC*, pp. 26-7.

[15] Lodge minutes, 15-21 April 1921; *VWC*, pp. 26-7.

[16] Lodge minutes, 7 April 1921; *SWS*, March 1937.

[17] Interview Tom Watkins…

[18] *GV*, pp. 62, 63 & 93; Returns of Trade for Western Section 1920-22 in Congress Reports, 1921-1923. The 1921 lockout remains a gaping hole in the historiography of South Wales.

[19] William Brown, who was a school attendance officer, replaced Hazell as President in 1922, and held the post until 1935, when Hazell was once again elected President, upon Brown's death.

[20] My emphasis in italics. *Co-operative News*, 23 October 1920, p 8.

[21] 'Cash or Credit Trading', *The Producer*, June 1922, p 241.

[22] See Peter Gurney, 'Labor's great arch: Co-operation and cultural revolution in Britain, 1795-1926', in *Consumers against Capitalism? Consumer Co-operation in Europe, North America and Japan, 1840-1990*, eds. E. Furlough and C. Strickwerda, (Maryland, Rowman & Littlefield, 1999) pp. 158-9; *CN*, 13 January 1923 & 31 December 1927; 'An Able Administrator…', pp. i-ii; Lodge minutes, 28 November 1920.

[23] Emphasis in original. 'Cash or Credit…', p 241.

[24] Returns of Trade for Western Section in Congress Reports, 1920-1926; *GV*, p 62.

25   *CN*, 18 April 1925.

26   Fiftieth Annual Co-operative Congress, Central Hall, Liverpool, 20-22 May
      1918, p. xxxv; 'Twenty Five Years...', p 387; See for example *CN*, 9 April
      & 23 July 1927; 28 January & 13 October 1928; Sectional Board Retirements
      "W Hazell of Ynysybwl", *CR*, June 1959, p 135.

27   'A Democratic Romance', *SWS*, July 1930, p i.

28   See John F Wilson, Anthony Webster & Rachel Vorberg-Rugh, *Building
      Co-operation: A Business History of the Co-operative Group, 1863-2013,* Oxford,
      2013.

29   *CN*, 11 November 1924, 17 October 1925, p 3 & 7 July 1926; 'Twenty Five
      Years in College', p 387.

30   'Is the Co-operative Congress Unwieldy?', *CO*, Vol. VIII No. 85, April
      1927, p 145.

31   'A Democratic Romance, pp. i-ii.

32   'Twenty Five Years...', p 387.

33   *CN*, 13 May 1922.

34   'Lessons Learnt on Welsh Hills', *The Colliery Workers' Magazine (CWM)*, Vol.
      1 No. 4, April 1923, p 90.

35   'Lessons Learnt...'.

36   *CN*, 23 September 1922, quoted in Helen Thomas '"A Democracy of
      Working Women" The Women's Co-operative Guild in South Wales,
      1891-1939', *Llafur*, Vol. 11 No. 1, 2012, p 158.

37   *CN*, 20 September 1924.

38   *CN*, 23 May 1925.

39   'Sentence – Twenty Five Years Hard', *SWS*, December 1948, p i; UDC, 9
      October 1923. 'Twenty Five Years in College', p 387.

40   'Sentence...'; Eds. Joyce M Bellamy & John Saville, Dictionary of Labour
      Biography, Vol. II, 1974, pp. 25-30.

41   'A Leaf from a Councillor's Diary', *CWM*, Vol. II No. 10, October 1924, p
      260.

42   'A Leaf...', pp. 260-1.

43   'A Labour Councillor's Dairy: Public Health (Meat) Regulations, 1924',
      CWM, Vol. III No. 11, November 1925, p 255.

44   'Notes from A Labour Councillor's Diary', *CWM*, Vol. IV No. 1, January
      1926, pp. 15-16.

45   'A Page of Mining History', *CWM*, Vol. II No. 7, July 1924, pp. 180-1.

46   'A Full Life', *CWM*, October 1923, pp. 254-5.

47   'Smiling Land of Gwent', *SWS*, December 1952, p ii; 'There's Magic to be
      Found on the Highway', *SWS*, October 1956, p ii.

48   Lodge minutes, 3 & 18 May 1926; UDC, 7 May 1926; E W Edwards, 'The

Pontypridd Area', Margaret Morris, *The General Strike*, Penguin, 1976, pp. 413–5.

49 'The Art of Putting Things', *CO*, January 1947, p 12; *GV*, p 64.

50 *CN*, 19 June 1926. It was reported in July that there were 11 centres. ('The Co-operative Movement and the Miners', *SWS*, July 1926, pp. ii-iii). The account in *VWC* (p 27) is at odds with contemporary reports as it did not refer to the organising role of the Co-op.

51 'Miracle of the Valleys', *CR*, Vol. IX No. 51, May 1935, p 111.

52 *GV*, p 29; UDC, 19 October 1926; Hywel Francis and David Smith, *The Fed: A History of the South Wales Miners' in the Twentieth Century*, 1980, Lawrence and Wishart, p 57.

53 Lodge minutes, 3 July 1926; UDC & MCWC, 10 August 1926.

54 'Miracle...', p 111.

55 Lodge minutes, 26 August & 15 November 1926.

56 *VWC*, pp. 27-30; Joint meeting of UDC and MCWC, 10 August 1926.

57 UDC, 26 October 1926.

58 General Annual & Ordinary Meeting of UDC 3 May 1927; 1 May 1928; 29 April 1930. UDC, 26 March 1929; EC, 21 April 1931.

59 Lodge Minutes, 23 December 1926.

60 '"Strictly Non-Political"', *CWM*, Vol. V No. 7, July 1927, p 114.

61 'Nuffieldism in Practice', *SWS*, March 1937, p ii.

62 'Effect of Falling Prices in Trade', *SWS*, April 1931, p iii.

63 *CN*, 3 December 1927 & 16 June 1928; *GV*, pp. 124-5.

64 'Some Aspects of Stamp Club Trading', *The Producer*, April 1939, p 102.

65 *GV*, p 61.

66 *GV*, p 59.

67 'An Able Administrator...', pp. i-ii; *CN*, 3 September & 31 December 1927, 5 January 1929; *Ocean and National Magazine*, *(ONM)*, January 1930, p 30.

68 *CN*, 5 January 1929.

69 Marjorie, 11 November 2007 & 16 January 2008.

70 *ONM*, April 1929, pp. 123-4; 'Unanimity Achieved at Lady Windsor', *ONM*, February 1931, pp. 43-44'; See Neil Evans and Dot Jones, '"A blessing for the miner's wife": the campaign for pithead baths in the south Wales coalfield, 1908-1950', *Llafur*, Vol. 6 No. 3, 1994, pp. 5-28.

71 *ONM*, February 1931.

72 'Unanimity...'.

73 *ONM*, April 1929, p 124, April 1932, p 133, September 1932, p 318, October 1933, p 343, 'Twenty Five Years...', p 387.

74 *CN*, 28 July 1928; UDC, 26 February 1929; Sanitary and Public Health

Committee (SPHC), 9 July 1929; EC, 5 March 1929. See '"Summer Meadow": A "Noble" Quarter Century', *SWS*, April 1953, p iv.

[75] See *CN* for 1929, especially 26 October 1929.

[76] Report of School Medical Officer, 30 April 1929; EC, 3 February 1931 & 1 December 1936.

[77] *VWC*, p 31.

[78] *GV*, p 63.

[79] "Summer Meadow".

[80] Letter Hazell to Lilian, 13 November 1932.

[81] Letter Hazell to Lilian, 13 May 1933.

[82] *ONM*, June 1930, p 198.

[83] *ONM*, March 1932, p 98.

[84] *ONM*, Xmas 1936, p 426.

[85] *CN*, 26 July 1930; he was still a magistrate in 1944, *AL*, 18 November 1944.

[86] SPHC, 13 September 1927; Municipal Undertakings Committee (MUC), 13 December 1927.

[87] UDC, 11 November 1928. Report of School Medical Officer for term ended 30 April 1929 & 1 July 1930; EC, 6 & 13 January 1931.

[88] UDC, 16 September 1930; *ONM*, September 1931, pp. 305-6 & September 1933, p 304; *CN*, 5 April 1930.

[89] MCWC, 1 July 1930, 20 October 1931, 7 June & 19 July 1932.

[90] *CN*, 5 October 1929.

[91] The Sixty-Third Annual Co-operative Congress, 1931, p 262; The Sixty-Fifth Annual Co-operative Congress Report, Birmingham, 1933, p 270.

[92] 'Co-operators on Local Authorities', *SWS*, April 1935, p iii.

[93] 'I Remember', pp. i-ii.

[94] 'Magic of the Hills', *SWS*, May 1957, p ii.

[95] *CN*, 2 & 30 May 1936; 1936 Co-operative Congress Report.

[96] *CN*, 14 November 1936.

[97] 'Outlines for Speakers', *The Producer*, October 1929.

[98] Letter William Hazell to Lilian, 13 November 1932; *ONM*, January 1930, p 30; *ONM*, December 1932, p 427; 'The Philosophy of Henry Ford', *CN*, 24 May 1947, p 9.

[99] 'What of Amalgamation', *CO*, December 1929, p 459.

[100] 'Amalgamation – An Alternative', *SWS*, June 1930, p ii.

[101] In 1942, Hazell seemed to reverse his earlier position. See 'Sixteen to One', *SWS*, May 1942, p iii.

[102] *CN*, 13 May 1922.

103 'Miracle…', p 111.

104 *CN*, 25 January 1930.

105 Italics in original. 'Amalgamation – An Alternative… p iii.

106 'Amalgamation – An Alternative', p ii.

107 *CN*, 26 July 1930.

108 Information provided by Gillian Lonergan, 20 August 2010.

109 Letter William to Lilian, 11 September 1932.

110 Letter William to Lilian, 13 May 1933.

111 Letter William to Lilian, 13 May 1933.

112 Information provided by Gillian Lonergan.

113 See for example December 1929, pp. 363-4; June 1930 p 198; February 1931 pp. 43-4.

114 *ONM*, May 1929, p 153.

115 Letter William to Lilian, 11 September 1932.

116 Letter William to Lilian, 13 May 1933.

117 Letter William to Lilian, 13 November 1932.

118 Letter William to Lilian, 13 May 1933. Emphasis in original.

119 Letter William to Lilian, 13 May 1933.

120 Letter William to Lilian, 11 September 1932.

121 Letter William to Deborah Elizabeth, 7 February 1933.

122 Letter William to Lilian, 13 May 1933.

123 Letter from W George to Lilian, 'Thursday', undated.

124 Memorial card for Deborah Elizabeth.

125 'Don't Remember', *CN*, 13 November 1948, p 6.

126 'Exaltation of Literature', *CN*, 25 September 1946, pp. 8-9.

127 'Don't Remember'.

128 Employer references from Dr Davies of Ynysybwl, 18 November 1936 and Dr Harold Coultard of Cardiff, n.d..; *ONM*, March 1937, p 100.

129 *ONM*, January 1934, p 20, Xmas 1936, p 426; *CN*, 15 September 1934; 'In This Year's…'.

130 'Sudden Death of Co-operative Stalwart', *PO*, 21 November 1964. For a brief history of Glyn Street Chapel see Alan Vernon Jones, *Chapels in the Cynon Valley*, Cynon Valley History Society, 2004.

131 *CN*, 20 April 1935 and 28 November 1936; Lodge Minutes, 3 February 1937; *ONM*, July and September 1937.

132 'Miracle…', pp. 112, 111 and 109.

133 'Miracle…', pp. 111-2.

134 See for example 'Thomas Hughes', *CR*, December 1946, p 239.

135 'In This Year's…'.

136 'The Western Mail Looks at Distribution', *SWS*, March 1955, pp. i-ii.

137 'Practical Propaganda…', p 311.

138 Collins, 'Hazell of Ynysybwl', pp. i & iv.

139 'The President', *Agenda*, March 1955, pp. 35 & 38.

140 *GV*, p 107; *CN*, 17 April 1937, p 9; 'Taken as Read.', *CO*, October 1933, p 425; 'The President', pp. 36-7.

141 'Gateways to the Boardroom: 3 – Employee Representation and the Popular Gate', *CR*, August 1957, p 175.

142 *CN*, 24 September 1927; 'Committees'; *SWS*, March 1939, p ii; *GV*, p 96.

143 'Committees'; 'In Defence of Committees' *SWS*, November 1949, pp. i-ii.

144 'In Defence of Committees'.

145 'Committees'.

146 'Committees'.

147 *GV*, p 115; *CN*, 23 April 1938, pp. 14 & 15; 14 January 1939, p 15; 'Committees'. Hazell returned to the theme in 1957 in 'Gateways…3', pp. 174-6.

148 'Forty Years at the Table', *CR*, February 1957, pp. 41-2.

149 '"Taken as Read."', *CO*, October 1933, p 425.

150 *VWC*, p 9; 'The President', p 35; 'Forty Years at the Table', p 4.

151 See photograph section. *GV*, p 65; "The Gateway of the Rhondda", *SWS*, March 1933, p i; The Magic Carpet of National Membership, *CN*, 2 July 1949, p 6.

152 *GV*, p 67.

153 *GV*, p 61.

154 Returns of Trade for Western Section, 1920-1940 in Co-operative Congress Reports, 1921-41.

155 Michael Lieven, The Universal Pit Village, 1890-1913, Gomer, 1994, p 350; *CN*, 3 August 1929; *Home Magazine*, October 1939, quoted in *GV*, p 70. *CN*, 29 September 1956.

156 *CN*, 22 November 1930; EC, 1 December 1931 & 2 February 1937.

157 'Miracle…'; Collins, 'Hazell of Ynysybwl', pp. i & iv; '1889-1939', 'Ynysybwl Society's Half Century of Co-operation', *SWS*, November 1939, p i.

158 *VWC*, p 31; *SWS*, Dec 1936 p iii; *CN*, 2 January 1937, p 6, & 6 August 1938, p 9; 'Nuffieldism…', p ii; FC, 30 August 1938.

159 *CN*, 22 & 29 June 1935; EC, 2 September 1930, 7 May & 3 September 1935; The Cardiff Citizen, No. 1, Sept 1935.

160 'Co-operators on Local Authorities', *SWS*, April 1935, pp. iii-iv.

161 'Sentence…', p ii; FC, 27 September 1938.

162 EC, 5 November 1935, 6 October, 3 November and 1 December 1936.

163 Marriage certificate, Margaret West papers; *ONM*, Xmas 1936, pp. 425-6.

164 EC, 6 October 1936.

165 Margaret.

166 See writings in her 1950s journals; *ONM*, Xmas 1936, pp. 425-6 & September 1939, p 300. Her first cousin was Herb – later Lord Justice – Edmund Davies. W W Price index cards, Aberdare Library on William Hazell, cards 1 and 3; 'A Good Word…', p 6.

167 'The Green Corn Ripens', *SWS*, February 1958, pp. ii–iii; A R Davies, 'Hazell of Ynysybwl', pp. 224-5.

168 Marjorie, 11 November 2007.

169 *ONM*, March 1937, p 100.

170 *ONM*, August 1938, pp. 285-6; Letter Elizabeth and Will[ie] to Lilian and David, 18 August 1966.

171 Margaret, 10 November 2007.

172 'Don't Remember'.

173 Letter Gwlad to Lilian, 25 January 1972.

174 *CN*, 4 December 1937, p 8; 1 January 1938, p 6, and 22 January 1938, p 2.

175 *CN*, 26 October 1935 & 25 July 1936.

176 *CN*, 24 October 1936.

177 *CN*, 18 September 1937, p 12.

178 *CN*, 9 October 1937, p 10.

179 *CN*, 25 September 1937, p 12.

180 *CN*, 23 October 1937, p 12.

181 *CN*, 22 January & 23 July 1938.

182 *CN*, 28 January, 1 & 22 April 1939, p 9.

183 'Practical Propaganda…', p 312.

184 *CN*, 22 July 1939, p 7; 19 August 1939, p 1; 2 September 1939, p 10.

185 *CN*, 16 January 1932; 'The Voice that is Silent', *SWS*, November 1938, pp. i & iv.

186 'Outcast of the Air', *CN*, 23 September 1944, p 10.

187 'Why Not a Statue Here?, *SWS*, November 1958, p i.

188 *CN*, 20 June 1936. In 'Looking Back…' he incorrectly gave the date as 1935. UDC, 26 May 1936.

189 'Miracle…', p 112.

190 Emphasis in original. 'A Co-operator on the People's Outlook', *CN*, 14 November 1936, p 2.

191 'A Co-operator on the People's Outlook'.

192 See *PO*, 16 February 1935. (Thanks to Daryl Leeworthy for this reference.) *CN*, 28 November 1936.

193 Notes and Comments by the Editor, *SWS*, June 1938.

194 *ONM*, March 1938, p 102; *CN*, 19 September 1936 and 10 April 1937, p 17, & 22 January 1938, p 15; *GV*, pp. 73-4; MUC, 21 February 1939; UDC, 24 January 1939.

195 'Cavalcade', *CN*, 1 March 1952, pp. 8-9.

196 'Co-operation Fights Capitalist Exploitation: Transforming Wage Slaves into Financiers and Employers', *SWS*, August 1937, p i.

197 Programme in J E Morgan papers.

198 'Book Titles What's in a Name?', *CN*, 8 November 1947, pp. 9 & 10.

199 '"Omitting Personalities" Some Reflections on Peace Alliance or "Popular Front"', *AL*, 20 May 1939.

200 *ONM*, June 1939, p 209.

Chapter 3: Wartime

1 Air Raid Precautions Committee (ARP), 21 February 1939; EDC, 4 April, 31 May, 6 June & 7 November 1939.

2 UDC, 27 September 1938 & 15 May 1939; ARP, 29 September 1938 & 21 February 1939; EDC, 7 February 1939.

3 ARP, 9 May 1939; UDC, 29 August & 12 September 1939.

4 'The Challenge of '1984'', *CN*, 15 December 1954, p 2.

5 *GV*, p 69; *CN*, 7 October 1939 & 14 October 1940, p 9.

6 '1889-1939', p i.

7 *CN*, 21 October 1939, pp. 1 & 2, 28 October 1939, p 4 & 14, October 1940, p 9; *GV*, p 69.

8 *CN*, 2 November 1940, p 2, 29 June 1940, p 12 & 1 June 1940, p 2.

9 Letter Sgt Will in Cairo to Lilian, 4 June 1940.

10 Photo dated 1940 held by Margaret.

11 *ONM*, June 1940, p 128.

12 Letter from Roy to 'Lil', no date, but after 13 December 1939; *AL*, 29 June 1940; W W Price card index.

13 Letter from Sgt Will in Cairo to Lilian, dated 4 June 1940, (emphasis in original). Austen was in tanks in North Africa and was in Siena in Italy in 1944 and Rome in April 1945. At one point all three brothers met in the desert. Willie, forever running himself down, said his work in the Education Corps meant that he was 'a bit of a coward' compared to his other brothers who had seen fighting. All three brothers survived. (Comments from Margaret and Bob West).

14   *ONM*, June 1940, p 128.

15   *ONM*, June 1940, p 128; Article on Roy's funeral, *AL*, 29 June 1940, in W W Price card index.

16   UDC, 25 June 1940; EDC, 4 June, 2 July & 5 November 1940.

17   ARP, 3 & 17 July 1940; MUC, 3 July & 17 December 1940; Public Health Committee (PHC), 9 July 1940 & UDC, 4 September 1940.

18   'Sentence…', p ii.

19   'Ration Anomalies, *CR*, September 1940, p 302.

20   *CN*, 27 July 1940.

21   *CN*, 9 December 1939, p 5; 6 January 1940, p 1; *GV*, p 72.

22   'Ration Anomalies', pp. 302-3.

23   Maternity and Child Welfare Committee (MCWC), 29 October 1940; UDC, 22 October & 11 December 1940; EDC, 4 June, 2 July & 5 November 1940, & 6 October 1942; FC 22 April 1941.

24   PHC, 10 September & 12 November 1940.

25   *CN*, 26 April 1941, p 5.

26   See, for example, *CN*, 16 March 1940, p 4; 23 March 1940, p 11 & 23 November 1940, p 11. Also minutes of Western Section of CCTA, 1940-41, and, for example, Minutes of the Co-operative Coal Trades Association National Executive for 12 July & 12 December 1940.

27   *GV*, p 103; *CN*, 4 November 1939, p 4.

28   'Phantom of Piccadilly, *CN*, 15 September 1945, p 9.

29   'Why Britain Needs Books', *CR*, January 1949, pp. 17-8; 'Shrines Where Sanity Rules', *CN*, 13 July 1946, p 7.

30   *CN*, 6 July 1940.

31   UDC, 28 January & 25 February 1941; FC, 25 February 1941; *CN*, 11 January 1941, & 5 April 1941.

32   'The Treasure of Swansea', *SWS*, January 1949, pp. i-ii; 'The Sun Shone on Swansea's Opening Day', *SWS*, August 1956.

33   MUC, 20 May 1941.

34   FPC, 7 & 14 May 1941; MUC, 17 June 1941 & ARP, 7 May 1941.

35   PHC, 10 June 1941.

36   Richmal Crompton, 'William and the Bomb', *William Carries On*, Newnes, 1942, p 42.

37   UDC, 3 June 1941; FPC, 26 June 1941.

38   FC, 22 July 1941; PHC, 13 May, 8 July, 17 June & 16 September 1941; MCH, 21 May 1941; UDC, 27 May 1941 & 22 September 1942; *CN*, 25 October 1941, p 6.

39   Communal Feeding Committee (CFC), 10 December 1941 & 16 April 1942;

UDC, 24 April 1942; 'Are They British Restaurants?', *CN*, 22 November 1941, p 2; *CN*, 27 December 1941, p 5, & 23 March 1946, p 10.

40 MUC, 17 June 1941 & 15 November 1938; FC, 24 June & 28 July 1941.

41 Juliet Gardiner, *Wartime Britain 1939-1945*, Headline, 2004, p 74.

42 *CN*, 29 August 1942, p 11; 'Mignonette and Onions', *CO*, April 1942, pp. 109-10.

43 'Pan-Celtic National Anthem', *SWS*, December 1941, pp. i-ii; *CN*, 2 November 1940.

44 *CN*, 5 September 1942, p 3; 25 October 1941, p 6, & 8 January 1944, p 5; *GV*, pp. 73-5.

45 'Marx and Robert Owen: A Gibe at "Reactionary Humbug"', *SWS*, April 1940, pp. i & iv.

46 'Honouring a Practical Saint: St. David's Perfect Life', *SWS*, Feb 1950, p i.

47 'Why Did Robert Owen Leave Manchester for Lanark?', *CN*, 13 September 1947, p 9.

48 'Owen's Kindergarten', *CR*, October 1941, pp. 306-7.

49 'Pan-Celtic...', pp. i-ii.

50 *CN*, 15 February 1941, p 8; 'Co-operators and the Peace', *CN*, 1 March 1941, p 2.

51 Emphases in original. *CN*, 21 November 1942, p 10.

52 *CN*, 6 November 1943, p 2.

53 Quoted in Maurice Bruce, *The Coming of The Welfare State*, B.T. Batsford, 1961, (1974 reprint), p 306.

54 'Beveridge Report is Ambulance Work', *CN*, 13 February 1943; editorial, 16 January 1943.

55 Emphasis in original. *CN*, 18 December 1943, p 9.

56 'A Jewel...', p iii.

57 'We Are Coming to Worship', *CN*, 26 December 1942, p 7.

58 'The Whole Nation is In Debt to "Strikers"', *CN*, 10 June 1944, p 2.

59 'In Wales Now', *Co-operative Party Monthly Letter (CPML)*, June 1955, pp. 12-13.

60 PHC, 8 February 1944; CFC, 24 February 1944.

61 UDC, 4 August 1943 & 28 March 1944; FC, 18 July 1944.

62 *CN*, 22 July 1944, p 4.

63 UDC, 27 February 1945.

64 UDC, 27 September 1944; MUC, 20 February 1945; FC, 27 February 1945; PHC, 13 March 1945; CFC, 30 January 1945; PHC, 13 March 1945.

65 HC, 9 March 1944; FC, 23 May 1944; *SWS*, June 1944, p ii; UDC, 25 April 1944.

66 Housing Sub Committee, 14 March 1944; UDC, 1 August 1944; HC, 29 August, 10 October, 14 November & 12 December 1944.

67 *SWS*, July 1943, No. 238, p I; Minutes of Western Section of CCTA, 12 July & 18 October 1944; *CN*, 28 October 1944, p 4, 2 December 1944, p 10 & 28 April 1945, p 5.

68 "A Co-operator at the Westminster Conference of Urban Authorities', *CO*, March 1945, pp. 77 & 79; Slum Problem: Co-operators Welcome Government Action', *CN*, 5 April 1930.

69 'A Co-operator at…', pp. 77 & 79.

70 *CN*, 30 September 1944, p 1, & 6 January 1945, p 11; 'Movement Hamstrung, *CN*, 9 July 1949, p 10; 'Chippenham', *CN*, 13 August 1949, pp. 8-9; *GV*, p 74.

71 *GV*, pp. 74 & 78.

Chapter 4: Socialism in Our Time

1 Alan Allport, *Demobbed: Coming Home After the Second World War*, Yale, 2009, pp. 111-2, 122 & 126.

2 'Midianites – Merchantmen', *The Producer*, October 1945, pp. 27-8.

3 'Vitamins in Politics', *CN*, 6 April 1946, p 10. They were Arthur Pearson (Pontypridd); Ness Edwards (Caerphilly); D T Jones (West Hartlepool) and A J Champion (Derby); *CN*, 23 July 1945 p 3.

4 'Gas: Review of an Industry Which is Down for NATIONALISATION', *CN*, 30 March 1946, p 9. See my *Co-operation A Post-war Opportunity Missed? A Welsh Perspective*, Bevan Foundation, 2012, for a fuller analysis of Hazell's writings and actions in relation to Labour's post-war programme.

5 'Vitamins in Politics…'.

6 *CN*, 22 December 1945, p 11; 'Rebecca of Wales', *SWS*, March 1946, p i.

7 *CN*, 28 July 1945, pp. 4 & 5; October 1945, p 16; 23 February, 1946, pp. 1 & 2; March 1946, p 8, & 22 November 1947, p 4.

8 UDC, 3 September & 5 November 1946 and 7 January & 4 November 1947.

9 'The South Welcomes the National Eisteddfod – pageant of song', *SWS*, July 1946, p i; UDC, 24 October & 28 December 1944; 18 April 1946 & 5 November 1946; FC, 27 January 1948.

10 *GV*, p 75; *CN*, 5 May 1946, p 8, & 8 May 1954, p 13; 'Cavalcade', pp. 8-9.

11 'Sentence…', p ii. UDC, 16 April & 4 June 1946; Victory Celebrations Committee, 6 May 1946.

12 HC, 3 December 1946; UDC, 7 January 1947.

13 HC, 18 March & 1 April 1947; Council Houses Management Committee (CHMC), 24 March & 24 May 1949.

[14] 'Rebecca…', p. i; 'First Welsh Jones in Robert Owen's County', *SWS*, March 1953, p ii.

[15] 'Progress Report from Ynysybwl', *The Producer*, June 1948, p 11; *GV*, pp. 90, 109 & 111.

[16] 'The Most Important…', p i; Ynysybwl Society's Diamond Jubilee, *SWS*, May 1949, pp. i–ii.

[17] 'Ynysybwl Society's Diamond Jubilee', pp. ii–iii.

[18] Megan E Morgan, aged 38, of 15 Thompson Street, Ynysybwl, Mass-Observation Archive: Topic Collections 66/20/F Ynysybwl 1947.

[19] Raymond Fletcher, 'Ynysybwl is the word for it!', *Tribune*, 21 August 1953.

[20] 'Nutritive Value of Canned Foods', *CR*, June 1946, pp. 116-7; 77th Co-operative Congress, Blackpool, 1946, p 349; Sectional Board Retirements "W Hazell…", p 135.

[21] 'Midianites…', pp. 27-8.

[22] 'This Nation of Shopkeepers', *SWS*, November 1953, pp. i–ii.

[23] 'The Origin, History, and Practice of Functionalism', *CO*, July 1941, pp. 261-2.

[24] 'May Day is a Challenge, *CN*, 3 May 1947, pp. 9 & 10.

[25] 'May Day…'.

[26] 'After Two Wars – A Comparison', *CN*, 11 January 1947, p 9.

[27] 'May Day…'.

[28] 'Cavalcade', pp. 8-9.

[29] 'Incentive', *CN*, 6 May 1950, p 8.

[30] Emphases in original. 'After Two Wars…', p 9.

[31] 'Co-operation Must Remedy New Coal Problem', *CR*, November 1946, pp. 215-16.

[32] 'Honouring a Practical Saint', *SWS*, p i.

[33] 'The Pioneers Fifth Objective', *CN*, 19 July 1947, pp. 9 & 14.

[34] 'If you Are Forestalled Do Not Despair', *CN*, 30 August 1947, p 9.

[35] 'The Pioneers' Fifth Objective', pp. 9 & 14.

[36] 'Intelligent Boy's Guide to Parasites', *CO*, Vol. XXX No. 345, January 1949, p 22.

[37] 'Old Man Datum – Movement Hamstrung', *CN*, 9 July 1949, p 10. While only bearing the initials 'W.H.', the article reads as his, both in style and content.

[38] See for example *CN*, 15 October p 1; 22 October 1949, pp. 1 & 2.

[39] 'The Thunder of a Falling Feather', *The Scottish Co-operator*, 23 December 1950, p 11; Lord Beveridge, *Voluntary Action*, George Allen & Unwin, 1948, and Lord Beveridge and A F Wells, *The Evidence for Voluntary Action*, George Allen & Unwin, 1949.

40   'LOST A Co-operative Commonwealth', *CN*, 9 December 1950, p 10.

41   *CN*, 2 December 1950, p 16.

42   'Is the Labour Party 'NEUTRAL'?', *CN*, 7 July 1951, p 10. Peter Gurney looks at this critical issue in 'The Battle of the Consumer in Postwar Britain', *The Journal of Modern History*, Vol. 77, No. 4 (December 2005), pp. 956-87.

43   'Cavalcade', pp. 8-9.

44   '1900 and all that', *CN*, 6 January 1951, p 8.

45   See for example PHC, 9 July 1946 & 7 January 1948; UDC, 1 June 1948; MUC, 17 February 1948; 'Sentence...', p ii.

46   UDC, 20 April 1948; MUC, 20 July & 15 September 1948, 26 April 1949; 'Effect of Local Planning on the Local Store', *CN*, 5 January 1946, p 9; 'Planning of East Glamorgan – Significant Trends discussed', *AL*, 10 April 1948; 'Future Development of Aberdare Valley: Mountain Ash Lacks Building Sites', *AL*, 17 April 1948.

47   Road Safety Committee, 9 December 1946; Entertainments Committee, 17 November 1948; FC, 28 January 1947; '1900 and all that...', p 8.

48   'Sentence...', p ii; UDC, 15 April 1947.

49   Local Government (Boundary Commission) Committee, 2 February & 29 March 1949; D. Ben Rees Chapels in the Valley, The Ffynnon Press, 1975, p 38.

50   Davies, 'Hazell of Ynysybwl...', pp. 224-5; 'Sudden Death...'.

51   *CN*, 17 May 1947; 'On Being Burgled', *CN*, 17 July 1948, pp. 8-9.

52   'Away With Discretion', *CN*, 8 January 1949, p 6.

53   *CN*, 4 June 1949, p 11.

54   'What is this Means Test?', pp. i-ii.

55   W W Price card index 1.

56   'The Virtue of Economy is Mainly Ancestral', *CN*, 14 January 1950, p 10; 'I'm All in Favour of the South Shore', *CN*, 28 April 1951, p 10; 'Silence is Not Always Golden, *CN*, November 1949, pp. 2 & 14.

57   'The Virtue of Economy...', p 10. UDC, 1 November 1949.

58   Margaret conversation 13 January 2014; 'Let's Do A Spot of Grumbling', *CN*, 19 July 1952, p 8.

59   Handwritten draft, 'History of Lady Windsor Lodge (contd) Part II' and JEM private papers; conversation with Hywel Francis, 4 October 2013.

60   Morgan's personal notebooks.

61   '1900 and all that', p 8.

62   'Tiger', *CN*, 27 October 1951, p 8.

63   'What is this Means Test?', pp. i-ii.

64   'Calendar Time Comes Around Again', *CN*, 7 January 1950, p 10.

[65] 'Land of Beautiful Bridges', *SWS*, June 1956, p iv; 'Something for Nothing in Pontypridd', *SWS*, April 1952, p i; *GV*, p 58.

[66] *GV*, p 90.

[67] *CN*, 29 May 1948, p 8; Western Section CCTA minutes, 11 June 1947 & 30 June 1948; Welsh Sectional Board (WSB) minutes 3 May 1952, 3 July 1954, 4 June 1955 & 9 June 1956; Davies, 'Hazell of Ynysybwl', p 224. 'Sectional Board Retirements, "W Hazell..."', p 135.

[68] Hazell came second in the ballot with 246 votes to J T Roberts 278 votes, reflecting his position in the movement. None of the other five candidates received more than 31 votes. Report of the 82nd Annual Co-operative Congress, Blackpool, 1951, p 429; Report of the 83rd Co-operative Congress, Margate, 1952, pp. 400-408; *CN*, 26 April 1952, p 1.

[69] ' "...and our education...", pp. 11 & 13.

[70] *CN*, 19 May 1951, p 16 & 30 August 1958; 'Flintshire Pilgrimage', *SWS*, p iii; 'The Railways of Wales, *SWS*, Dec 1956, p i; WSB minutes, 2 February & 2 August 1952, 5 March 1955 & 7 March 1959; 'N.H.S. – What it Means to Glamorgan', *SWS*, Sept 1955, p i.

[71] 'In Wales Now', *CPML*, June 1955, p 14.

[72] 'The White Saint and the Fountain of Light', *SWS*, Sept 1957, p I; 'A Lakeland Day', *SWS*, August 1957, p I; 'Vaynor Could be Excused for Vanity', *SWS*, Feb 1953, p I; 'Magic of...', *SWS*, May 1957, pp. i-ii; 'St Tudno Speaks', *CN*, 29 March 1947, p 9; 12 April 1947, p 2; 'W. Hazell Looks At the Congress Town', *CN*, 19 May 1953, p 10; 'Pryce Pryce-Jones Also From Newtown', *CN*, 1 July 1950, p 10; 'Robert Owen Speaks Again', pp. i-ii.

[73] Davies, 'Hazell of Ynysybwl...', pp. 224-5.

[74] 'The South Welcomes...', p i.

[75] 'So Caerphilly is Shining Its Shoes', *SWS*, July 1950, pp. i-ii.

[76] 'Roar of Dragons, or Was it Only a Purr?', *SWS*, August 1958, p I; 'First Welsh Jones...', p ii; 'Epstein and Llandaff', *SWS*, March 1958, p i.

[77] 'Something for Nothing in Pontypridd', *SWS*, April 1952, p i; 'It was the Singing That Did It', *SWS*, January 1956, p iii; 'Labels', *CN*, 8 September 1951, p 10; 'Hooray...', pp. 9 & 10; 'Real Film of Welsh Mining', *SWS*, August 1949, pp. iii-iv.

[78] Margaret, 31 March 2007; 'Be Yourself', *CN*, 29 November 1947, p 7.

[79] 'Headaches...', p 178.

[80] 'The Pioneer Co-operators of South Wales', p ii.

[81] The Pioneer Co-operators of South Wales', p ii; Co-operative Triumph in Tredegar, *SWS*, Nov 1951, p i.

[82] 'History And All That', *CN*, 24 June 1950, p 8; 'The Fortifications of Wales', *SWS*, April 1956, p ii; 'Headaches...', pp. 178-9.

[83] 'First Lodgings', *SWS*, January 1953, pp. i–ii.

[84] 'Invasion by the Monster – Coal' *SWS*, November 1957, pp. i–ii; 'Headaches…', pp. 178-9.

[85] 'Beyond the Chains', *CR*, Feb 1959, p 34; 'A Page of…', pp. 180-1; "The Gateway of the Rhondda".

[86] Emphasis in original. 'Chartism in Owen's Country', *SWS*, April 1948, p ii.

[87] See for example, 'The New Capital and the New "Capital"', *SWS*, March 1949. pp. i–ii; 'There's a Welcome on the Hillside', *SWS*, February 1951, p ii.

[88] 'The Fortifications…', pp. i–ii.

[89] 'Notes from…', p 15; 'Flintshire…', p iii.

[90] See for example 'Gold Coins Stretched for a Mile', *SWS*, May 1956, p iii, and for gavelkind 'Why John Jones Married His Cousin', *SWS*, May 1946, pp. i–ii.

[91] My emphasis. 'Honouring a Practical Saint…', *SWS*, p ii.

[92] 'Glamorgan's Greatest Wonder', *SWS*, January 1955, p iii; 'Honouring a Practical Saint', *CN*, 2 March 1946, pp. 9 & 14; 'Honouring a Practical Saint…', *SWS*, p ii.

[93] 'The New Capital and the New "Capital"', *SWS*, March 1949. p ii.

[94] 'The Fortifications…', pp. i–ii.

[95] 'The Fortifications…,'pp. i–ii; 1891 census; 'Pan-Celtic…' pp. i–ii; 'Welsh Literary Weapons of Yesterday and Today', *SWS*, April 1951, p ii; 'Wales Produces Her Flashbacks, *SWS*, July 1949, pp. i–iii; 'Was Daniel Owen the Welsh Dickens?', *SWS*, October 1953, p iv; 'Story of a Vanishing Society', *SWS*, November 1956, p iii. See also 'Wooden Walls of Wales', *SWS*, June 1956, p ii; 'Why Britain…', pp. 17-8.

[96] 'The Fortifications…', pp. i–ii.

[97] 'One Hundred Years of Wild Wales', *SWS*, June 1954, p i.

[98] 'The Fortifications…', pp. i–ii.

[99] 'The South Welcomes…', p i.

[100] 'Llangollen…', p i.

[101] 'Llangollen…', p iii.

[102] 'Links Across the Channel', *SWS*, September 1948, p ii.

[103] 'Movement Would Gain by Decentralisation', *CN*, 17 April 1954, p 10.

[104] 'In Wales Now', *CPML*, April 1955, pp. 6-9.

[105] 'Atomic Bomb May Give Savages a Chance', *CN*, 27 October 1945, pp. 11 & 13; 'Britain's Power in Moral Leadership', *CN*, 26 April 1947, p 9; 'In Defence of Compromise', *CN*, 14 February 1948, p 9; 'Calendar Time…', p 10; 'An Eighteenth Century "New Deal"', *CN*, 19 January 1946, p 9.

[106] 'Such a Friendly Town', *SWS*, July 1952, p i.

[107] 'Glorious Fifth!', p 9.

108 'A Thing of Beauty', *SWS*, January 1955, p iii.

109 'The President', p 38.

110 'Hooray...', pp. 9 & 10; 'In Search of Miss Wales', *SWS*, April 1953, pp. i-ii.

111 Davies, 'Hazell of Ynysybwl...', p 225.

112 See for example 'A Jewel...', p iii; 'Wales and the Lake Poet', *SWS*, April 1950, p iii; 'The Treasure...', pp. i-ii.

113 'Book Titles...', pp. 9 & 10.

114 '...and our education...', pp. 11 & 13.

115 'Forest of the White Saint', *SWS*, June 1946, pp. i-ii.

116 'N.H.S. – What it Means...', p i.

117 'Robert Owen Speaks Again', pp. i-ii.

118 'Does the Rhondda Make Sense?', *SWS*, Oct 1955, p ii.

119 'New Books About Wales', *SWS*, June 1958, p iii.

120 'Music, Teachers, Coal – the Rhondda exports all three', *SWS*, July 1958, pp. ii-iii; 'Secrets of the Rhondda', *SWS*, August 1946, pp. i-ii.

121 'I Remember...', pp. i-ii.

122 'Some Problems of the Five Day Week', *SWS*, July 1947, p i.

123 'Magic of...', *SWS*, May 1957, p ii.

124 Emphasis in original. 'Music, Teachers, Coal...' p iii.

125 'Revolution...', p i.

126 'Just Sitting', *CO*, August 1947, p 223.

127 *CN*, 25 December 1943.

128 'Is It a Mirage?', *CN*, 22 December 1945, pp. 9-10.

129 'Atomic Bomb...', p 11.

130 'Social Suicide', *CN*, 26 October 1946, pp. 9-10.

131 'Pools Without Healing', *CN*, 8 July 1950, p 10.

132 WW Price index card 6 on William Hazell; 'Sudden Death...'; Presbyterian Church, Certificates of Merit, 1949,1953,1954 and 1957; conversation with Margaret, 13 January 2014.

Chapter 5: *Consumers Arise!*

1 'Distribution in Europe', *CR*, March 1955, pp. 64-6; 'The Western Mail Looks at Distribution', *SWS*, March 1955, pp. i-ii.

2 'The Western Mail...'; 'Distribution...; 'The Miner – No Longer...', pp. 258-60.

3 'Distribution...', p 65.

4 'The Miner – No Longer...', pp. 258-60.

5   'Distribution…', p 66; See *CN*, 3 February 1951, p 2; 24 March 1951, p 7; the comments of H J Twigg, 10 February 1951, p 2; 10 July 1954, p 1.

6   'Derationing Brought Gains', *SWS*, March 1955, p ii; *CN*, 19 May 1956, p 4.

7   A R Davies comments, *GV*, p 11.

8   'They All Went to the Show', *SWS*, October 1954, p iv; 'The Next South Wales Borough?', *SWS*, November 1954, p i.

9   WSB minutes, 9 May & 11 August 1956.

10 'The Sun Shone…'.

11 *GV*, p 82.

12 *CN*, 29 September 1956.

13 'Ynysybwl Society's Diamond Jubilee…', p i; *CN*, 19 May 1956, p 4, 10 May 1958, p 5, 6 December 1958, p 5.

14 *GV*, p 11.

15 'Co-operative Youth – Was W.L. Stedman Right?', *SWS*, August 1947, pp. iii–iv.

16 'W. Hazell's Appeal to Maturity', *CN*, 20 June 1953, p 10.

17 'Promotion', *SWS*, February 1955, p iv.

18 'Promotion'.

19 *GV*, pp. 94 & 96.

20 'Gateways to the Boardroom, 2 – Municipal Service and Trade Unionism', *CR*, p 134.

21 'Gateways… 2', pp. 134-5.

22 'Are Chances Missed in New Towns', *CN*, 20 February 1954, p 12.

23 'This "Rest" is no "Rest"', *SWS*, March 1954, pp. i–ii.

24 'There's a Welcome…', p i; 'W. Hazell's Appeal…', p 10.

25 'A Congress Creed: Democracy for Man – Not Man for Democracy', *CR*, April 1953, pp. 82-3.

26 'Howells' Ducats…', *SWS*, May 1954, p iv.

27 'A Congress Creed…'.

28 'Are Chances Missed…', p 12.

29 'Movement Would Gain…', p 10.

30 *GV*, p 124.

31 'I Remember…', pp. i–ii.

32 'Vale of Clydach (IV): Invasion by the Monster – Coal', *SWS*, November 1957, pp. i–ii.

33 Emphasis in original. 'Dictatorship of the Proletariat', *CN*, 11 May 1946, p 9.

34 'Co-operators and the Peace', p 2.

35 'Beyond the Chains', p 34.

36   'First Welsh Jones...', *SWS*, March 1953, p i.

37   'In Wales Now', *CPML*, April 1955, p 9 & June 1955, pp. 12-13.

38   'Dictatorship...', p 9.

39   'Logic Which Can Be Terribly Inhuman', *CN*, 20 October 1951, p 10.

40   'Logic...', p 10.

41   'Gateways...1', p 106.

42   'Logic...', p 10.

43   'The Challenge of '1984'', p 2.

44   *CN*, 8 January 1955, p 14.

45   'Incentive', p 8.

46   'Robert Owen Memorial', *CR*, September 1953, pp. 206-7.

47   Bernard Crick, 'Introduction', George Orwell, *The Lion and the Unicorn*, 1982, Penguin edition, especially pp 8-9 & 25-6.

48   *CN*, 28 March 1953; 'Are Chances Missed...', p 12.

49   'Is the Movement Going Totalitarian?', *CN*, 27 February 1954, pp. 2 & 13.

50   This debate still continues in the 21st Century.

51   'Movement Would Gain...', p 10.

52   'The Unity of the Co-operative Mosaic', *CN*, 14 April 1956, p 14.

53   'Gateways...1', p 106.

54   Report of the 89th Annual Co-operative Congress, Scarborough, 1958, pp. 267-8.

55   *CN*, 19 July 1958, pp. 4 & 5.

56   *CN*, 6 December 1958, p 9.

57   *CN*, 29 November 1958, p 6.

58   'Beyond the Chains', pp. 34-5.

59   'Amalgamation Road', *CR*, March 1959, p 69.

60   *CN*, 7 June 1958, p 3.

61   *CN*, 30 August 1958; W W Price index card 9 on William Hazell; 1958 Congress pp. 350-60; Report of Central Executive, 90th Annual Co-operative Congress, Edinburgh, 1959, p 71.

62   WSB, 7 April, 7 May, 7 July & 6 October 1956; *CN*, 11 May 1957, pp. 14 & 19.

Chapter 6: Last Words

1   Minutes of South Wales Group, Co-operative Party, 22 June 1957; The Cymric Democrat, July 1956, p 7; conversation with Hywel Francis, 4 October 2013.

2   *CR*, May 1959, pp. 103-5.

3   'A Good Word...'

4   'Spoken on Co-operative Day', *CR*, July 1959, p 152.

5   'Gateways...3', p 176.

6   'Gateways...1', p 107.

7   'Men and Events of 1956', *SWS*, Feb 1957, p i.

8   *CN*, 20 March 1937, p 4; *CN*, 28 May 1955, p 16; Co-operative Party Conference Agenda & Reports 1956-9; 'Men and Events of 1956', p ii; Co-operative Party National Committee Minutes, 20 April 1957.

9   Brecon, Monmouth and East Glamorgan Federation of the Co-operative Party Executive Committee (BMEG EC) minutes, 23 October 1954, 25 June 1955 & 8 December 1956.

10   'Men and Events of 1956', p ii.

11   *CN*, 18 August 1956, p 6; BMEG EC Minutes, September 1958 & 26 September 1959.

12   'Aberystwyth', *SWS*, October 1958, p iii.

13   *CN*, 9 May 1959, p 4.

14   Co-operative Party AGM Minutes, 20 February 1960.

15   Report of the 92nd Annual Co-operative Congress, Scarborough, 1961, p 329.

16   Co-operative Congress Report, 1961, p 357.

17   Ynysybwl Co-operative Society, Report and Balance Sheet for 27 weeks ended 7 September 1964.

18   *CN*, 29 September 1956.

19   Letter William to Lilian & Dd., n.d., but probably 28 December 1963.

20   Letter William to Lilian & Dd., n.d., but probably 28 December 1963; letter to Lilian & Dd., n.d. but 1964.

21   Letter William to Lilian, Dd., dated 2 July [1964].

22   Letter 'Dad' to Lilian, undated but April 1964.

23   Letter 'Dad' to Lilian, undated but April 1964; *Observer, Leader & Free Press*, 17 October 1964.

24   Letter from Dad and Auntie to Lilian, 5 November 1964; Sectional Board Retirements "W Hazell...", p 135; 'Sudden Death...'; 'Just Plain Eighteen', *CN*, 12 August 1950, pp. 8-9.

25   Letter signed from Dad and Auntie (but from Gwlad) to Lilian, 5 November 1964.

26   'Sudden Death...'. (Death certificate held by Graham Brooks, grandson.)

27   YCS Report and balance sheet for the period up to the 7 September 1964.

28   YCS, Supplement to Good Shopping, December 1st 1964, Lilian Price papers.

29   *GV*, p 100.

30 'Sudden Death..'. WSB, 2 May 1959; Ynysybwl Industrial Co-operative Society Limited programme, Lilian's papers; *CR*, November 1964, p 342. Hazell was cremated to avoid issues about with which of his two wives he should be buried.

31 Letter from A. Glad to Lilian, 25 January 1972.

32 Probate Registry document dated 18 December 1964; Proceeds of sale in the estate of Gwladys Sarah Hazell; Schedule of sale dated 15 February 1973.

33 Letter from Will[ie] and Elizabeth to Lilian, 11 November 1964. William had moved back to Britain and was living in Leigh on Sea by July 1977. (Letter from Will[ie] to Lilian dated 18 July 1977).

34 Comments to author by Margaret's husband Bob, as reported to him by Bill, and of Margaret, Ynysybwl, 31 March 2007.

35 YCS Report and Balance Sheet for 27 weeks ending 7 September 1964.

36 Co-operative Union, *The Co-operative Directory*, 1961, pp. 368-9.

37 YCS Report and Balance Sheet, Year Ending 3 September 1979, p 2.

38 John Butler, ex-Secretary Co-ops UK, conversation with author, Cardiff, September 2006.

Index

William Hazell's Gleaming Vision is just one of
a whole range of publications from Y Lolfa.
For a full list of books currently in print, send
now for your free copy of our new full-colour
catalogue. Or simply surf into our website

www.ylolfa.com

for secure on-line searching and ordering.

TALYBONT CEREDIGION CYMRU SY24 5HE
e-mail ylolfa@ylolfa.com
website www.ylolfa.com
phone (01970) 832 304
fax 832 782